Frank Knight and the Chicago School in American Economics

T0330750

Frank Knight occupies a paradoxical place in the history of Chicago economics: vital to the tradition's teaching of price theory and the twentieth-century re-articulation of the defense of free enterprise and liberal democracy, yet a critic (in advance) of the empirical and methodological orientation that has characterized Chicago economics and the rest of the discipline in the post-war period, and skeptical of liberalism's prospects. This edited collection focuses on the tension between economic science – with its assumption of stable, known preferences necessary for predictive power (the *de gustibus non est disputandum* assumption of the Chicago School's approach) – and economics as one element of a social philosophy befitting a free society. Knight's emphases – uncertainty, the exploratory nature of human choice, the role of religion, and democracy as "government by discussion" – clearly resonate through the volume.

Spanning 20 years of Emmett's work in the history of economics, the majority of the chapters collected here examine Knight's work on economic theory, social philosophy and uncertainty. Accounts of Knight's relationship to the Chicago School are woven throughout the volume, which includes previously unpublished material examining topics such as whether Chicago implicitly rejected Knight's philosophy of economics even while embracing his price theoretic orientation in economic theory, and how Chicago economists were educated as the Chicago approach was solidified through the educational and research agenda of the department.

This book will be of use to students interested in Knight's economics and philosophy, the nature of Chicago economics, the relation of the history of economic thought to the discipline of economics and the relation between economics and religion.

Ross B. Emmett is Associate Professor of Political Economy and Political Theory and Constitutional Democracy, and co-director of The Michigan Center for Innovation and Economic Prosperity at James Madison College, Michigan State University.

Routledge Studies in the History of Economics

Frank Knight and the Chicago School in American Economics

Ross B. Emmett

LONDON AND NEW YORK

First published 2009
by Routledge
2 Park Square, Milton Park, Abingdon, Oxon OX14 4RN

Simultaneously published in the USA and Canada
by Routledge
711 Third Avenue, New York, NY 10017

Routledge is an imprint of the Taylor & Francis Group, an informa business

Typeset in Times New Roman by
Value Chain International Ltd

First issued in paperback in 2013

British Library Cataloguing in Publication Data
A catalogue record for this book is available from the British Library

Library of Congress Cataloging in Publication Data
Emmett, Ross B.
  Frank Knight & the Chicago school in American economics /
Ross B. Emmett.
     p. cm.
  Includes bibliographical references and index.
  1. Knight, Frank H. (Frank Hyneman), 1885–1972. 2. Chicago school of
economics. 3. Economics. I. Title.
  HB119.K59E46 2008
  330.15'53092–dc22
                                                      2008036637
ISBN13: 978-0-415-74596-3 (pbk)
ISBN13: 978-0-415-77500-7 (hbk)
ISBN13: 978-0-203-88174-3 (ebk)

For Lydia, David, and Thomas

Contents

Preface

The purpose of this volume is to collect in one place my essays on Frank H. Knight, Chicago economics, and economics and religion written over the 20-year span between 1987 and 2007. Most of the essays have been previously published, but are scattered across a variety of publications which make it difficult for scholars in the history of economics and others to see the interconnections among the various strands of my work.

The collection begins with two historiographic essays that reflect my long-standing interest in the interpretation of texts and the relation between that activity and what economists (or historians or theologians) do. One of the lessons I've learned from both historiography and my research on Knight is that authors ultimately do not control their texts. Thus, I will not try here to provide some overarching meta-theory or meta-narrative that provides insight into how my work fits together. I will, however, provide a little information about the provenance of the essays.

The first of the historiographic essays is the result of an invitation from Warren Samuels to contribute a piece to the *Companion* he was editing with John Davis and Jeff Biddle: Warren gave the piece its title, and the essay is one of my favorites. The other historiographic essay was the result of observing so many historians of economic thought responding negatively to Margaret Schabas's suggestion that they consider "breaking away" from economics and associating more with the history of science (1992). When I was invited to the 1995 University of Manitoba Departmental Conference on the "History of Economics: Is it 'History' or 'Economics'?," held at the Delta Marsh Field Station, I used the opportunity to finish my reflections on the topic. The essay is largely taxonomic, although I use the careful delineation of terms to steer a middle course in the debate, which continues to surface in discussions among historians of economics (as recently as the June 2008 History of Economics Society conference at York University in Toronto).

The oldest essays in the volume are the first and last essays in section II (Chapters 3 and 8). They were both written about the time I completed my dissertation: the third chapter is a condensed version of the dissertation chapter on *Risk, Uncertainty, and Profit* (combined with some material from other chapters); the eighth chapter was my first attempt to extend the argument of the dissertation to the latter part of Frank Knight's work. My dissertation (Emmett 1991) had historically reconstructed Knight's work up to the mid-1930s, and I knew I would need to work past that point in order to complete my study of his relation with American social science. When I decided that my description of Knight's orientation as "therapeutic" was not going to work for his later writings, chapter 3 was never revised and resubmitted; thus chapter 8 is the only published version of the "therapeutic orientation" argument prior to the publication of chapter 3 in this volume.

My one previously published interpretation of *Risk, Uncertainty, and Profit* (Chapter 4) is, therefore, not an interpretation that comes from my dissertation. Instead, the origins of "The Economist and the Entrepreneur" lie in my interdisciplinary teaching at Augustana University College (now the Augustana Faculty of the University of Alberta) and reflection on Deirdre McCloskey's encouragement to economists to tell better stories (1998). In interdisciplinary settings, economists sometimes argue that novels and other forms of art may embody a theory of individual behavior and social coordination that can be teased out and modeled using economic tools (Cowen 2008). In this case, I argued that the opposite could also be the case: a 1920s-era economics book could be treated as a novel of the same era. The larger-than-life characters of the Economist and the Entrepreneur have the same tragic qualities as Jay Gatsby: dreams so obviously close to realization that they can hardly fail to grasp them; and then they slip away.

Chapter 5 is an extended version of an essay prepared for a project on the question: what constitutes dissent in economics? Because most of the essays in the volume focused on theorists who were known as heterodox or dissenters from the orthodoxy of neoclassical economics, I suggested that the inclusion of Knight would help to show that dissent can run in other directions. My original essay included a section in which I used the Rational Dissenters of eighteenth- and nineteenth-century England as models for understanding dissent (in order to distinguish dissent from disagreement). Although that section was not included in the original publication, I have restored it here.

History of Political Economy hosts a yearly thematic conference at Duke University, and uses some of the essays presented to produce an annual supplement to the journal. I have attended the *HOPE* conferences fairly regularly, and a number of the papers included here reflect the themes of the conferences over the years. "Maximizers vs. good sports" (chapter 7) was written for the 1993 conference on "Higgling." "'What is truth' in capital theory" (chapter 6) was completed for the 1996 conference that John Davis organized to profile younger historians of economics and their innovative methods, although I had been playing around with the theme for several years before that in earlier presentations (and ended up putting an extended version of the article online at https://www.msu.edu/~emmettr/capital/). Steve Medema would think me remiss to not mention that my 1996 Duke presentation began with a playing of Mozart's "Ave Verum Corpus," because one metaphor Knight uses in his articles on capital theory is that of the economy as a choral performance. Finally, "Entrenching disciplinary competence" (chapter 10), my first paper on the Chicago workshop system, was presented at the 1997 *HOPE* conference.

Few doubt that Frank Knight was a Chicago School economist: indeed, he is widely thought of as the School's co-founder (with Jacob Viner). Even Chicago economists, however, recognize the tension between Knight's role in the department of economics at the University of Chicago and his call for a social science that is broader than that usually associated with Chicago economics. I have tried a number of ways to tackle this tenuous relationship. Most recently, in an essay published here for the first time, I asked if the Chicago School had implicitly rejected Knight. Previously, I examined Knight's relationship to the one thinker he often said he admired, Max Weber, and also wrote "Knight's response" to the *de gustibus* methodological principle articulated by Stigler and Becker that forms one of the twin bases for the Chicago approach to economics (the other being Friedman's essay on positive economics). All of these essays try to interpret in various ways Knight's argument that the economic approach captures part of human life, but that "Life must be more than economics" (Knight 1951: 4). Ironically, the way I differentiate Knight from subsequent Chicago economists is related to his longstanding criticism of institutional economics; an approach to economics that Knight's colleagues at Chicago also criticized (see Chapter 5). The argument is that, for Knight, both institutionalism and the Chicago School make the mistake of reducing economics to a science.

I originally entered economics to understand how it had come to occupy in the modern world the role that religion often assumed in pre-modern ones. Knight provided one lens through which to investigate that question, although he also led me into a wider investigation of the discipline of economics, economic philosophy, and the history of Chicago economics. But I've returned to my original interests in several essays, which are included here at the end. Along with my interpretation of Knight on religion (Chapter 12), I've included two essays written in 2003. Warren Samuels asked me to review Robert Nelson's *Economics as Religion* (2001) at the same time that I was working on an essay for Anthony Waterman's *festschrift* (and undertaking my move from Alberta to Michigan State University). The two essays together almost form a whole: while one argues that economics plays a role in the modern world analogous to religion without itself becoming religion, the other argues that liberal society must be secular in the sense that its formal institutions are religion-neutral even if people themselves are devout.

Several words of appreciation to institutions, organizations and people are appropriate here. The essays included in this volume were written at: St. John's College, The University of Manitoba; Augustana University College (Camrose, Alberta); and James Madison College, Michigan State University. Each of these institutions provides a wonderful environment to teach, research, and write. Many of my colleagues at Augustana have heard versions of these papers (often at colloquia organized by the Center for Interdisciplinary Research in the Liberal Arts), and my new colleagues at James Madison are becoming familiar with them as well. The contribution of my recent students at James Madison to my scholarship is not seen in the essays published here, but they are making a significant difference in my work both through the quality of class discussion and through their independent research on topics close to my own. All three of the universities mentioned, as well as the Social Sciences and Humanities Research Council of Canada and the Earhart Foundation, provided financial support for the research that informs these essays.

Anthony Waterman and Warren Samuels read and commented on many of these essays prior to publication. Both have provided advice as mentors and friends, and I also wish to thank them for writing forewords to the volume. Others have provided comments or assistance with research questions on one or more of the essays here: Jeff Biddle, Jack Birner, Peter Boettke, Richard Boyd, Maria Brouwer, Jim Buchanan, Bill Buxton, Marc Casson, John Coates, Avi Cohen, John Davis, Alexander Ebner, Philippe Fontaine, Wade Hands, Dan Hammond, Bruce Janz, Bryce Jones, Robert Leonard, David Levy, Steve Medema, Phil Mirowski, Mary Morgan, Claus Nopenney, Greg Ransom, Malcolm Rutherford, Eric Schleisser, Karen Vaughn, Richard Wagner, and Roy Weintraub.

Several of the essays included here were presented at the annual History of Economics Society meeting, which remains my favorite professional conference setting because the community of historians of economics provides constructive criticism, both at the conference and through email throughout the year. Two essays were presented at organizations that participate in the annual ASSA meeting: the Association for Social Economics (Chapter 8) and the Association of Christian Economists (Chapter 11); and chapter 9 was presented at the invitation of the UK Economic History Society, at the University of Birmingham in 2001. Unfortunately, the history of economics community has lost several venues for presentation and discussion since I started presenting my work: chapter 4 was presented at the Thorstein Veblen Society (Chicago area), chapter 6 at the Kress Seminar (Boston area) and the first European Conference in the History of Economics, and chapter 11 at the History of Economic Thought and Methodology Seminar at Michigan State University. None of these seminars or colloquia continues in existence today. Presentations of these essays at departmental seminars include the University of Alberta (Chapter 4), St. Mary's University in Halifax (Chapter 5), George Mason University (Chapters 9 and 11), Miami University in Ohio (Chapter 11), and New York University (Chapter 4).

Permission to use material from the Frank H. Knight Papers at the University of Chicago Special Collections Research Center, The Frederick D. Kershner Papers at the Christian Theological Seminary Library in Indianapolis, the Talcott Parsons Papers at the Harvard University Archives, and the Jacob Viner Papers at Princeton University Library's Department of Rare Books and Special Collections is gratefully acknowledged. I also want to thank participants in the Chicago Economics Oral History Project for their willingness to allow me to use material from their interviews.

Quite a few of the essays refer to Knight's famous book *Risk, Uncertainty, and Profit*. I have used the acronym *RUP* for the book throughout the volume. Also, I have standardized all the citations to the various essays of Knight's which have been reprinted in volumes devoted to his work. In each case, the original publication date is used in the citation, and where page numbers are cited, they refer to the most recently reprinted version of the essay. In many cases, those citations are to my two-volume collection of Knight's essays. The reference list provides both the original and the reprint information.

Original publication information

All previously published articles reprinted with the kind permission of the copyright holder. If the current copyright holder is different than the original publisher, the original publisher information is also included below.

"Exegesis, Hermeneutics, and Interpretation" was published in *A Companion to the History of Economic Thought*, edited by Warren J. Samuels, Jeff E. Biddle, and John B. Davis, 523–37. Oxford: Blackwell. Copyright: Wiley-Blackwell, 2003.

"Reflections on 'Breaking Away': Economics as Science and the History of Economics as History of Science" was published in *Research in the History of Economic Thought and Methodology*, edited by Warren J. Samuels and Jeff Biddle, Vol. 15: 221–36. Greenwich, CT: JAI Press. Copyright: Emerald Insight, 1997.

"The Economist and the Entrepreneur: Modernist Impulses in Frank H. Knight's *Risk, Uncertainty and Profit.*" *History of Political Economy* 31 (Spring): 29–52. Copyright: Duke University Press, 1999.

"Frank Knight's dissent from progressive social science" was published in *Economics and Its Discontents: Twentieth Century Dissenting Economists*, edited by Steven Pressman and Richard Holt, 153–64. Copyright: Edward Elgar, 1998.

"'What is Truth' in Capital Theory?: Five Stories Relevant to the Evaluation of Frank Knight's Contribution to the Capital Controversy" was published in *New Economics and Its History* (supplement to *History of Political Economy*, volume 29), edited by John B. Davis, 231–50. Copyright: Duke University Press, 1997.

"Maximizers vs. Good Sports: Frank Knight's Curious Understanding of Exchange Behaviour" was published in *Higgling: Transactors and their Markets in the History of Economics* (supplement to *History of Political Economy*, volume 26), edited by Neil De Marchi and Mary S. Morgan, 276–92. Copyright: Duke University Press, 1994.

"Frank H. Knight on the Conflict of Values in Economic Life" was published in *Research in the History of Economic Thought and Methodology*, edited by Warren J. Samuels, vol. 9: 87–103. Greenwich, CT: JAI Press. Copyright: Emerald Insight, 1992.

"Frank H. Knight, Max Weber, Chicago Economics, and Institutionalism" was published in *Max Weber Studies*, Beiheft 1: Weber and Economics, 101–19. Copyright: 2006.

Foreword

Warren J. Samuels

For over 50 years, Frank Hyneman Knight has been one of a group who have principally influenced my thinking. The others include, in alphabetical order, John R. Commons, Robert Lee Hale, Vilfredo Pareto, Adam Smith, Max Weber and Edwin E. Witte. Although I never met Knight personally, it was good for me that I had him to read and, in my mind, to argue with. It was also good for the Department of Economics at the University of Chicago that it had Knight as a member for twenty-seven years (1928–55), along with Jacob Viner (1916–46), overlapping during 1928–46, and Henry C. Simons (1927–46), overlapping during 1928–46. It also was good for the discipline of economics that it had Frank Knight as a member. And it was also good that throughout the world people could read him, even if the political authorities were upset. I will express why in the next few paragraphs.

Some time ago it occurred to me that, at a certain level of abstraction, I encounter two types of mentality. One type requires determinacy and closure; the other type is comfortable with ambiguity and open-endedness. Knight was of the second type modified by the first. He would have preferred determinacy and closure but knew that he had to settle for ambiguity and open-endedness. (In this he was, to my mind, close to Adam Smith. Smith, in his "History of Astronomy" (1795), writes that philosophers and scientists, on the one hand, and the average man or women on the other, would prefer to know truth but often had to settle for what would soothe the imagination or set minds at rest.)

Knight knew – really knew – that the world is a complicated place, that problems and issues are not uni-dimensional, that everything worth thinking about had many ifs, ands, and buts, or assumptions and limitations. He saw that problems of freedom, for example, had a multiplicity of rival strands, and that most people who discussed them did so on a superficial level and thought that they had said something meaningful. Knight was not happy with Wisconsin Institutionalists; he thought that they often asked the correct question but came up with a wrong-headed answer. Of course, the Institutionalists, he might go on to say, were not alone in doing that, for most people did likewise. If the Institutionalists recognized social control (the framework of Lionel Robbins' market plus framework approach), they tended to be overzealous in putting it to work; theirs were the sentiments of control and change. He recognized social control but his sentiments were those of free-dom and continuity. These sentiments were "only" sentiments. But freedom and continuity required social control. Both Commons and Knight would have agreed with the propositions that there was a law covering all aspects of life in society; that law represented the formation and structure of freedom, at least at first cut, and that mankind had to have both continuity and change. He might have added that the conservatives could be overzealous too. Every problem solu-tion, therefore, could be faulted and could have different oxen being gored. For Knight, institutions mattered; they govern who would have what freedom and who, because they did not have their relevant interests protected, would be exposed to the decisions made by those who did have their interests protected – willy-nilly, by law. But they mattered in a certain way. They were conservative because, when push came to shove – an interesting trope is it not?! – they were not happy to have much if any change, especially legal change. Freedom was the absence of legal change of law. Most conservatives – less so Knight – however, knew that one set of laws and of rights yielded one set of freedoms, and that another set of laws and of rights yielded another set of freedoms. If an existing law was replaced by another law, then government was only doing under the new law what it had been doing under the old law. By changing the law, government was only changing the interests to which the law was giving its promotion. It generally was not intruding into an area in which it hitherto had been absent. When it intruded in this way, for exam-ple, when a new technology (say. surrogate motherhood), new law was required to establish the relative rights of the parties involved, including determining who was involved and whose interests needed protection as rights. By the same token, the rules that govern who can do what to whom on the football field or in a baseball stadium would be performing the same function if the rules were reversed; different rules would protect different interests with the rules serving the same function.

Knight, Viner and others of his Department of the 1920s and 1930s were deep thinkers along the foregoing lines, even if they expressed themselves differently and even if, like Knight, they would have preferred that certain points not be widely publicly discussed (as he said in Knight 1932). They knew that conservatives have their own agendas for government, their own candidates for legal change of law; and that those who were arguably not conservative had their own lists of what to retain. The classic example of the period of my youth was labor unions – either you wanted them or you wanted to do away with them. The questions, whether capital-ism remained capitalism if there were unions, and what would warrant collective action by investors in corporations and not collective action by workers, were rarely so baldly stated. The various litmus tests of those years on the trade union issue were typically less subtly comprehended and expressed.

As I have explained elsewhere, I soon tired of the dismal languages of liberal-ism and conservatism in politics and in academia. The two positions had many things in common and yet were opposed in many ways. It was something of a revelation to read Frank Knight and learn that, even though he often came out on issues in a predictable way, he knew, he deeply knew, certain problems and fundamentals that I had come to know from Commons, Hale, Pareto, and Witte. It should come as no surprise that, well within a decade after receiving my doctorate, I gave a graduate seminar on Knight. It was no surprise to me, a few months ago, to hear from a student in that class, now, like me, a retired professor, that studying Knight in depth was for him a life-changing experience.

Knight was not happy, to put it mildly, with organized religion. He would have bristled, I imagine, if he had been told that his religiosity was both secular and on a different, higher, level from most other people's. Having written that, I am reminded of the professor from the Harvard Divinity School, whose visiting lectures I attended, who said that if people knew what theologians meant by God, they would think the theologian was an atheist. One can understand, therefore, how it is possible for some people to think that Milton Friedman is a socialist.

Most economists have a love–hate relationship with the faculty of the department of economics of the University of Chicago. From what I have learned, Knight may have had such a dual relationship with them himself. At any rate, I wonder what Knight felt about Jim Buchanan's efforts to have economics provide a moral defense against interventionism and about George Stigler's promotion of a Coase "Theorem" that maintained the very opposite of what Ronald Coase had been trying to say, namely that institutions matter. Both efforts (Buchanan's and Stigler's) were in the nature of what Knight had called, in his review of Lionel Robbins' study of the theory of economic policy of the English classical economists (Knight 1953), a propaganda for economic freedom. Two characteristics of the Chicago department are, first, that its members are on the cutting edge of neoclassical price theory, and, second, that its members have dedicated their careers as polemicists and as technicians to the search for a suitable, i.e. effective, propaganda for economic freedom.

The difference between the pre- and post-World War I Chicago School in view of the foregoing is striking. The older School generally did not play games with policy. They did not over-simplify and exaggerate in order to produce certain desired results. The younger School is noted for doing the opposite. The younger School has not had its Frank Knight; or, rather, it had its Frank Knight (who retired in 1955) but the sophistication of his policy analysis was lost on them. They preferred to be polemicists rather than policy analysts working at arm's length from the material they studied. For them, academia was a preacher's paradise.

If it was good for me to have Frank Knight to read, if it was good for people generally to have Knight to read, especially for Chicago economists and for the discipline of economics to have Frank Knight to read, then it has been good for all these folks, too, to have had Ross Emmett as the primary scholar studying the Chicago School. It has been good for Frank Knight to have Ross concentrating his attention on his ideas.

I have known Ross since I went to the University of Manitoba as his external examiner on his doctoral dissertation, written under Anthony Waterman. Ross proved to be the virtuoso intellect claimed by Anthony, who himself is a foremost virtuoso performer. And Ross has since then done nothing to reverse or lower that judgment.

There is no younger economist of whom I have a higher opinion and greater respect than Ross Emmett. There are several, including two of my own doctoral students, who, in my judgment, share the highest rank. More important, I have learned a great deal from Ross. I have been able to interact with him in numerous ways. Of the 15 essays comprising this volume I have been involved, in one way or another, with the creation and/or publication of no less than six of them. He has become a co-editor of my three-volume annual publication, *Research in the History of Economic Thought and Methodology*. I have chosen him to lead a small group that will finish my enormous project on the use of the concept of the invisible hand, should I not be able to complete it myself, as seems likely. My only serious regret is that I am not his colleague at Michigan State University, having retired (and relocated) shortly before his arrival there at James Madison College.

The essays are evidence of the brilliance of Frank Knight. They are similarly evidence of the brilliance of Ross Emmett. A number of other historians of economics and methodologists are studying Knight. The enormity of Ross's quality work on Knight is compelling. And his work on Knight is but one part of his total output. All this is because Ross can think and analyze on the same level as Knight.

I have known several scholars, not only historians of economics, who have each worked principally on one earlier person. They knew what their subjects thought and wrote, they knew the evolution of their subjects' thinking, they knew the context of other people's work with which their subject interacted, and they knew the larger field with respect to which their subject has to be understood. I have worked with one of them on a set of lecture notes taken by a student in a class taught by John Dewey, some seventy years earlier. In a discussion with my colleague, I raised a point. My colleague told me about Dewey's thinking on the point in general. He was able, with neither difficulty nor need to resort to anything but his memory, to relate what Dewey was doing on matters both pertinent and not pertinent to my point, during a certain two-week period when Dewey was working on my point. Ross Emmett is well along the path of comparable knowledge about Frank Knight.

The 15 essays comprising this collection are exceedingly insightful about the topics on which Knight worked, on what Knight thought, and on the deep historiographic issues which inevitably arise in such matters. Scholars working on Knight and others seeking to relate Knight to various important issues, will find these essays by Ross Emmett mind-expanding.

In the meantime, let me say a few words about one of the essays you are about to read, one of the deepest and most important. In the eleventh essay, Emmett examines Knight in relation to the postwar Chicago School. He concludes that the School "can be said to owe everything, and nothing to Knight." One reason for this is that Knight took price theory seriously and while the later Chicagoans also took it seriously they did so in different ways. One part of the important story is that while Knight assumed the necessity, but also the insufficiency, of price theory, the later Chicagoans assumed its sufficiency for explanatory purposes. Another part of the story was that later price theorists assumed that the economy is not only competitive – markets are, in their view, inherently competitive – but Knight had argued that monopoly was a key problem, that the serious operation of ethics and the law was important in sustaining the propriety and effectiveness of competition. A quite different part of the story concerns the rejection of Knight's views on methodology, one view being that predictive power is too weak to place the burden assumed for it by Milton Friedman, another view being that democracy required agreement through discussion and not some standard of value produced by valuers positioned, as Emmett puts it, "outside the 'discussion' that defined democracy itself." If one asks, to what do the parts of the story add up, it is that Chicago's "price theoretic way of seeing the world" is unbelievably narrow. On other grounds, Knight was prepared to go only so far as to believe in "relatively absolute absolutes," whereas his later colleagues could, by assuming away anything to the contrary, seriously limit price theoretic explanation under the aegis of taking it seriously. (I am not sure that Knight's view on discussion would prevail. The discussion in the real world includes all sorts of positions and all sorts of stratagems in their support. (What I take to be) Knight's description of the later Chicagoans' model is correct; but even a myopic approach should be able to join the conversation.)

Something like this story has been sensed by many who have studied Chicago with an open mind. Ross Emmett has examined what was going on at Chicago and provided a brilliant and comprehensive account. The irony of it all is that George Stigler and his colleagues apparently successfully identified Chicago economics with a particularly narrow interpretation of Adam Smith's *Wealth of Nations*. This could be done by first interpreting Smith along late Chicago lines. But it was with Knight's version that Smith could properly be identified.

It has been said of Michael Jordan, the basketball player, that his performance in his field, with respect to other basketball players, is further ahead than any other person with respect to others in his or her field. The essays in this collection suggest that some day, not too far off, one will be able to say that about Ross Emmett. As should be evident, I consider Frank Knight to have been one of the world's greatest economists. By virtue of the quality and quantity of his work, Ross Emmett will some day lay claim to be one of the world's greatest historians of economic thought.

Foreword

A. M. C. Waterman

The late Paul Heyne, who was trained in both theology and economics, spent most of his life wrestling with the seeming dissonance between the two. At an early stage in his career he determined to pursue his studies at the University of Chicago. At "Chicago I focused on the theological and philosophical presuppositions of economics. My goal was to refute Frank Knight. I lost" (Brennan and Waterman 2008).

Ross Emmett, himself one of Paul Heyne's many friends until the latter's untimely death in 2000, made a somewhat similar start. He wished to study the relation between economics and theology in order to investigate the coherence and validity of Christian social ethics and Christian "social thought." Believing that I might be able to help him in this, he came to the University of Manitoba and enrolled under my supervision in a doctoral program in economics. At an early stage, while we were still discussing the conceptual problems of combining the insights of economics with those of Christian theology, I suggested that he might read Frank Knight's famous – or notorious – article "Ethics and Economic Reform: III Christianity," in which Knight argued, as he continued to do in subsequent writing, that "evil rather than good seems likely to result from any appeal to Christian religious or moral teaching" (Knight 1939a: 47).

As in the case of Paul Heyne, Emmett's sharp encounter with Frank Knight's abrasive dismissal of Christian moral teaching shaped the whole course of his subsequent thinking, scholarship and research, though in a characteristically different way. Heyne accepted Knight's account of the inevitably limited scope of Christian economic ethics, and of the necessity for impersonal rules in coordinating individual, self-regarding actions in any society much larger than the family or clan. For the rest of his life, he continued to preach this message, in and out of season, to his fellow Christians in America and elsewhere. Like Heyne, Emmett began with "the desire to tell a particular dead person (namely Frank Knight) why he was wrong about a number of fundamental issues regarding the relation between Christianity and democratic capitalism" (Emmett 1991: v). But he immediately recognized that "conversations with the dead, like those with the living, require one first to listen and to seek to understand" (ibid.: v). His first task was therefore to understand what Knight had wanted to do in his voluminous, heteroge-neous and by no means fully coherent writings; to consider the extent to which Knight's thinking had changed or "developed" over the decades; and to investigate the religious, social, political and intellectual context of that work – in particular, the culture of the University of Chicago in the first half of the twentieth century.

Though Emmett's doctoral thesis contains two chapters that dealt with religion and science in relation to political thought, they are embedded in a large-scale consideration of "The Economist as Philosopher" much influenced by Richard Rorty's conception of the "therapeutic" function of at least some recent philo-sophical writing. The finished product, "Frank H. Knight and American Social Science during the Twenties and Early Thirties" (Emmett 1991) located Knight's most famous work, *Risk, Uncertainty, and Profit* (Knight 1921a) in the context of "therapeutic" philosophy, related Knight's economic "value" theory to ethical and political theory, and thoroughly examined the evolution of American social discourse, especially at Chicago, up to the 1930s. This is "intellectual history" in the spirit of the "Cambridge" School of Peter Laslett, John Dunn, J. G. A. Pocock, and Quentin Skinner: a study of ideas with careful attention to context and genu-ine respect for the quiddity of all dead authors. Emmett's thesis was awarded the History of Economics Society prize in 1992 for the best doctoral dissertation in the history of economic thought. It is the seed plot of all his subsequent work on Knight and Knight's context.

I

In order to sustain any exchange with another that deserves to be called a "conver-sation" one must "listen" and one must "seek to understand." In practice the two are often carried on at the same time, since listening to another's utterances will quickly lapse into boredom and indifference if the language is unknown or unintel-ligible. But mere familiarity with the words may not be enough. We need to know what our interlocutor is trying to do with his words. That in turn implies that we must know the background of allusion, of literary, scientific, political and histori-cal context, and of the polemical or ideological disposition of that interlocutor. The phrase "rational expectations," for example, means one thing when used by Robert Malthus in the 1800s, quite another when used by Robert Lucas in the 1970s.

In any "conversation" with the dead, the importance of these contextual mat-ters is acute. We can ask Lucas if we have correctly understood his meaning: we can't ask Malthus. Historical imagination is therefore at a premium. If our aim is faithfully to represent certain ideas that some dead thinker (were we able to resur-rect and interrogate him) could be brought to agree were those he had intended to express when he wrote the text we are examining, we must try so far as may be possible to see with his eyes and hear with his ears. And in doing the latter we must attempt to "eavesdrop upon the conversations of the past" (Collini 2000: 15). This is by no means uncontroversial. The proper "interpretation" of biblical texts, for example, has been a matter of dispute at least since the Alexandrian Fathers

(see vol. III of Quasten 1953). The art of exegesis and the corresponding discipline of hermeneutics which is its methodological rationale, have been extended
in recent centuries beyond biblical literature into all fields dealing with written
material from the past, notably including the "history of ideas" in general and the
history of economic thought in particular.

Because historiographic method is a minefield of controversy, it is necessary
that the serious historian should declare and defend his methodological commitments. This Emmett does in Section I of this collection: chapter 1 on "Exegesis,
hermeneutics, and interpretation" and chapter 2 on "Economics as science and the
history of economics as history of science." The former criticizes Stigler's influential doctrine of "scientific exegesis" in light of Quentin Skinner's "mythology of
coherence", questions Stigler's assumption that hermeneutical authority resides in
the relevant scientific community, and repudiates "whig history" of which not only
Stigler but also Frank Knight himself had been guilty. Chapter 2 asserts the "need
for an historiographic framework which enables us to distinguish … between participation in a disciplined conversation … and the study of the ideas and practices
of the disciplined conversation." [p. 27 in this volume]

II

In light of these methodological affirmations and disclaimers, how does one go
about "Interpreting Frank Knight" (part II, containing Chapters 3, 4, 5, 6, 7, and
8)? Emmett's most important contribution to Knight scholarship has been to per-
ceive clearly, and to explain more thoroughly than any previous author, that "systematic analysis and anti-systematic ruminations on the limitations of analysis are
never far apart in Knight's work," and that this was intentional (Emmett 1989).
What previous authorities such as Stigler have rejected as "at best incoherent, and,
at worst, inconsistent" was in fact a carefully constructed program for their own
re-education. For Knight's

> primary purpose was edification – he wanted to preserve the health of that
> great conversation we call human society by showing economists their inabil-
> ity to encompass the dynamic complexity of human experience within the
> confines of a single intellectual system and the necessity of accepting the
> responsibility their intellectual limitations placed upon them.
>
> (Emmett 1989)

Building on ideas first introduced in his doctoral thesis (1991, Chapters 1 and 2),
Emmett characterizes Knight's method – or at any rate his intentions – as "therapeutic" in the sense associated with the philosophy of Richard Rorty. According to
Rorty, there is no ideal vocabulary which contains all genuine discursive options:
there are no inescapable forms of description. It is the business of the philosopher to pursue the implications of this insight and to subvert, or at any rate call in
question, all attempts to foreclose options in science, religion, politics – and philosophy itself – by appeal to "foundations" or other authority. The philosopher is thus

a "gadfly" and his activity "therapeutic" in that it heals thinkers of their delusions and opens their minds to the inescapable limitations of human knowledge.

It is now generally agreed that Frank Knight was a notable example of "The Economist as Philosopher." But he was utterly unlike his most famous predecessors, Adam Smith and John Stuart Mill – each of whom, perhaps, might more accurately be described as "The Philospher as Economist." For Smith and Mill, "political economy" was a branch of moral and political philosophy, and the economic analysis that gave it its shape was unproblematically congruent with their general philosophical positions. What some have seen as a dissonance between Wealth of Nations and Theory of Moral Sentiments is sufficiently contradicted by Smith's continual attention to the latter long after Wealth of Nations first appeared.

For Knight however, economic analysis and its implications may be inconsistent, or even at variance, with other ways of conceiving human social phenomena. We may understand his often puzzling and seemingly mixed-up writings if we are willing to assume that the "anti-systematic ruminations" they so often contain are there for a purpose: that Frank Knight saw his vocation, in part, as that of disturbing the easy epistemological assumptions of his fellow-economists.

The first essay in Section II, on "The therapeutic quality of *Risk, Uncertainty, and Profit*" (Chapter 3) deals directly with this matter and arises out of corresponding material in Emmett's thesis (1991, Chapter 5). Chapter 4 deals with "modernist impulses" in that famous work, begins by noting that "The culture of modernism springs from the unsettling but liberating experience of uncertainty", and explains that in a "Modernist" work of art or literature "the quest for a unified aesthetic expression is fragmented by its own quest for unification" (Emmett 1999c). Chapter 5 shows how and why Knight dissented from the generally accepted ideology of "Progressive social science"; which was "an ideology giving unique authority to science and appointing social scientists as the guardians of public discourse about social problems" (Emmett 1998c). Knight's characteristic and unique style is illustrated by his interventions in the capital theory debate of the 1930s (Emmett 1997a). For Knight at any rate, it was "impossible to separate scientific activity from other activities." For "at what point is Knight qua economist separable from Knight qua social philosopher or Knight qua educator or even Knight qua spouse/ex-spouse and father?" (Emmett 1997a). Knight's ambiguous relation to orthodoxy and "dissent" is further illustrated by his ability to see that participation in the market is often regarded by many as a game, which it is good to win if possible – but only by being a "good sport" (Emmett 1994b). Knight had "spearheaded a newly emerging American neoclassicism" by defending the assumption of a rational, utility-maximizing individual, necessary to safeguard the scientific status of economics. But by allowing the "good sport" to play, Knight admitted moral considerations into an account of market processes and subverted his own assumption of instrumental rationality. The final chapter of section II continues several of the themes of previous chapters in the context of Knight's conception of "value" as encompassing both (economic) "price theory" and (ethical) "value theory." Here too the seeming incoherence resulting from Knight's conflation of the two is interpreted as an example of his "therapeutic orientation" (Emmett 1992) and of his recognition that "social problems" are, at least in part, moral problems.

III

Place is part of context. The universities of Oxford and Cambridge emerged and grew at the same time and in the same way, and are only 80 miles apart. Yet for more than three centuries their intellectual, religious and political culture was markedly different. It is hard to imagine a Newton, or a Paley, Malthus, Darwin, Russell,or Keynes having been formed at Oxford; or a Laud, a Pusey, or a Ruskin thriving in Cambridge.

The University of Chicago was founded neither by church nor by state but by the entrepreneur and arch-capitalist John D. Rockefeller, more than two centuries after the Ivy League colleges of the original colonies. And it is about 800 miles distant, in the heart of the American Mid West. The city itself had long been a home, almost a symbol, of all that is not "East Coast" in American culture: populist, turbulent and – perhaps because of its large number both of German and Irish immigrants – fiercely anti-British at least until the Second World War. From the first its university was distinguished by Rockefeller's desire to foster a meritocracy in America, by the admission of women on equal terms with men, and by the importance of its graduate research institutions established on the German model. The Divinity School that Rockefeller endowed quickly became a centre of "liberalism" in religion and a thorn in the flesh to "fundamentalists."

Frank Knight was born and raised in rural Illinois, and though he went to Cornell for post-graduate study, returned to his home state in 1917 as a lecturer in economics at the University of Chicago. "Despite ... a secure position at the State University of Iowa" which "lured him away from Chicago for eight years", Chicago was "the center of his intellectual universe" for much of his life (Emmett 1991: 28). Emmett has shown in his thesis that the "discursive context" of Knight's work at Chicago in the 1930s was the "Re-Orientation of American Social Discourse" arising out of the confrontation of the formerly dominant scientific naturalism by a new, critical rationalism (ibid.: Chapters 3, 7). The local, Chicago debate arose out of curricular reforms introduced by a new President, Robert Hutchins. At stake was "authority in a democratic society." Like all participants in the debate, in Chicago at any rate, Knight took the need for "democracy" – however threatened by its internal contradictions – as given and beyond dispute. For Knight "democracy" meant "a conversation about what wants and values we should have ... in which all members of society were deemed eligible to participate" (1991: 263).

These high considerations were an important part of the intellectual context of economic studies at Chicago, and in particular of Knight's participation in those studies. Section III of this collection (Chapters 9, 10, 11 and 12) therefore contains four of Emmett's essays on Knight's place in "Chicago Economics."

Knight knew German, had visited Germany in 1913, and "had read extensively in the work of the German historical school, including Weber" in the 1920s (Emmett 2006b). Chapter 9 reports Knight's use of Max Weber's approach to scientific methodology in the former's "efforts to create a social science that transcended the terms of the neoclassical-institutionalist debate during the 1920s and 1930s" (Emmett 2006b). As a consequence, although Knight was known as a champion of neoclassical theory between the wars, "by the postwar period his work was relegated to the non-scientific realm of "social philosophy" (Emmett 2006b). In chapter 10, Emmett locates changes in the teaching of economics in the context of the "Great Debate" following the Hutchins reforms of the early 1930s. "Chicago economics refined a disciplinary self-critique that entrenched a particular set of competencies ... in its researchers" (Emmett 1998b). Chapter 11 is historical fiction: an imaginative reconstruction of Frank Knight's posthumous "Reply to George Stigler and Gary Becker's 'De Gustibus Non Est Disputandum'" (Emmett 2006a). The Stigler–Becker assumption is central to methodology of the Chicago school in postwar years. And in view of the dominant importance of Knight in interwar Chicago economics, the mythology of an "oral tradition" in that school advanced in particular by Milton Friedman, and abandonment by his younger colleagues of Knight's approach to economics after the Second World War, the question must arise: "Did the Chicago School reject Frank Knight?" This Emmett addresses in Chapter 12.

IV

According to Lord Keynes, the decade of the 1860s "was the critical moment at which Christian dogma fell away from the serious philosophical world of England, or at any rate of Cambridge" (Keynes 1933: 168). Marshall, Sidgwick, Foxwell and Neville Keynes had become unbelievers by the end of the 1870s. Their influence, especially that of Marshall, was exerted to abstract "economics," as a scientific and professional discipline, from a traditional "political economy" that had generally included ethical considerations, including those derived from the Christian religion. Though a rearguard action was fought at Oxford, and though some economists at both universities and in Scotland remained Christian believers, religion had become actually, though not yet officially, privatized in Britain by the 1880s. Indeed, as early as 1832 the Oxonian Richard Whately had argued influentially for a sharp epistemological demarcation between "science" (including political economy) and religion. Sixty years later it was no longer held to be part of the professional duty of economists to reconcile their findings with Christian theology (Waterman 2008, part 4). Alfred Marshall's world-famous Principles (1890) is a landmark. By 1903, when Marshall succeeded in establishing an Economic Tripos at Cambridge, modern, secular economics was well launched in Britain.

This was decidedly not the case in the USA. During the early part of the nineteenth century American economists such as Francis Wayland (1796–1865) had thoroughly assimilated the analysis of the English School. But political economy of the English School was inescapably associated with an ideology of free trade, highly unwelcome to American protectionist sentiment for much of the century. Moreover, towards the end of that century, there was "an estrangement from British scholarly life" created by "a growing attachment to German thought" (Goodwin

1973: 297). Perhaps in part because of this, American religious thought was relatively insulated from those new ideas in science and philosophy that had dissociated economics and Christian theology in England. When the German-educated Richard T. Ely co-founded the American Economic Association in 1885, he did so with the intention that it should promote the Liberal-Protestant "Social Gospel" to which he and many of his colleagues were fully committed. Though the AEA soon took other directions, the climate of religious opinion changed but little until the First World War.

Frank Knight, who was 32 when he first went to Chicago in 1917 and 43 when he returned from Iowa in 1928, therefore "stood 'at a fundamental turning point' in the history of American economic thought" (Emmett 1994a). For

> Behind him lay the history of a community of economists who understood their discipline to be part of a larger social, historical, and even moral understanding, and whose world was shaped by the reality of God's providential presence.
>
> (Emmett 1994a)

Both Knight and his first wife had been raised in the Disciples of Christ, a relatively inclusive Protestant sect, many members of which (but certainly not Knight) were affected to the Social Gospel. After their move to Iowa they became Unitarian. Knight was President of the men's club, taught Sunday school and ran a young adults' group. When Knight went back to Chicago he left his first wife behind in Iowa City, replacing her with a woman who had been a member of his Unitarian young adults' group, and who remained an active Unitarian until her death. Knight himself occasionally attended and even preached, but did not become a member (Emmett 2008).

It is therefore no surprise to discover that Knight's writings on religion should be as ambiguous, and as hard to tie down neatly, as his writings on economics. For despite his genuine commitment to secular "modernity" and scientific rationalism, he was deeply aware of the inability of the merely rational to comprehend all of human existence. Both his understandable scepticism in face of religious dogma, and his less admirable prejudice against traditional forms of Christianity, obliged him to assume the absence of God from any worthwhile social discourse. But he was "acutely aware of what we have lost because God is no longer present" (Emmett 1994a).

In section IV (Chapters 13, 14, 15) of this collection, therefore, Emmett returns to the themes with which he began his studies 25 years ago: "Economics, religion and politics." Chapter 13 indeed, on "Economics vs. religion," goes right back to Square One: Knight's powerful argument against the ability of a Christian ethic to afford any guidance for public policy in a complex, industrialized economy. Emmett notes that Knight subsequently added a second, equally strong objection to Christian social ethics. The necessarily dogmatic character of Christian theology is incompatible, actually at war, with that free and general "discussion" which Knight took to be the essence of democracy.

As Arthur Vidich and Stanford Lyman (1985) claimed, however, and as Robert A. Nelson (2001) has more recently argued, the efforts of social scientists to prescribe for a secular society may itself become a "fundamentally theological" activity (Emmett 1994a). The purpose of chapter 13 is to show how Knight's work illustrates that claim. In the following chapter, "Is Economics a Religion?" Emmett examines Nelson's attempted "theological exegesis" of modern economic thought, based on the latter's plausible assumption that "economics provides for a modern secular society the types of answers and validation that various religions provided for prior societies" (Emmett 2003). Though Nelson's characterization of Knight shows points of agreement with Emmett, and though in many other respects his argument is sound or at least arguable, his enterprise fails in the end. For to say that the social function of economics in Anglo-American, secular society has been analogous to that of religion (which is true) is not at all the same thing as saying that it is religion.

The final chapter continues Emmett's engagement with Nelson, and considers the arguments of the English economist Denys Munby and the American theologian Harvey Cox with respect to a secular society – in which, by definition, no transcendent standards of virtue, morality or value can be publicly recognized. What then is the proper function of the economist, what is the duty of the Christian economist, and how ought the Christian churches to function in such a society? Emmett concludes that Munby was correct in resisting the temptation to develop a "Christian economics" that might differ in method and findings from "secular" economics; and also in arguing that the Church ought to assist the faithful to live the Gospel in what Alfred Marshall called "the ordinary business of life." This is the only essay in the entire collection which makes no mention at all of Frank Knight. Yet from all that Emmett has shown us in his writings here and elsewhere it is certain that Knight would have agreed with the first of these conclusions, and very possible that he would have agreed with the second.

Section I

Historical reconstruction in the history of economics

1 Exegesis, hermeneutics, and interpretation

Introduction

Before you on the desk sits an economics text. It may be the most recent article in a journal or a classic book in the discipline. If you are like most readers, your concern as you read is to make sense of what the text says. This is the central task of textual interpretation: to make sense of the meaning of a text.

The other two words of our title are closely associated with interpretation, although they are used less frequently in economics than in the humanities. "Exegesis" refers to the *critical analysis of a text,* and hence is an integral part of the interpretive task. Exegesis takes us beyond reading the text to attending to its genre, style, form, word choice, model assumptions, internal logic, and contextual issues. Because the exegetical task forces one to pay close attention to the text, an exegesis usually focuses on one particular passage (or, in the case of contemporary economics texts, one model) in an author's work. "Hermeneutics," on the other hand, most often refers to the study of the methods or principles of interpretation. It may be thought of as the *methodology of interpretation.* Because this essay will focus on the methodologies of interpretation in the history of economics, it is primarily an essay in hermeneutics.

The close relation of methodological studies to philosophy has led to a hermeneutic tradition in philosophy, which assumes the primacy of the interpretive stance. Hermeneutic philosophy is founded on the notion that all knowledge, not only knowledge of the meaning of a text, is a process of interpretation – there are only interpretations and their reinterpretations. While its philosophic roots lie in the nineteenth century, especially in the work of Wilhelm Dilthey (1976), twentieth-century hermeneutic philosophy is dominated by the contrast between the work of Hans-Georg Gadamer (1989) and Jacques Derrida (1976; see also Michelfelder and Palmer, 1989). Banished from economics during the positivist orientation of the postwar period, hermeneutic philosophy has made some inroads into contemporary economics, especially among Austrian economists. The interaction of hermeneutic philosophy and economics lies outside the scope of this essay, but the interested reader can consult Lavoie (1991) and Gerrard (1993).

But let us return to the text before you. Most readers obtain a satisfactory understanding of a text by reading it for themselves. Even if the text is written in a style that is unfamiliar to the modern reader, or uses some specific tools and terminology unique to a sub-field of the economics discipline, you probably picked it up with the confidence that its meaning would be clear to you, even if you have to do a bit of exegetical work to ferret the meaning out.

Yet while making sense of a text's meaning seems to be a simple process, it can be fraught with difficulty. One of the prime difficulties was expressed well by the Christian reformer Samuel Werenfels, about 400 years ago, with reference to the Bible: "Men ope this book, their favorite creed in mind; each seeks his own, and each his own doth find." Werenfels's observation is as true of the reading of canonical texts in economics as it is of sacred religious texts. One can find passages in many of the seminal works of economics that lend credence to any number of economic theories. And the literature of the history of economic thought is filled with "new" interpretations of classic texts, which demonstrate how a historical author agrees with one or another contemporary theory. Invariably, the contemporary theory the classical text is said to "anticipate" is the authors own! How can we distinguish between what we think these authors' works mean, and what they really mean?

Stigler's principle of scientific exegesis

One starting point for answering that question is found in the work of George Stigler. In "Textual Exegesis as a Scientific Problem," Stigler (1965) addressed the problem of choosing among competing interpretations of a portion of an author's work. Stigler clearly has Werenfels's problem in mind when he points out that one can find in many authors' works individual passages that seem to support widely different theoretical conclusions. How should those passages be interpreted? Which of them should be given prominence? Stigler likens the problem of textual exegesis in this regard to the problem of the single fact in statistical work. In order to increase your confidence in a statistical test, you increase the sample size. Similarly, in order to increase your confidence in a particular interpretation of a text, you increase the amount of the author's work taken into consideration. "We increase our confidence in the interpretation of an author by increasing the number of his main theoretical conclusions which we can deduce from (our interpretation of) his analytical system" (Stigler 1965: 448).

Stigler goes on to provide a method for applying his "principle of scientific exegesis" (Stigler 1965: 448), illustrated in figure 1.1. First, the "general position" of the author under study is established. A general position is the theoretical core of an author's work, restated in a manner compatible with contemporary economic theory. The general position will probably not be formally stated in the author's own work, but will have to be constructed by interpreters from the various elements of the author's work. Nevertheless, Stigler appears confident that, at any given time, the economics community will recognize what the general positions of past economists are, especially in the case of significant figures such as Adam Smith, David Ricardo, Karl Marx, Leon Walras, or John Maynard Keynes. Once the author's general position is identified, it can be stated in "a strong form capable of contradictions by the facts" (ibid.: 448).

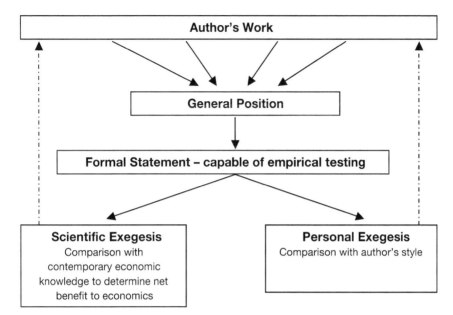

Figure 1

At this point, Stigler argues that two different interpretive activities can occur. First, contemporary theorists can examine the relation between the author's general position and what the modern discipline knows about the economy. The interpretation of the author's general position allows us to evaluate how it can be (has been) amended or improved to explain a greater portion of modern economic life. If the author's general position survives comparison with contemporary economic knowledge, we can say that the author has had a net positive impact on the modern discipline. On the other hand, if the modern discipline's knowledge falsifies the author's general position, the interpretation allows us to say that the author's work has made no lasting contribution to economics.

The other interpretive activity that can occur once the author's general position has been stated in a strong form is the evaluation of the consistency of the author's own conclusions. Theorists often make logical mistakes, or hold beliefs that are later proven false. Should the classical economists' "iron law of wages," or Stanley Jevons's sunspot theory of the business cycle, lead us to reject their entire theoretical work? Certainly not. While economic science may winnow this chaff through the process of testing the author's general position, some interpreters may be interested in figuring out exactly what the original author really believed, even when it is wrong by today's standards. Where contradictory passages in an author's work are encountered during this type of interpretive work, Stigler says his principle of scientific exegesis provides no guidance, because the net benefit to modern economics is not the interpreter's concern. In its place, he suggests that the interpreter choose as "decisive" an interpretation that fits well with the author's "style" of thought. Stigler calls this rule "the principle of personal exegesis" (Stigler 1965: 448). We will return to the theme of personal exegesis later in the essay.

Stigler and the hermeneutic circle

Stigler's principle of scientific exegesis provides a strong hermeneutic program for the evaluation of the contribution of past economic work to the current discipline. There is a fly in Stigler's exegetical ointment, however. Notice in figure 1.1 the prominent role that the author's "general position" plays. While this theoretical framework is derived from the author's work, it also plays a governing role in the interpretation of specific passages in the author's work (note the feedback loop from the general position to the author's work through both personal and scientific exegesis). Which comes first, the text or the general position?

In Stigler's formulation, there is an implicit assumption that the interpreter already knows the author's "general position" before she begins to interpret a specific passage of the text. This is a seemingly innocuous assumption, but actually points to one of the central issues in hermeneutics, which has generated much of the most interesting work in hermeneutic theory. Put differently, Stigler assumes that if you are to make sense of any portion of the text before you, you need to have some prior understanding of what the text is generally about. But how are you to acquire a general understanding of the text without understanding all the passages within the text? We call this dilemma the "hermeneutic circle": understanding any portion of a text requires knowledge of all of the text; understanding all of the text requires knowledge of every portion of the text.

Methodologically, the problem posed by the hermeneutic circle is a question of how you break out of the hermeneutic circle: is there a means of avoiding the trap? Stigler's assumption that the interpreter has prior knowledge of the author's general position comes quite close to the answer to this question provided by Paul Ricoeur (1981) in his synthesis of hermeneutic philosophy. Drawing upon the hermeneutic tradition of Dilthey, Gadamer, Martin Heidegger (1962), and others, Ricoeur accepts the dilemma expressed in the problem of the hermeneutic circle, but suggests that the dilemma's resolution lies not in the metaphor of "breaking out," but rather in one's "entrance into" the circle. He argues that the interpreter must enter the circle with the *right* pre-understanding of the text. You come to the text before you with an anticipation of what it may hold – an anticipation shaped by your familiarity with other texts and with an interpretive community. Quoting Heidegger, Ricoeur (1981: 58) says, "what is decisive is not to get out of the circle but to come into it in the right way." But this only pushes our methodological question back one level, for now we have to ask: What is the "right way" to come into the hermeneutic circle?

Stigler's response to the question of the "right way" for an economist to gain a pre-understanding of economics texts is best expressed in another essay (Stigler 1976). There, in an investigation of the possible uses of biography in the study of the history of economics, Stigler argues that the meaning of a text is determined not by the individual interpreter, or even the original author, but by the scientific community of economists, as they read and re-read the text over time: "The recipients of a scientific message are the people who determine what the message is …" (Stigler 1976: 91). *For economists,* then, the *right* pre-understanding of authors' general positions is provided to the interpreter by the economics profession. That scientific community is best positioned, Stigler argues, to understand the scientific meaning of a text. So the modern interpreter enters the hermeneutic circle as an economist with the profession's pre-understanding of the scientific meaning of the author's work in hand.

We have come full circle with Stigler: the methodological principle of scientific exegesis calls for us to use the author's text as a testing ground for the analytic framework that the economics profession has identified with the author. If we can show that the author's theoretical conclusions can be deduced from the general position ascribed to the author, and these theoretical conclusions stand up against what the modern profession knows of the economy, then we can say that the author has made a positive net contribution to modern economics. Where these conclusions need modification or improvement, we can show that the economics profession has progressed beyond the author's original work. Both history and progress, then, emerge from the exegetical work associated with identifying the author's general position.

The mythology of coherence

Stigler's argument that the interpreter's pre-understanding of an economics text should depend upon the general position ascribed to the author by the economics profession is problematic, however. The first reason we should be suspicious of Stigler's notion regarding the pre-understanding of the general position focuses on the problematic nature of the "general position" itself. Where does one find the general position within the author's work? It is rarely said to be in one specific passage; rather, one finds pieces of it scattered over the length and breadth of the author's career. But why choose those pieces and not others? What do you do with statements that modify parts of the general position, or with other statements that we can show to contradict the general position? We are, of course, right back to Stigler's original problem – the hermeneutic circle. But why, we ask, did the author not simply make her general position clear herself?

To use Stigler's own statistical style of discourse, the central problem with the notion of distilling a general position from an author's work is one of over-determination. Just as there are several hypotheses that can account for a specific set of data, there are always several possible general positions that can be constructed from any author's work. Increasing the sample size (the range of the author's work taken into consideration) simply increases the probability that competing general positions cannot be ruled out.

A general position, therefore, is an *abstraction* from the texts that comprise the author's work. In keeping with Stigler's characterization, Don Patinkin once described it as the attempt "to pass a regression line through a scholar's work that will represent its central message" (Patinkin 1982: 17) Ignoring the author's own interests and audience, the interpreter abstracts a general position from an author's texts, giving the author's work a coherent meaning that the author never actually thought at any particular moment in time – and could in fact disagree with. The search for a coherent general position for the purpose of evaluating scientific progress is labeled by Quentin Skinner (1969) as the construction of a "mythology of coherence." While we may assume that no author deliberately contradicts herself in order to make her contemporary or future interpreters confused, we must also accept the fact that no author's work is handed down to us from "on high" – written in a single moment and with a God-like recognition of all the interconnections among the work's many parts. Skinner remarks that such mythologies become histories "not of ideas at all, but of abstractions: a history of thoughts which no one ever actually succeeded in thinking, at a level of coherence which no one ever actually attained" (Skinner 1969: 40).

If we take the passage of time in an author's work seriously, and reconstruct specific passages on their own merits (even when they are at odds with passages written earlier or later in the author's life), it is unlikely that we will end up creating a mythical general position. Anthony Waterman caught Skinner's point well when he remarked, in responding to a criticism of his interpretation of a particular passage in Malthus:

> There is a great temptation to tidy up the creative mess left behind by men like Malthus. But Quentin Skinner … has warned historians of ideas to resist that temptation. For to succumb to what he called the "mythology of coherence" would be to impose a far greater distortion upon the material than that minimum that must inevitably be inflicted when we attempt to pin down *a coherent subset* of our author's work. Those of us who accept this methodological rule will content ourselves with lots of little snapshots, like "Mr. Keynes and the Classics"; and will remain unrepentantly skeptical of all attempts to inform us of "What Malthus (Keynes, Marx *et al.*) Really Meant."
>
> (Waterman 1988a: 206–7)

Interlude: "Little snapshots" – rational reconstruction

While there are a couple more problems with the search for general positions that need to be examined, Waterman's suggestion that we "content ourselves with lots of little snapshots" provides an opportunity to point out a positive hermeneutic application of Stigler's principle of scientific exegesis. You may, in fact, already have thought to ask this question: What if the interpretive goal is more modest than the construction of a general position that spans the author's entire work? What if you simply want to bring a subset of the author's work – one particular text, or a small group of texts – into dialogue with current economics? Could we thereby avoid the mythology of coherence trap that is inherent in a general position? In order to distinguish this less ambitious interpretive task from the construction of general positions, we will give it the label "rational reconstruction." Originally introduced by Richard Rorty (1984), the term rational reconstruction is used here in a narrower sense than it is by Blaug (1990), who applies it to any interpretation adopting the concerns of current economics as its primary hermeneutic stance, including the search for past authors' general positions.

As interpretive exercises, rational reconstructions differ from the construction of general positions in four important ways. First, rational reconstructions, as suggested by Waterman's phrase, focus on a subset of a past author's work. Whether it is one book or article, or a group of articles written at about the same time, the text chosen for a rational reconstruction is not chosen because it best represents the author's general position; the interpreter's goal is simply to bring that particular text into dialogue with present-day concerns. A narrower focus prevents abstractions that move too far away from the texts under consideration. In this sense, a rational reconstruction is still governed by the texts in a way that a general position may not be.

Second, the interpreter's task in a rational reconstruction is not the construction of a theoretical position from the past author's work that can be contrasted with current knowledge, but rather the reconstruction of the past author's argument in a modern theoretical framework. Mathematical modeling techniques and theoretical concepts unknown to the original author may appear in the rational reconstruction, and aspects of the author's argument that the interpreter knows to be mistaken may be replaced with more defensible propositions. Reconstruction, then, is an appropriate term for this interpretive exercise: the author's work will not appear as it did in the original, but will be rendered intelligible to the modern economic theorist.

Third, the selection of techniques and concepts used to cast the author's work in modern garb by each interpreter implies that multiple rational reconstructions of an author's work may be possible. We saw earlier that the possibility of multiple general positions from an author's work poses a problem for interpreters who are seeking an abstract coherent theoretical framework from the entirety of an author's work. In the case of rational reconstructions, the existence of differing interpretations emerges from the choices made by the interpreter. If one were to compare rational reconstructions, the relevant comparison would be which reconstruction makes the original author's work more useful to the needs of the modern economics community (Emmett 1997b).

Finally, because rational reconstructions focus on particular parts of authors' work, and bring that work into dialogue with contemporary scholarship, they are less likely to be used as an indicator of the degree of scientific progress from the past to the present. The connection between Stigler's principle of scientific exegesis, the search for general positions, and the notion of scientific progress will be mentioned in a subsequent section. Rather than setting the past author up for a damning comparison, a rational reconstruction makes the author our contemporary, and forces us to confront the fact that we may not know something that she did. Because rational reconstructions deliberately rewrite past authors' work in the language of current science in order to challenge current theory, we might think of them as the use of the past to advance toward the future, rather than a judgment upon the past from the standpoint of the present.

Hermeneutic authority and the hermeneutics of suspicion

A second reason why Stigler's notion of the pre-understood general position is problematic emerges from the role that it assigns to the economics profession as the final arbiter of meaning. If the economics profession governs the pre-understanding that we bring to the text before us, will that scientific community be willing to give a legitimate hearing to a new interpretation of a well-known text? ("We" know Adam Smith, and this is not the Smith "we" know.) Can a new interpretation of an author cause the profession to reevaluate a canonical author's position relative to contemporary work? Ricardo serves as a good example, because Stigler himself assumes that we "know" Ricardo. Yet even in Stigler's lifetime, a fundamental reinterpretation of Ricardo's work was under way, led by Samuel Hollander (1979). The new "Ricardo" is at odds with Stigler's own "Ricardo," and would likely be judged to have made a greater net contribution to modern economic thought than Stigler might have allowed. Stigler also dismissed the contribution of American institutionalists to postwar economics, but more recent studies have created linkages between them and the emergence of the New Institutionalism (Rutherford 1994a). If the scientific community determines the meaning of the text, can these studies change the community's pre-understanding?

The notion of the economics profession as the final arbiter of meaning is problematic, therefore, because it gives *hermeneutic authority* to one specific interpretive community (see Fish 1980). On what basis are we to accept the authority of the economics profession as an arbiter of meaning for economics texts? Are we to accept its authority because of the validity of current economics theory, its practitioners' knowledge of the texts, their interpretive skills and balanced appreciation for the net benefit of past theorists' work – or simply because we are economists? These questions were raised in an interesting way several years ago, when an English professor at Harvard University held a conference on Adam Smith. The title of the conference was "Who Owns Adam Smith?" and only a few historians of economics were among the invited speakers.

Similarly, why should economists yield hermeneutic authority to other disciplines over texts that might contribute to our understanding of economics? Historians of economics have sometimes been reluctant to accept the contribution of "noneconomics" texts to the history of economics. This reluctance may stem from another implication of Stigler's principle: economists are not the recipients of the message of noneconomics texts, and are therefore unqualified to interpret them. Unpublished manuscripts, correspondence, government reports, magazine articles, and teaching materials provide a rich resource for understanding the meaning of published texts (Weintraub *et al.* 1998), but were often ignored until recently, because historians of economics accepted Stigler's argument that biographical material would divert them from the task of assessing the scientific validity of the abstracted general position (Stigler 1976). In like manner, nonscholarly dialogue by economists and others on public policy has often also been ignored by historians of economics, because neither the economists' contributions nor other commentary were "economics" proper. The acceptance of this artificial dichotomy between economics and noneconomics texts left historians of economics handicapped in their efforts to interpret texts, because they missed opportunities to study sources that might assist them. A recent study of the origins of the "dismal science" by one of Stigler's former students provides an excellent example of the implications of our ignorance of this dichotomy (Levy 2001).

Even within the community of economists, there are problems with the hermeneutic authority of mainstream economies' interpretation of particular authors. The magisterial voice that Stigler adopts suggests to the historian of economics that the pre-understanding of an economics text comes from the economics profession because that scientific community speaks with one voice. The notion of *one community, one voice* is as problematic as that of hermeneutic authority, however. The various schools of economics interpret past authors quite differently, and historians of economics in the past 40 years have shown remarkable diversity in their interpretations of past economists' writings. The past is often the stage on which the debates of the present are contested. Once again, the interpretation of Ricardo is a good example, with at least two, if not three, different Ricardian theoretical frameworks articulated in the literature. Furthermore, the differences among these different "general positions" usually parallel the theoretical differences between different schools of economics (for a plea to make this contest the center of the history of economics, see Roncaglia 1996).

Is there a way to avoid the proliferation of "general positions" ascribed to canonical texts among competing contemporary schools of economics? As long as the focus of interpretation is on the construction of a general position that can be used to identify the author's net benefit to modern economics (Stigler's hermeneutic principle), the answer is probably "no." We can gain something by turning this question around somewhat, however, and looking at the issue from a different angle. Rather than looking at the various general positions ascribed to an author by the different schools of economics, and arguing over their relative merits, we might ask of any particular general position the following questions: What aspects of the author's work does this interpretation obscure from view? What does it hide? These questions engage the reader in what, following Ricoeur (1970: 32–3), might be called the "hermeneutics of suspicion." If interpretation is the act of focusing attention on certain themes in a work, then necessarily it is also the act of leading one's attention away from other themes in the work. One task an interpreter can undertake is that of uncovering in an author's work that which the "general position" ascribed to the author has missed.

Whig history

The third problem with Stigler's hermeneutic program relates to the issue of scientific progress and the present-day scientific community's appreciation of the past on its own terms. Stigler's mentor in the history of economics, Frank H. Knight, began his essay on classical economics with the words:

On the assumption that the primary interest in the "ancients" in such a field as economics is to learn from their mistakes, the principal theme of this discussion will be the contrast between the "classical" system and "correct" views

(Knight 1935c: 237)

Stigler's principle of scientific exegesis articulates the hermeneutic program behind these words, a program designed to interpret the contribution of authors and key works to the progress of economic science. By identifying the key interpretive question as the determination of an author's net benefit to modern economic science, Stigler implicitly sets a standard for scientific progress: present-day theory stands as the judge of the past. More than likely, no past author will escape the interpreter's knife entirely (for contrasting views of the importance of progress for the historian of economics, see Winch 2000; Hynes 2001).

A history that allows present-day theory to be the judge of the past is often called a *Whig history.* The term, picked up from Herbert Butterfield's (1931) study, has been a subject of debate among historians of economics since Paul Samuelson (1987) first introduced it. Much of the discussion has been complicated by the conflation of two different problems. The first, often called *presentism,* refers to a theme already introduced in this essay: the practically inevitable present-day concerns embedded in a pre-understanding that the interpreter brings with her to the study of past texts. But Butterfield's concern was not with presentism *per se;* he acknowledged that all history shares this problem, and that present-day concerns often do provide a motivation for historical investigation. Whig history is a particular type of presentism, one that makes the historian's present-day perspective the judge of the past. In a Whig history, the goal of the interpreter is to praise those who have made significant net contributions, and to condemn those whose contributions have been discarded on the waste heaps of historical progress. Although Stigler's principle of scientific exegesis need not be used for Whiggish purposes (rational reconstructions usually avoid the charge of Whig history), it often is. As Frank Hahn recently said, "What the dead had to say, when of value, has long since been absorbed, and when we need to say it again we can generally say it much better" (Hahn 1993: 165). Stigler would not have put it better.

Abandoning Whig history, and the search for general positions

So far, we have asked what sense *you as a member of the contemporary community of economists* can make of a past economist's work. Stigler's principle of scientific exegesis was our starting point, and we have examined the pitfalls such as mythologies of coherence and Whig history into which it may lead us. While the legitimacy of general positions, Whig history, and notions of progress in the history of economics remain topics of debate (see Henderson 1996; see also the discussion on history of economics readers in the August 2001 and September 2001 archives of the HES email list), some historians of economics have abandoned the attempt to assess the past in terms of the present, and opted instead for what has been called "historical reconstruction" (Rorty 1984). Choosing to make the past their present, these historians of economics focus on reconstructing the meaning of texts at specific moments in time in the past (for a contribution that helped to turn historians' attention in this direction, see Weintraub 1991).

Until recently, studies that focused on a text's relation to its own context were considered to be "external" or "relativist" history (Blaug 1985). The critics of external history condemned the deterministic linkage made in such studies between a text and its social, political, cultural, and intellectual contexts (for example, that Keynes's *The General Theory* arose from the Great Depression). Ideas, it was said, have their own history; telling the story of an idea's development was "internal" or "absolutist" history (Blaug 1985). There is a difference, however, between arguing that ideas are determined by their context and interpreting the historical meaning of texts. Rather than seeking the link between ideas and historical events, historical reconstructions seek to reconstruct the sense (meaning) that someone gave a particular text at some historical point. The most obvious form of historical reconstruction is the effort to understand the original author's meaning; but there are other forms of historical reconstruction as well. For example, we might want to ask what sense public policy-makers in the 1940s made of Keynes *The General Theory,* or what Piero Sraffa (1951) made of David Ricardo. We might also be interested in what contemporaries of the original author made of the text when it appeared. Our interest in these questions leads us to try to make sense of the meaning that *someone other than ourselves* (and in many cases, other than a present-day economist) gave to a text.

To examine the hermeneutic issues related to historical reconstruction, we will focus on the reconstruction of the original author's meaning. The same principles apply to other historical reconstructions. We can ask initially if Stigler's aforementioned principle of personal exegesis provides the basis for the historical reconstruction of the original author's meaning. Although we have concluded that scientific exegesis is problematic, might personal exegesis yet help us to construct a coherent account of the author's own theoretical conclusions (wrong as they may be!)?

Stigler, you may remember, suggested that, after determining an author's general position, it would be possible to go back and examine whether the conclusions of the general position match up with the author's own conclusions. Putting aside the issues that we have already addressed regarding the determination of a general position, we will focus here instead on Stigler's suggestion that the appropriate guide to follow in personal exegesis is the author's "style." Economists are not accustomed to analyzing a writer's style as part of their exegetical work, but style has reentered economics discourse in the rhetorical work of D. N. McCloskey (1998). McCloskey points out that every writer adopts an "ethos" or *persona* in her writing. A writer's "style" emerges from the authority or trustworthiness of the ethos to which she appeals. Nineteenth-century writers wrote in a plain style: educated readers addressing their equals. Modern economists adopt a style that deflects attention from the writer toward the authority of the "scientific ethos" provided by the community of economists (McCloskey 1998: 10–11).

Because style depends, at least in part, upon the author's rhetorical community, Stigler's notion of personal exegesis naturally takes us into an examination of the author's intellectual and social context. What concerns the interpreter interested in historical reconstruction is the range of meanings of words and concepts that were available to the author at the time she wrote her text. The term "uncertainty," for example, has a more specific meaning within economics today than it did in the early twentieth century, when Frank Knight (1921a) wrote his famous treatise on the subject. If we wish to reconstruct Knight's treatment of uncertainty historically, we will have to make ourselves aware of the range of meanings that he may have drawn on, rather than assuming that he shared the current discipline's understanding of the term (Emmett 1997b). While we may not be willing to go as far as Michel Foucault (1972: 129) in arguing that the linguistic structure in which Knight operated governed the possible meanings that could be assigned to his text, we can agree that the disciplinary discourse of uncertainty in the 1910s will have to be placed in the context of the term's meaning within a larger social and philosophic discourse (for examples, see Kloppenberg 1986). J. G. A. Pocock (1962, 1985) has made this type of linguistic contextualism the cornerstone of his historiography, which has made significant inroads into the history of economics, especially the history of its early period (see Winch 1996).

While we may agree with Pocock and Foucault that the discursive context and linguistic structure within which a past author worked limit the range of meanings and usages to which the author had access, the key issue for most historians of economics is what the author *did* with the meanings at her disposal; it is not just the meaning of concepts and structure of the language that are important, but their use. To return to the example of Knight's notion of uncertainty, we recognize that he took notions of indeterminacy and voluntary action that were attached to the notion of uncertainty outside the realm of economics and brought them together in the introduction of a new concept within economics. A historical reconstruction of his work would then recognize the new use within economics of a term previously associated with other discourses. Hence while we as interpreters cannot avoid the examination of an author's intellectual and linguistic context in the process of writing an historical reconstruction, we must in the final analysis make sense of the particular way in which the author used those concepts and spoke within that linguistic context to communicate to her contemporaries what she meant.

The guiding hermeneutic principle of historical reconstruction is Quentin Skinner's: "The relevant logical consideration is that no agent can eventually be said to have meant or done something which he could never be brought to accept as a correct description of what he had meant or done" (Skinner 1969: 48). To make it clear that hermeneutic authority is given here to the original agent, Skinner adds that his principle requires that "any plausible account" the interpreter may provide "of what the agent meant must necessarily fall under, and make use of, the range of descriptions which the agent himself could at least in principle have applied to describe and classify what he was doing" (Skinner 1969: 48). While this principle bears some resemblance to Stigler's principle of personal exegesis, Skinner argues that one should examine the authors *use* of words rather than the author's style (for comparison of Skinner's approach to Pocock and others, see Tully 1988; Bevir 1999). Skinner's question is: What was the author trying to do by using the words she used?

Answering Skinner's question often requires a richly textured study of the text that examines its relation to the author, the author's discursive community, and the social context within which the author lived at the time of writing the text. A wide variety of literature will assist the interpreter, including published texts (scholarly and otherwise), unpublished manuscripts, correspondence, curricular materials, pictures, interviews, and other materials. The anthropologist Clifford Geertz (1973) has called such studies "thick" descriptions – the term is an appropriate contrast to the thin abstractions of general positions.

Conclusion

At the beginning, we considered an economics text sitting on the desk in front of you. Making sense of that text appeared to be a straightforward problem of reading carefully. By now, however, you may wonder what sense, or how many senses, you can make of the text! The problems that we have considered challenge any interpretation you may attempt, be it the construction of a general position along Stiglerian lines, a rational reconstruction, or a historical reconstruction. In conclusion, then, perhaps it is appropriate to summarize and emphasize the positive aspects of the issues we have considered.

First, as interpreters, we cannot escape the concerns of the times in which we live, i.e. the present, and our historical interests are often animated by our present-day concerns. But the interpreter does have a choice as to whether she will interpret the text from the perspective of the present. Where the interpreter's interest is in bringing an historical author's work into dialogue with current economics, Stigler's principle of scientific exegesis is an appropriate guide. There is a thin line, however, between rationally reconstructing the author's work in a way that enables the interpreter to identify its relation to modern thought and adopting the judgmental voice of Whig history. The latter should be avoided when the former is undertaken.

Second, whether the interpreter seeks to reconstruct the contemporary meaning of a text (rational reconstruction) or a historical meaning (historical reconstruction), less is more. The creation of a general statement of the author's position inevitably leads the interpreter to create a mythology – an abstraction from the author's work that will be upheld by appeal to some texts, but almost certainly falsified by others. Careful exegesis of specific texts – considering the range of meanings that they might have, the context in which they were created, and the purposes to which the author (or past interpreter) may have put them – will serve the interpreter well. Ironically, perhaps, abstract general positions turn out to be thinner representations of an author's work than either the contemporary rendering provided by a good rational reconstructions or the richly textured accounts that emerge from a good historical reconstruction.

Finally, the act of interpretation is a humbling experience. When we recognize the contingencies that shape the texts that we interpret, we also realize that our own ideas are limited by the context in which we live. And when the past speaks to us, we learn that others thought well – sometimes even better than we do.

2 Reflections on "breaking away"

Economics as science and the history of economics as history of science

Why do historians of economics still attempt to speak to economists first and foremost?

Schabas 1992: 196

Margaret Schabas's recent article on the history of economics and the history of science (Schabas 1992) questions the longstanding relation that exists between historians of economics and the economics profession, and calls on historians to switch over and join the historians of science, with whom the historians of *economics* have had comparatively little to do until recently. In the set of responses printed with her article, several historians of science echoed her call (with varying degrees of enthusiasm), while acknowledging that there may be good financial reasons for staying within economics (Keyssar 1992; Porter 1992; Proctor 1992; Sylla 1992; Wise 1992). On the other hand, those historians of *economic thought* (note the slight, but significant, difference in identification from that used by Schabas) who were invited to respond unanimously rejected Schabas's call. They argued that although historians of economic thought can learn from the history of science, they should stay within the fold of economics (Caravale 1992; Coats 1992; Hollander 1992; Ménard 1992; Mirowski 1992; Moggridge 1992; Negishi 1992; Patinkin 1992; Walker 1992). The following reflections emerge from my reading of Schabas's article, the responses of her critics, and a number of other recent essays on the historiography of economics (Backhouse 1992, 1994; Bellofiore 1994; Blaug 1990; Clark 1994; Ingrao 1994; Porta 1994; Samuelson, Patinkin, and Blaug 1991; Screpanti 1994; Vaughn 1993).

The assumptions behind Schabas's argument

"As I see it, [historians of economics] might as well break away and form an alliance with historians of science" (Schabas 1992: 197); Schabas's call for historians of economics to abandon departments of economics and join departments of the history of science (or form independent departments of their own) is based on two assumptions: first that economics as a discipline is fundamentally different from the history of economics as a discipline; and second that the history of economics and the history of science are fundamentally the same.

Because the history of economics has so little in common with economics, and so much in common with the history of science, what prevents historians of economics from breaking away and joining the historians of science? Schabas simply suggests that historians of economics feel like prodigal sons, "self-indulgent but still yearning for the approval of their authoritative fathers," and – with flagrant disregard for her own biblical simile – calls them to seek independence and self-sufficiency (Schabas 1992: 196, 200).

The comments made by Schabas's critics emerge from their rejection of the first of the two assumptions on which she bases her call – the distinction between the history of economics and economics. In short, her call to leave economics and join the historians of science is rejected on the grounds that *the history of economic thought is part of economics.* The remarks of Coats, Hollander, Ménard, Mirowski, Moggridge, Negishi, Patinkin, and Walker all echo, at least in part, the comment Giovanni Caravale (1992: 206) makes: "being a historian of economic thought and an economist ... are to a very large extent the complementary sides of the same coin."

The debate between Schabas and her critics raises a number of fundamental questions regarding the historiography of economics. Toward what purpose should the history of economics be studied? By whom? Does the scientific status of economics imply that economists can largely ignore the history of economics? How should the history of economics be studied? What are the relative merits of "historical reconstruction" as opposed to "rational reconstruction" or *"geistesgeschichte"* in the history of economics (Blaug 1990; Rorty 1984)? And what of the potential impact that the sociology of science literature holds for the study of the history of economics (Hands 1994; Latour 1987)?

In order to pursue these questions, let me state at the outset that, while I am uncomfortable with Schabas's psychoanalytic suggestions regarding historians of economics, I am quite sympathetic to the general line of argument she develops in her article. The history of economics is distinguishable from economics, just as the history of science is distinguishable from science. Historians of economics may well find themselves more at home in conversation with historians of science – who share their purposes, methods and conventions – than with economists, with whom (or with some of whom, at any rate) they have less in common. At the same time, however, Schabas's presentation of the argument leaves several questions unresolved. A further clarification of these issues will serve to heighten the tension between her position and that of her critics.

Economics and science: The history of economics and the history of science

Buried beneath any discussion of the relation between economics and the history of economics will be assumptions about the nature of economics as a social science and the nature of the history of economics. Let me begin by identifying explicitly the assumptions about these issues under which I work (Table 2.1 provides a summary).

First, science is a form of *disciplined conversation.* That is to say, science is a conversation among the members of a community of scholars who share a common purpose and follow a common set of rules and conventions. There could be no science without a community of scholars in which the conversation could occur; and the conversation could not progress without the acceptance of certain conventions (some known as "facts" and others as "methods") by which the contributions of members could be judged and evaluated. There are other forms of disciplined conversation: for example, most of the humanities share a common set of purposes, rules, and conventions that are distinct from those of the sciences; the same could be said about the arts and the historical disciplines. For our purposes here, however, I will assume that the disciplines we commonly identify as sciences,

Table 2.1

Science	*History of science*
Disciplined conversation: common set of purposes, rules, and conventions	Disciplined conversation: common set of purposes, rules, and conventions
Distinguishable from other disciplined conversations	Distinguishable from economics by purposes, rules, and conventions it shares with intellectual history
History of scientific thought	
Self-reflection on tradition of scientific conversation, guided by purposes, rules, and conventions of	Disciplined conversation about a different disciplined conversation – in this case, science
Common techniques: rational reconstruction and *geistesgeschichte*	

Economics	*History of economics*
Disciplined conversation: common set of purposes, rules, and conventions	Disciplined conversation: common set of purposes, rules, and conventions
Distinguishable from other disciplined conversations by the purposes, rules, and conventions it shares with science	Distinguishable from economics by purposes, rules, and conventions it shares with intellectual history
History of economic thought	
Self-reflection on tradition of scientific conversation in economics, guided by purposes, rules, and conventions of science	Disciplined conversation about a different disciplined conversation – in this case, economics
Common techniques: rational reconstruction and *geistesgeschichte*	Common technique: historical reconstruction

both social and natural, share enough significant conventions to distinguish them as a group from these other forms of disciplined conversation.

Second, *economics is a science,* to the extent that it shares the purposes, methods, and conventions of the group of disciplined conversations we call science. The conversation among scholars of economics proceeds according to scientific conventions that are widely accepted within the economics community, despite continuing dispute over some of the "facts" and "methods," and perhaps even the purposes that govern it. When the dispute is too crucial to the conversation to enable the community to continue, it either splits the community apart or is resolved by a reevaluation and shifting of the community's shared rules and conventions.

Before moving over to my assumptions about the history of science, I might point out that economics is usually described as a *social* science, and sometimes referred to as *a policy* science. In the parlance used here, referring to economics as a social science can be read as the equivalent of saying that it is disciplined conversation according to scientific rules and conventions about the social consequences of economic behavior (however defined). To refer to economics as a policy science can be read as the equivalent of saying that the conversation we call economics does not, or cannot, exist separately from the larger social conversation about the control and guidance of the economy (Coats 1992). In either case, the social nature of the subject matter and/or the policy-oriented purpose of the conversation raises the question as to whether or not economics is distinguishable from the "natural" sciences in a way that is relevant to the study of its history. Some of Schabas's critics suggest that the differences between economics and the other sciences are significant and are relevant to the relation between economics and its history. I will take up this question in the third section.

Third, the history of science (and here we speak of both the history of particular sciences and the history of the entire group of disciplines that share scientific conventions) is also a disciplined conversation. There is a community of scholars who wish to converse about the history of science, and they do so according to an agreed set of rules and conventions. If there is anything that separates the historians' conversation from the scientists' conversation, it is the fact that the history of science is *a disciplined conversation about a different disciplined conversation.* As an historical discipline, the history of science is a conversation, conducted according to the conventions of intellectual history, about the work of particular scientists and the tradition of conversation in present and past scientific communities.

Fourth, the history of science can usefully be distinguished from the *tradition of self-reflective discussion* that occurs within any particular scientific community. In some disciplines, the self-reflective discussion is known as "theory." Hence political theory is the self-reflective exercise of discussion about the tradition of political discourse by political scientists; in other disciplines it is known as the "history of thought." Whatever it is called, the tradition of self-reflective discussion is distinguishable from the history of science because, as separate disciplined conversations, the history of science and science have different purposes, and hence different rules and conventions. Within any particular scientific discipline, there will be discussion about the extent to which past ideas and the rules and conventions inherited from the tradition of conversation enable the community to pursue its ends. When there is a fair degree of unity among the members of a scientific community (as has been the case in physics and chemistry), the self-reflective discussion will not occupy a significant amount of their time. In other cases, there will be more extensive self-reflective discussion because of an underlying lack of common agreement on the usefulness of traditional ideas, rules, and conventions (as is the case in political science, and to a lesser extent in biology). The important point to realize, however, is that the tradition of self-reflective discussion within a scientific community is guided by the purposes, rules, and conventions that define the community's existence, and therefore *is part of the conversation we call science.* Thus, the "history of scientific thought" is separate from the "history of science."

By combining my second and third assumptions, we can conclude that the history of economics is also a disciplined conversation: scholars converse about the work of particular economists and the conversation of past communities of economists according to an agreed set of rules and conventions. Defining the "history of economics" in this way identifies the similarity between the history of economics and the history of science that Schabas wants us to see. Each is a disciplined conversation about other disciplined conversations. As she points out, historians of economics should not be surprised, therefore, to discover that their conversation shares quite a number of conventions and rules regarding its progress with the conversation that occurs within the history of science.

Recognizing the difference between the history of science and the self-reflective discussion within a scientific tradition identifies one of the key differences between Schabas and her critics. Caravale's remark about economics and the history of economic thought being two sides of the same coin is correct when one recognizes that his understanding of the "history of economic thought" is that of the self-reflective exercise of economists discussing the tradition of economic discourse. But this is not a criticism of Schabas's argument, because she and Caravale are talking about two different things: *the "history of economics" and the "history of economic thought" are not identical.* They are not identical because they have different purposes, employ different methods, and are conducted within different disciplined conversations.

An example to help clarify the distinction

Before moving on to consider some of the implications of the difference between the history of economics and the history of economic thought, consideration of a specific example can highlight the difference and introduce the methods associated with the two disciplines. Borrowing from my own area of research, I will briefly compare the questions that are asked by "historians of economic thought" with those asked by "historians of economics" in the process of interpreting Frank Knight's distinction between risk and uncertainty, introduced in his classic treatise *Risk, Uncertainty, and Profit* (Knight 1921a; hereafter *RUP*).[1]

Consider, then, the relations among the following three questions about Knight's treatment of risk and uncertainty:

(1) What did Knight mean by risk and uncertainty, and why did he use the terms?
(2) What did Knight's distinction between risk and uncertainty contribute to modern economics?
(3) Can Knight's distinction between risk and uncertainty be reconstructed in a way that avoids the criticisms brought against it?

The first two questions occupy the attention of historians of economics (the inclusion of the second question in the history of economics will undoubtedly surprise some readers); the latter is an example of a question often posed within the history of economic thought.

In order to answer the first question, one needs to know two things. The first is the range of meanings for the terms "risk" and "uncertainty" that Knight's context would have enabled him to draw on. Characterizations of Knight's distinction that draw on meanings that Knight could not in principle have had at his disposal (e.g. those drawing on Bayesian theory or modern decision theory) must be ruled out.[2] The second thing one needs to know is how Knight employed his distinction. Here I am speaking not only of the important position he gave it in his treatment of the theory of profit, but also of the role it played in his response to the central issues of his intellectual context. An answer to the first question, therefore, will provide a reconstruction of the historical identity of Knight's distinction; a task we can call *historical reconstruction* (Rorty 1984; Skinner 1969).

One of the more common mistakes in the history of economic thought is the assumption that the second question requires a prior answer to the first question. Before we can assess Knight's contribution to modern economic theory, must we not first know what Knight meant by his distinction between risk and uncertainty, and how he used it to construct a theory of profit? The short answer is "No." The second question is independent of the first. In order to explain why this is the case, let me ask the following: What difference would it make for our answer to the second question if a historian showed that what Knight meant in *RUP* was significantly different from the meaning generally attributed to him? The answer, of course, is "No difference." Knight's contribution to modern theory is not determined by what he was trying to say in saying what he did, but rather by how he has been read. Once his works circulated among economists, his words were no longer his own – they belonged to the scholarly community that sought to interpret them. What the second question requires, then, is knowledge of the ideas and contexts of Knight's interpreters, rather than of Knight himself. Thus an answer that directly addresses the question about the contribution to modern economic theory of Knight's distinction between risk and uncertainty will reflect the evolving pattern of conversation among economists more than it reflects what Knight said. Difficulties will abound if one tries to answer the second question through a reconstruction of the distinction's original identity.

Despite their differences, there is nevertheless a striking parallel between the examination required to answer the second question and the historical reconstruction carried out in determining the answer to the first question. The only difference between them is the discursive context with which one is concerned. In order to understand what Knight meant, one looks at how his context shaped his work. In order to understand how economists have read Knight, one looks at how their contexts have shaped their interpretations. The similarity implies that both of these examinations are historical reconstructions. Because they are concerned with uncovering the meaning of Knight's work for different discursive contexts, however, they are conducted independently of each other.

The third relevant historiographic question is whether it was possible to reconstruct Knight's distinction between risk and uncertainty in a way that avoids the criticisms brought against it by modern theory. This question calls for a different type of examination from that required by either of the first two. Rather than providing a reconstruction of the historical identity of an author or of the author's interpretive community, an answer to the third question provides a contemporary identity for the author. Thus another way in which the third question can be posed is: What might Knight say about risk and uncertainty if he knew what we know now about the relation between probability theory and rational choice? Would his distinction then differ in any way from contemporary usage? To ensure a contrast between answers to the third question and those provided in response to the first two questions, I will identify the former as examples of *rational reconstruction* (Rorty 1984).

One of the more interesting aspects of rational reconstructions is that several different reconstructions of the same work can exist simultaneously with no necessary contradiction. Because the concerns of the contemporary conversation among economists directs the reconstructive effort in a rational reconstruction, different parts of the contemporary economics community may seek to draw a past author's work into their conversation in different ways. In Knight's case, contemporary interest in his work has resulted in several excellent rational reconstructions that, while differing significantly, each provide a means by which Knight and some portion of the contemporary economics community can converse (compare Barzel 1987; Foss 1993; Langlois and Cosgel 1993; LeRoy and Singell 1987). Although their authors sometimes make the mistake of arguing about which rational reconstruction is better (by what standard could that argument be settled?), these reconstructions each play a significant role in contemporary theory: an author's work is only worthy of rational reconstruction if the theorist who reconstructs it thinks that it has something to contribute to current theoretical discussion in the economics discipline.

Despite the fact that rational reconstruction and the reconstruction of the historical identity of an author's work (question 1) are decidedly different tasks, they are similar in one regard: they both share a concern for the author's original text that is not shared by the reconstructive effort required to provide an answer to the second question above. The primary "text" for an answer to the second question is the standard account of Knight's distinction between risk and uncertainty provided by a particular interpretative community; this "text" may have little to do with *RUP* itself. Reconstructions aimed at answering either the first or third question, on the other hand, seek to identify a meaning for Knight's text itself. Answers to the first question provide the text's historical identity; rational reconstructions provide it with a contemporary identity. Even though the second and third questions are often assumed to be related, they are, in fact, quite different.

Before concluding this interlude, I should point out that there is another form of self-reflective discussion common to the history of economic thought besides rational reconstruction. For lack of a better term, this alternate form can be described by Richard Rorty's term *"geistesgeschichte."*[3] Rather than addressing the work of one economist or a small group of economists in order to reconstruct either its historical or contemporary identity, *geistesgeschichten* address a broad range of economics texts across a longer timeframe in order to tell a story about the development of economic ideas that either justifies or challenges the guiding disciplines of the economics community. As Rorty suggests, *geistesgeschichten* articulate the canon for a particular branch of economics. When they are written to justify a community's purpose, rules, and conventions, *geistesgeschichten* provide contemporary economists with a credible defense for their participation in the community, and tell them who the important figures in the tradition of that community are (or should be). When they are written to challenge the scholarly community, *geistesgeschichten* will often rewrite the tradition, arguing that at some point the community took a turn that should be reversed. Approaches to economics were overlooked that ought not to have been overlooked, while the ideas that were followed have led the community astray. Keynes's story about Malthus and the classical economists is one famous *geistesgeschichte*; Phil Mirowski's (1989) *More Heat Than Light* is a more recent one that is also highly controversial, and which may conceivably have some effect on the canon of modern economics.

Finally, the differences among the three forms of intellectual history discussed here highlight the chief failures of textbook treatments of the history of economics/economic thought. Intended to provide an overview of the contributions of the great past theorists to modern economic theory (the canon of economics, so to speak), history of economics/economic thought textbooks ignore the difference between assessing the contribution of a work to its interpretative community and providing the work with its historical identity, and only rarely engage in either rational reconstruction or *geistesgeschichte*. Instead, the textbooks assume a set of concerns that are supposed to apply to the work of all economists (nowadays, from Aristotle to Lucas), and briefly explicate the portions of famous authors' works traditionally identified as having some relevance to these concerns [Rorty's (1984) term for such histories is "doxography"]. No effort is made to reconstruct the works covered in the textbooks either historically or rationally, and few textbooks take seriously the task of writing a *geistesgeschichte*. No wonder economists claim to have lost interest in the history of economic thought – its textbooks speak to no-one and make few, if any, claims with which the contemporary theorist can engage.

Further questions to consider

We can now return to the questions that remain unanswered by my analysis of Schabas's call for historians of economics to "break away." Some of my responses to those questions will strengthen her argument; others will require some modification. The first is a theme mentioned earlier: the social or policy-oriented nature of economics, and the implications of this for the relation between economics and its history. Is it possible that history is essential to economics as a social/ policy science, and hence that the "history of economics" cannot be as separate as the history of science from the disciplined conversation it seeks to explain? Second, there is the question of whether the history of science provides the only other disciplined conversation that historians of economics might turn to. Does Schabas's willingness to classify economics as a scientific discipline (which we have accepted without question so far) also lead her to ally the history of economics with the history of science, to the exclusion of other possible allegiances? What of intellectual history, the history of the other social sciences, the emerging interest in the sociological analysis of scientific knowledge and practice, or even economics itself?

Does it matter if economics is a social/policy science?

I outlined earlier the ground on which Schabas's critics attack her call to align the history of economics with the history of science: economics and the history of economic thought/economics are like two sides of the same coin, and therefore cannot (or ought not) be separated. Implicit in most of these critical responses, and explicit in some, is the assumption that the relation between economics and its history is somehow different from the relation between the natural sciences and their respective histories. Because economics is a social or policy science, the critics argue, the history of economics is an essential part of ongoing theoretical discussion. Contemporary theory in the natural sciences is less intimately connected with its history, and the division of the history of science from the natural sciences is therefore acceptable. In its more extreme forms, this argument bases a refusal to join historians of science on the ground that historians of economics can re-historicize the economics discipline.

Part of the problem here is that several issues have been rolled into one because Schabas's critics mistakenly equated the "history of science" with the "history of scientific thought." But if we accept the distinction between these two different disciplines that I proposed in the first section of this article, then we can disentangle the issues embedded in the comments of Schabas' critics. In particular, we can distinguish between two questions that, while fundamentally different, are often confused: (1) how essential is the "history of thought" for a scientific discipline as opposed to a social scientific discipline?; and (2) does economics, as a social science, share enough rules and conventions with the historical disciplines to be considered as much "history" as "science"? I shall address the second question first.

Central to the arguments offered by some of Schabas's critics is the claim that economics, though it shares significant conventions with the other sciences, is also closely allied with the historical disciplines. To explain the economy and its relation to society, one must think historically, because economic activity is rooted in particular historical moments. Philip Mirowski put the argument succinctly: "I hope it is not the case that economists have 'lost the means to think historically,' [a quote from Schabas (1992: 197)] for that means they have lost the means to think about the economy and about social life. To prevent such a debacle, HET [history of economic thought] must keep one foot in the economists' camp" (Mirowski 1992: 223; see also Clark 1994; Keyssar 1992; Ménard 1992: 219; Proctor 1992; Wise 1992).

We can see in Mirowski's remarks the claim that economics is (or at least ought to be) as much history as science. Perhaps unfortunately, this claim does not currently correspond to the existing repertoire of rules and conventions in the economics profession, and the argument Schabas's critics mount therefore appears to many economists as a case of special pleading from the margins of the scientific conversation. Like scholars in other scientific disciplines, economic theorists have largely abandoned historicist explanations of social processes, and are unlikely to change the basic methodological conventions of the discipline to please those with antiquarian interests. Perhaps one of the reasons why history of economic thought courses are disappearing from the economics curriculum is because they have too often represented the last vestiges of historicism in economics (the most vigorous recent historicist argument about the historiography of economic thought is found in Clark 1994).

Rejecting historicism does not require one to separate the history of economic thought from the science of economics, however, because the relation between a disciplined conversation and its tradition is independent of any relationship between scientific study and historical study. The relation identified in the first section between economics and the history of economic thought was based not on the historical nature of economics, but on the argument that every disciplined conversation is constantly in dialogue with its tradition. Whether economics is "science" or "history," it is a disciplined conversation, and therefore engages its tradition at every turn. The same is true of physics and political theory – the engagement is simply more obvious in the latter than in the former; the history of scientific thought is as important to science as the history of historical thought (historiography) is to history.

Rather than building their arguments for inclusion in the contemporary conversation of economic scientists on historicist grounds, then, historians of economic thought would be wiser to continue, *qua* economists, engaging their tradition in ways that other economists will pay attention to. Writing good rational reconstructions and *geistesgeschichten* would make a good start.[4]

What of alternative approaches?

Return, for the moment, to the assumption that the history of economics is a disciplined conversation about a different disciplined conversation – namely, economics. Margaret Schabas suggested that the fact that the history of science is a disciplined conversation about science makes the history of economics and the history of science twins, so to speak. But there are a variety of disciplined conversations about other disciplined conversations and there is no mention of these in her work. Might historians of economics be able to draw from these other disciplines as well?

The answer to this question can be approached in two steps. First, I have implicitly assumed throughout this chapter that the history of economics is an aspect of intellectual history, and hence that its guiding rules and conventions are shared with other aspects of intellectual history, among them the history of science. Here I differ somewhat from Schabas. For her, the close affinity of the history of economics and the history of science is derived from her assumption of an underlying affinity of economics with science. In my case, both the history of science and the history of economics, as forms of intellectual history, are disciplined conversations about the history of other disciplined conversations.[5] I see no reason, therefore, for historians of economics to limit their possible contacts outside the economics profession to historians of science. For example, recent studies of American intellectual history by Ross (1991), Hollinger (1985), and others [see the essays collected in Ross (1994a)] provide rich resources for historians of North American economic traditions.

The second step in our answer requires a reconsideration of the assumption that the history of economics, as a disciplined conversation about a different disciplined conversation, is necessarily confined to being an aspect of intellectual history. There are, of course, other forms of disciplined conversation that also take as the object of their study a different disciplined conversation. The fundamental reorientation that is required of the historian of economics in order to see the usefulness of these other disciplines is a shift, from looking at the history of economics as a scholarly conversation about ideas, to looking at it as a conversation about the practices of a scholarly community. The shift from ideas to practices is central to recent efforts to incorporate the methods of the sociology of science into the history of economics (Hands 1994; Sent 1998). Historians of economics may have much to learn from sociologists of science, and also from social historians, who are bringing a similar concern for practice into the literature of intellectual history (an excellent example is Bender 1993).

Conclusion

The shift from ideas to practices brings with it two implications that, in a sense, return us full circle to the questions with which we began this essay. Thus, they provide a appropriate set of concluding thoughts.

First, interest in explaining the practices of scientists have led several historians of science toward economics rather than sociology [Hands (1994) contains a number of examples]. After all, if the activity of a scientific community is viewed as a social practice, then there is no reason in principle why economics cannot provide an explanation. There has been some interest in providing economic explanations of the history of economics – for example, the efficient market hypothesis has been applied to the "life-span" of ideas in economics (Anderson, Levy, and Tollison 1988). But there is much that could be done, and economists would be remiss in losing an opportunity to enter a growing field of study. The ironic twist, for our purposes in this chapter, of course, is that as the historians of economics recognize the separation between their discipline and economics, they may have to become economists in order to explain the social processes of the economics discipline.

Second, Schabas's argument, and my reconstruction of it here, depend on the notion that the scientific disciplines can be distinguished from other forms of human intellectual activity (the humanities, history, etc.). The shift from examining ideas to explaining practices calls this assumption into question, however. Viewed as a practice, all intellectual activity is alike, and furthermore (the real punch line) intellectual activity is no different from any other human action (Latour 1987). If we make the shift from ideas to practices, therefore, science loses its privileged status (which is sometimes called the "postmodern turn"). The ironic twist here is that the success economics may, by explaining its own practices, have called into question the privileged status that economics has sought by identifying itself as a science.

To conclude, Schabas's call for historians of economics to "break away" from the economic discipline and ally themselves with historians of science raises a number of issues, not all of which her own assumptions enable her to resolve. My response has been shaped by the need for an historiographic framework that enables us to distinguish, not between science and nonscience, but between participation in a disciplined conversation (regardless of whether it is scientific, hermeneutic, historical, etc.) and the study of the ideas and practices of a disciplined conversation. Many historians of economic thought resist Schabas's call because they seek to participate in the disciplined conversation of economics – they recognize that a part of any disciplined conversation's work is its continual engagement with, and redefinition of, the conversation's tradition. But Schabas's call is not therefore irrelevant, because alongside the self-reflective element of the economics profession's conversation (which I have called the "history of economic thought") is the historical study of the economic profession's ideas and practices. This historical study, which is similar to the history of science, draws on the methods and resources available for the study of any other disciplined conversation, whether they are historical, sociological, literary, or even economic. Hence historians of economics – in this deliberately, and I hope usefully, stipulative sense – should heed Schabas's call to ally themselves with historians of science, but they should also look around for whatever resources they can find for the study of the practices of disciplined conversations. Should they leave economics departments? Perhaps, but historians of economics may also find in economics itself some of the means by which to enrich their studies.

Section II

Interpreting Frank Knight

3   The therapeutic quality of Frank Knight's *Risk, Uncertainty, and Profit*

When Alvin S. Johnson suggested that Frank H. Knight take up the theory of profit as his dissertation topic in the spring of 1914, Johnson undoubtedly expected that "the keenest student of theory" he had ever taught (Johnson 1952: 227) would be able to clear away the intellectual stubble and chaff that surrounded the existence of profit and provide it with a theoretical basis consistent with marginal productivity theory. Knight's success at fulfilling Johnson's expectations is attested to by the longevity of the dissertation's reputation within economics. As George Stigler said, *RUP* is "still a part of the living literature of general economic theory" (Stigler 1971: ix).[1]

As is usually the case in Knight's writing, however, there is more going on in *RUP* than simply the systematic analysis of the role of profit in the theory of competitive enterprise. Systematic analysis and anti-systematic ruminations on the limitations of analysis are never far apart in Knight's work, and *RUP* is no exception. The theory of profit merely provided a field on which the tug-of-war between these two sides of Knight's thought could be played out. But the theory of profit did not play an entirely passive or inactive role, for it is in his development of the notion of uncertainty, which is the "ground and cause of profit" (Knight 1916a: 9)[2] that Knight ensured that the tug-of-war would have no winner, and that the tension between the two sides of his thought would be sustained throughout the book.

The tension between Knight's systematic and (what I will term his) therapeutic sides has often contributed to the difficulties that interpreters have had in determining exactly what Knight meant in *RUP*. Consider, for example, the trouble interpreters have had with Knight's famous distinction between risk and uncertainty. Although the distinction has generally been connected to the applicability of the probability calculus, it has never been clear exactly what the connection is, nor why it is so important to the theory of profit. The conceptual confusion surrounding attempts to identify clearly Knight's systematic contribution to the theory of uncertainty led two recent revisionist interpreters to go so far as to suggest that there is no connection at all in *RUP* between uncertainty and probability theory – according to Stephen LeRoy and Larry Singell (1987), Knight's distinction is based solely on the existence, or non-existence, of insurance markets.

One way of accounting for the difficulties that interpreters have had in determining what Knight's distinction means has been suggested by George Stigler.

Because Stigler believes that the latter portions of *RUP* lack "substantive structure" (Stigler 1987: 56), he suggests that "any specific interpretation … constitutes an overinterpretation of a text that was simply not completely thought through" (quoted in LeRoy and Singell 1987: 402). If Stigler is correct, no reconstruction of Knight's distinction is possible because the textual evidence is at best incoherent, and, at worst, inconsistent.

Before we accept Stigler's judgment, however, we need to consider one obvious difficulty with the claim that *RUP* was not carefully thought through. That difficulty is, of course, the fact that Knight thought that the book was coherent and carefully thought through. While we must be careful not to make the mistake of attributing logical coherence to Knight's work simply because it was published (see Skinner 1969: 38–43), it certainly seems fair to say that Knight believed the book was coherent and thought that others would be able to understand his argument. Can we provide a reconstruction of *RUP* that shows why Knight thought the book was clearly thought through, even if modern economic theorists do not think it was?

The central thesis of this chapter is that such a reconstruction of *RUP* is possible, but only if one shows how the systematic and therapeutic sides of Knight's thought were constantly intertwined throughout the book. The first task, therefore, is to convince the reader that Knight was as much a therapeutic thinker as he was a systematic one. Once that it completed, we can examine how the tension between the two sides of Knight's thought shaped *RUP*. In order to do that, it will be necessary to begin not with Knight's book itself, but rather with the evolving nature of the debates over social and economic organization that Knight participated in as he wrote, and revised, *RUP*. Then, having established the discursive context within which Knight was writing, we can explore the way in which Knight shaped *RUP* as a therapeutic response to its central debates. Toward that end, we will examine not only Knight's notion of uncertainty, which has attracted so much attention recently (see, e.g. Langlois and Cosgell 1993; and LeRoy and Singell 1987), but also, and more importantly, the general purpose and structure of the book.

Knight's therapeutic orientation

Frank Knight is often identified as a philosophical economist: "Knight," remarked James Buchanan, "is the economist as philosopher, not the economist as scientist" (Buchanan 1968: 426). However, the nature of his philosophical reasoning is often misunderstood. Some interpreters identify Knight's work as philosophical because they believe he built his account of economics and society upon a coherent understanding of the relations among epistemology, ethics, and metaphysics (e.g. Gonce 1972; and McKinney 1967). However, while it is true that certain basic philosophical themes run throughout his work, it is also true that these themes serve less as a foundation upon which he builds than they do as directions toward which he points – over and over again. There is a questioning and ruminating character to Knight's work that is fundamentally different than the philosophical system-building of other philosophically-oriented economists.

In order to distinguish Knight's ruminations on basic questions from the style of systematic reasoning commonly associated with economists (and philosophers), I have found it helpful to borrow a term from Richard Rorty and describe Knight's work as *therapeutic*. Rorty uses this term to distinguish the basic orientation of philosophers such as Nietzsche, Dewey and Wittgenstein from that of philosophical systematizers (Rorty 1979: 357–94). The therapeutic philosophers were not primarily interested in the construction of progressive philosophical research programs, but rather in the edification of the intellectual community. Their purpose was to upset the course of normal philosophical discourse and remind philosophers and anyone else who would listen of the need for humility in the face of the dynamic complexity and novelty of human experience.

To speak of Knight as a therapeutic philosopher of economics is to suggest that his question-oriented ruminations were intended to have a similar disruptive effect upon the course of normal economic discourse. His primary purpose was edification: he wanted to preserve the health of that great conversation we call human society by showing economists their *inability* to encompass the dynamic complexity of human experience within the confines of a single intellectual system and the necessity of accepting the responsibility their intellectual limitations placed upon them. In a comment that tells us as much about Knight as it does about the philosophers he describes, Rorty says, "Edifying philosophers can never end philosophy, but they can help prevent it from attaining the secure path of a science" (Rorty 1979: 372).

The identification of Knight as a therapeutic thinker has a profound effect upon the historiographic perspective required to understand his work. Because Knight's primary purpose was edification, the interpreter cannot rely solely upon the text, but must always attend to the discursive (or rhetorical) context within which he operated in order to understand why he asked particular questions at certain points in time. Indeed, even when Knight is writing as "systematically" as he can, the interpreter cannot ignore the discursive context, because one must understand how his systematic thinking is shaped by his larger therapeutic purpose.

RUP is a case in point. Rational reconstructions of the book's contributions to the development of a system of economic thought encounter obstacles because they inevitably fail to capture the richness and, yes, ambiguity that emerge from the mixture of systematic and therapeutic purposes lying behind it. In order to understand *RUP*, one must move beyond the text to explore the way in which it was shaped by the therapeutic nature of Knight's participation in his discursive context. The main feature of that context is the evolving contemporary debate over the possibility of intelligent control and organization in a liberal democratic society.

Knight's lifelong participation in the debate over social organization and control is generally recognized as one of the distinguishing features of his work (see Buchanan 1968; and Stigler 1987). Standard interpretations of his contribution to the debate often impose a consistency upon his contribution, however, which obscures a great deal of diversity. Failure to observe the diversity of responses within Knight's work emerges from two things. First, guided by the historiographic assumption that the interpreter's chief task is to construct a system out of Knight's work, interpreters seek only for unifying themes. Secondly, because Knight's general position is taken to be anti-positivist and anti-reformist, interpreters look only for themes that re-inforce that general position, and fail to notice the themes that he shared with those who are usually assumed to be his opponents.

For a number of reasons (most of which will be identified in the next section), the failure to observe the diversity of Knight's responses to the debate over the organization and control of American society is particularly damaging to the task of interpreting Knight's early work, including *RUP*. Knight wrote and revised *RUP* between approximately 1915 and 1920, a time during which the American debate over social organization and control, and Knight's participation in that debate, underwent significant change. Only by examining the relation between Knight's text, his therapeutic intentions, and the evolving pattern of discourse with which he was engaged can we understand why Knight said what he did in *RUP* about economic theory and the connection between rationality, uncertainty, and organization at both the individual and social level.

The Evolving Pattern Of American Social Discourse In The Early Twentieth Century

Until the very end of the nineteenth century, discussion of social organization in America largely drew on two traditional themes. One was the language of individualism, expressed in the beliefs that prosperity was largely the result of character and hard work, poverty the result of intemperance and indolence, and good government the result of placing men of trust and integrity in office. The other was the language of antimonopolism (Rodgers 1982: 123); that distrust of privilege and concentrations of wealth deeply rooted in the American consciousness, which found expression around the turn of the century in the journalistic endeavors of the muckrakers, the campaigns of the single taxers, and public reaction to the manipulation of the market by financiers.

After the 1880s, another, somewhat alien, language – that of interdependence and social cohesion – was increasingly intertwined with the two more traditional ones of individualism and antimonopolism (Rodgers 1982: 124). The historical contingencies of America's origin and subsequent development had allowed the nation to use the language of Lockean social contract without recognition of the "dense and complex structure of constraint and obligation" within which that language had originally been set (Hawthorn 1987: 192–3). In the 1880s and 1890s, however, notions of social structure, social obligation and responsibility, and social integration became significant themes in American social thought.

Although its origins in American thought are unclear (see Rodgers 1982: 125–6), the language of social cohesion was reinforced by the emergence of an academic social science nurtured in the tradition of German thought. For reform-minded American graduate students in the social sciences, the historicist and institutionalist orientation of the German historical school provided a compelling approach to the study of human society that seemed more compatible with their desired role as social advocates than the *laissez-faire* orientation of the older American economists (see Church 1974; Furner 1975; Novick 1988; and Ross 1991). The resulting *Methodenstreit* during the 1880s and 1890s is well-known and often the focus of attention for historians of economics. What is less frequently recognized, however, is that the language of social cohesion survived within the discipline of economics despite the eventual "defeat" of the American historical school by marginal productivity theory.

One form in which the language of social integration survived was, of course, its re-emergence as a central organizing theme (albeit with a non-German form of evolutionism) in the work of Thorstein Veblen and the American Institutionalists. Closer to the center of the profession, however, were the large number of econo-mists who entered the discipline during the first or second decades of this century out of concern for issues related to the fragmentation of society, and who then accepted marginal productivity theory without giving up their desire for social reform (included in this group were Alvin Johnson, Allyn Young, and Herbert Davenport, all of whom were associated with Frank Knight early in his life). In fact, the emerging hegemony of marginal productivity theory greatly increased their ability to directly contribute to social reform because it gave the discipline the seal of scientific approval necessary for its practitioners to be considered experts (Church 1974; Ross 1991: 172–204).

The seal of scientific approval that professionalization provided is closely con-nected with the final theme in the evolving pattern of early twentieth-century debate over social organization and control; namely, the language of social effi-ciency and control (Rodgers 1982: 126). Although this theme emerged later than the language of social cohesion–only gaining significant public recognition around 1910 (Rodgers 1982: 126; Bannister 1987: 5; and Ross 1991: 301–470), the two soon became so intertwined that one could not speak of social integration without also being drawn into the dialogue on social control.

The language of social efficiency developed most rapidly in the social sci-ences, where it was connected with the call to objectivity that emerged from the pragmatists' revolt against formalistic philosophy. The call to objectivity involved three interwoven themes (Purcell 1973: 21–4; see also Ross 1991). The first was the term "objectivity" itself, which although variously defined during the period, was increasingly used to describe the replacement of "rationalist" speculation and deductive theorizing ("armchair speculation") with empirical techniques that minimized or eliminated personal judgments. The second attribute was a nomi-nalistic outlook that refused to go beyond the observable particularities of things, in order to avoid the teleological orientation of earlier social thought. Finally, the third attribute was behaviorism (understood broadly) or functionalism – i.e. the assumption that the meaning and importance of an action lie in its practical (and observable) consequences, rather than in its place in a system of logic or morality. Taken together, these themes defined a new methodological approach to the social sciences that was intended to move the study of society beyond moral subjectivity to scientific objectivity. Objectivity, in turn, was expected to provide the basis for a more intelligent organization and control of society than had previously been experienced. In short, social scientists came to believe that classical liberalism (i.e. the languages of individualism and antimonopolism) was hopelessly inadequate for the problems of twentieth-century American life, and that the hopes and aspirations of liberalism had to be completely re-written in the languages of social cohesion and efficiency in order to be realized. As Dennis Smith (1988: 5) said of the Chicago sociologists of the period, American social scientists were primarily concerned with the question, "how could social science be used in order to realize liberal values and goals in modern American society?" Objective social science became the means by which one might simultaneously describe, critique, and reform society.

Risk, Uncertainty, and Profit and the evolving debate over social organization and control

It is now time to return to *RUP* in order to see how Knight constructed it as a therapeutic response to the debate described above. There will be two parts to this reconstructive task. The first part will concentrate on the general purpose of the book in order to show: (1) how the debate over social organization and control provided the circumstances for Knight's writing; (2) that the intended audience for his book was the expanding group of economists and other social scientists, of which Knight considered himself a member, engaged in the process of reformulating the pattern of social discourse in American life; and (3) that Knight's message to that group emphasized both the need for, and limitations of, theoretical reasoning in the process of social reform. The second part will bring in Knight's treatment of uncertainty, in order to show how his understanding of that notion both supported the general purpose of his book and raised a number of paradoxical tensions for it.

Knight's evolving debate with American social science

The first section pointed out that, although Knight's participation in the debate over social control is commonly accepted as a dominant theme throughout all his work, most interpreters consider it to be largely all of one piece and, hence, tend consistently to emphasize the type of classical liberalism Knight's later work is known for. The first section also suggested that such an interpretation was a mistake because the nature of Knight's participation in that debate did change, both as the debate itself evolved and as his own understanding of the implications of the debate for both social theory and social practice grew. One of the periods during which both the debate and Knight's participation in it were changing was the period of five to seven years during which he wrote *RUP*. In order to understand *RUP*, therefore, we need to examine the way it expressed the tension between the themes that brought him into economics, and continued to play a role in his thinking until well into the 1920s, and the themes that emerged as he studied economics and began critically to reflect on the nature of the objectivist program for social science.

One of the most widely recognized aspects of Knight's early work is his critical assessment of the defects of the free enterprise system, summarized most completely in his essay "The Ethics of Competition" (1923a). Many find it paradoxical, if not ironic, that the man who wrote that essay, described by one student as "among the most radical ever written in economics" (Patinkin 1973: 36), was also in no small measure responsible for the resurgence of pro-market sympathies among American economists in the middle of this century.[3] The reason economists find this paradoxical, however, is because they tend to view Knight's work in the early 1920s from the perspective of his *later* work, instead of looking at it from the perspective of his *earlier* work in order to understand the concerns from which it originated. The historiographic perspective that is usually adopted has prevented us from seeing that Knight's early work was largely shaped by a number of rather activist concerns. Judging from a survey of his early work (both published and unpublished), and the little information we have about his career choice (see Dewey 1990) these concerns appear to be the ones that led Knight into economics in the first place. Perhaps more importantly, their prominence in his early work imply that there is a much closer relation between his work and that of the objectivist social scientists with whom he eventually clashed in the 1920s than we have previously allowed.

Although a complete survey of Knight's early work is beyond the scope of this chapter, two issues of central concern to it can be identified. The first was his belief that the competitive mode of social organization was an important contributor to social fragmentation in American society. Knight desired a society in which things would be arranged "so that people will find their lives interesting and will grow into such personalities that they can respect themselves, admire others and enjoy their society, appreciate thought and beauty, and in general look upon creation and call it good" (1919b: 806). However, in the society around him, the exact opposite was often the case. Knight placed part, if not all, of the blame upon the market itself.

> In the existing system, the serpent's tail is always in his mouth; all the inequities of the system aggravate themselves cumulatively around an unbreakable vicious circle. It is supposed to give us a social value scale made of up of individual desires, but in reality the purchasing-power factor in demand ever more overtops the desire or need factor; in the agitator's phrase, the money is placed ahead of the man. In addition, as we have already noticed, the system places a high premium on the corruption of tastes; and this also works cumulatively. And at the same time that the progress of civilization is throwing men closer together and calling ever more insistently for an enlightened social consciousness and conscience, competitive business breeds individualism, narrowness, and selfishness of outlook. …
>
> The highest wants, and in rightly developed men the strongest, are not individual at all, and do not directly depend on material means for their satisfaction. They are the wants for ideal human relations for their own sake. And it is from this point of view that the existing social system makes its worst showing of all. It turns every man's hand against his brother, compels him to

think in the hard, lifeless terms of material means and ends, makes him value things because others cannot have them instead of things that can only be enjoyed in common, gaudy, vulgar, despicable things which waste the precious resources of life instead of the costless treasures of the inner soul, and in general turn his vision and his life downward instead of upward.

(Knight 1920b: 32, 35)

The second concern that Knight brought to his early study of economics was the hope of progress toward a more integrated social order through reform of the basic structures of society. In the essay just quoted, Knight continued with the following paragraph:

From the falsity of the atomistic-individualistic view of human nature and human desires it is an easy inference that any mechanical theory of social organization is subject to very narrow limitations. The most potent agency of social control, even today, in spite of all the obstacles thrown in its way by an antiquated and wooden system of association, is the moral control of the individual's sense of decency and the pressure of the opinions of his fellows. We must therefore assume, as well as hope, that when the shackles of competition are finally broken, and industry based upon the general principles of conscious co-operation in some form, the now seemingly insuperable problems of administrative control will progressively solve themselves through the common recognition of the common good as the only worthy or profitable object of endeavor. The difficulties in the way of realizing a large part of the dream of a moral world so eloquently pictured by saintly idealists like Kropotkin and Tolstoy are, like those which confront a democratic system of industry, more imaginary than real. The first step in any progress toward this grand consummation is to replace our present so-called system, which directs a large part of its energies to the corruption of mankind with some sort of more truly social order under which attention can be directed toward the improvement instead of the degradation of tastes and ideals.

(Knight 1920b: 35–6)

Similar remarks appear repeatedly throughout his essays, book reviews, and public addresses until the latter half of the 1920s. After reading these remarks, it is not surprising that Knight later described his entrance into economics by saying, "When I took up Economics as a career, I thought of it in terms of doing good in the world" (Knight 1939b).

Despite Knight's desire for a social order that would promote social cohesion and support the quest of individuals for better values, his belief that such a world was possible was gradually offset during the first part of his career by three related things. The first was his growing awareness of the uncompromising reality of scarcity. In an early public address to his college class, Knight said that "we are placed in a universe capable of satisfying our every natural want" (Knight 1911: 3). He went on to relate poverty and misery to defects in the present social system for ordering choices. As his study of economics began, however, he began to revise the assumption of plenty underlying his concern for social reform. In a letter to his first wife Minerva, written from Chicago in the summer of 1919, his comment on the social unrest in that city was brief and to the point: "And back of the kind of folks people are is the kind of world it is. … for some to live others must die and for any to live decently most must live very indecently" (Knight, quoted in Dewey 1990).

The second thing that began to offset Knight's desire for social reform was his study of various proposals for reform. He had begun to read reformist literature in his student days (Stigler 1987: 56; Knight 1914), and continued to read widely in the field during the early years of his career (see book reviews from the period such as 1919b). Despite Knight's desire for reform of the contemporary system, he found reformers

> over-sanguine in [their] estimate of the amount of authority which it will be necessary to exercise over individual human nature and of the intrinsic difficulties of the unescapable [sic] problems of social organization, the amount and complexity of the machinery probably requisite for securing any fairly effective direction and co-ordination of human activities under the conditions of modern life.
>
> (Knight 1919a: 228)

Finally, I suspect that Knight's desire for social progress was also tempered by his first experience of objectivist social science at the University of Chicago, during the years 1917 to 1919. The University of Chicago at the time was fast becoming the center of practical and reform-oriented social science in America, and Knight was actively involved in discussions with individuals and groups from across the social sciences.[4] While at Cornell, Knight had locked horns with neo-Hegelian idealists such as philosophers James Creighton and Ernest Albee, while being trained in economics by economists such as Alvin Johnson, Allyn Young, and Herbert Davenport – none of whom were particularly wedded to the objectivist program. He had also gained a healthy dose of scepticism regarding the prospects for statistical method in social science from Walter Wilcox (see Knight's comments in Working 1927: 19). What Knight found at Chicago were social scientists firmly committed to the objectivist program, and intent on applying their new-found knowledge to the task of providing a more intelligent and responsible society. Because this was also the problem that occupied the center of Knight's attention, there was a certain affinity between his goals and those of Chicago social science. However, as he began to explore the objectivist program with its foremost proponents, he became increasingly concerned with the ethical implications of its method. Was not the objectivist program simply another "mechanistic theory of social organization" subject to all of the same objections as the economic theory of pure competition? The eventual result of Knight's ruminations on this question, of course, was the significant series of essays that he published in the early 1920s (Knight 1925a, and the essays collected in Knight 1935a) on various aspects of the relation between the objectivist program and ethics.

The general purpose of Risk, Uncertainty, and Profit

"The present essay," Knight said in the first chapter of the dissertation, "may ... be called a study in pure economic theory with a special view to its theoretical limitations" (Knight 1916a: 6; also see 1921a: 11). According to Knight, economists had become so concerned with the practical application of fundamental economic principles that they had avoided the basic tasks of isolating, coordinating, and defining the conditions under which those principles ideally worked, and contrasting those idealized conditions with the actual conditions of contemporary society (Knight 1916a: 4; for a more complete explication, see Knight 1921a: 3–10). The result, which Knight described as "evil" (Knight 1921a: 10), was that those interested in applying economics to the practical problems of society drew "sweeping and wholly unwarranted conclusions" from principles whose idealizing conditions they did not fully recognize (Knight 1916a: 5; 1921a: 11). The inevitable failure of the practical applications of theoretical economics led many to believe that the theory itself was fundamentally flawed. But this, Knight believed, was also unwarranted: the failure of practical economics did no more discredit to theoretical economics than the failure of perpetual motion schemes did to theoretical mechanics (Knight 1916a: 5–6; 1921a: 10–11; for comments along a similar line from the same time period see Knight 1921b and 1921d). The only difference between the two sciences was the simple fact that the physicists had carefully separated effects and familiarized individuals using their theories with the contrast between their simplifying assumptions and the complexity of actual experience, whereas the economists had not.

Knight's defense of theoretical reasoning, however, was not a defense of the market, for in the limitations of the theory he saw also the limitations for the market itself as a form of social organization. As he said in his preface: "The net result of the inquiry is by no means a defense of the existing order. On the contrary, it is probably to emphasize the inherent defects of free enterprise" (Knight 1921a: xii). Comments on the limitations of the market are scattered throughout *RUP*, appearing most notably in chapter VI, on the "Minor Prerequisites for Perfect Competition" and chapter XII, "Social Aspects of Uncertainty and Profit." The themes of the latter chapter, which was added in the process of revision, will be examined in more detail below.

The primary purpose of Knight's book, therefore, was to draw economists' attention to both the enormous distance between the idealized conditions required by economic theory and the complex reality of actual human experience, and the serious limitations that distance presented to the viability of the market as a form of social organization, in order to help them recognize both the nature and limitations of the contribution their theoretical reasoning could make to social reform. "The 'practical' justification for the study of general economics is a belief in the possibility of improving the quality of human life through changes in the form of organization of want-satisfying activity" (Knight 1921a: xi).

Although *RUP* appears, from the perspective of our own time, to have brought Knight into direct conflict with the method of the objectivist program in social science, it is important to realize that at the time he wrote and revised it he still shared the objectivists' goals and viewed his book as a contribution to their debate on how to proceed with the reform of American society. Thus, *RUP* was not intended as an attack on the objectivist program, as his work during the 1920s increasingly became, but rather as a kind of internal critique, speaking within the broad framework of the languages of social cohesion and efficiency to persuade other social scientists that theoretical reasoning was not "idle speculation," but a necessary part of understanding the inner workings of the liberal democratic, market-based system of the day, the prospects for its reform, and the limitations various reform proposals might encounter.

Uncertainty and the general purpose of *Risk, Uncertainty, and Profit*

One mark of the breadth of Knight's interests in writing *RUP* is the fact that I have not yet needed to refer in a significant way to either the central theoretical topic of the book – i.e. profit – or to the notion of uncertainty which Knight developed to explain it. But, of course, Knight understood the theory of profit to be intimately bound up with his general purpose in writing *RUP*, and, hence, we need to examine the relation between the two. In the process, we will also see how Knight used the notion of uncertainty as a part of his therapeutic purposes in *RUP* and how, at the same time, the notion of uncertainty raised several issues that created tension between his understanding of its role in social organization and his larger purpose in writing the book.

"The problem of profit," Knight said in the first chapter of the dissertation, "*is* in fact this very problem of the divergence of actual business conditions from the theoretical assumptions of perfect competition" (Knight 1916a: 7, italics in original; also see Knight 1921a: 19). Under perfectly competitive conditions, the value of a good would exactly equal its costs and no profit would exist. Only when the conditions of perfect competition were removed would the possibility exist for the value of a good to exceed its costs and, thus, for profit to arise. The fact that profit did exist in business life suggested that actual business conditions departed from the conditions for perfect competition. "Hence, the study of profit … and of the forces and conditions which give rise to it, is the study of the contrast between the ideal situation presupposed in economic theory on the one hand and real economic life on the other" (Knight 1916a: 7; also see 1921a: 19).

The central assumption that produced the conditions of perfect competition, Knight argued, was that of perfect knowledge. Because the absence of perfect knowledge was the essential condition of actual business life, and the existence of profit was the major effect of the change in conditions, the uncertainty that arose from the imperfection of human knowledge was "the ground and cause of profit" (Knight 1916a: 9).

> The general nature of the conclusion may be stated at the [outset]. … It is that perfect competition depends on perfect knowledge. All the essential elements of current industrial society may be present without destroying the ideal

no-profit resultant of competitive forces. The one fatal element is *uncertainty*, the imperfection of the knowledge upon which economic conduct is based.

(Knight 1916a: 9, italics in original)

The suggestion that uncertainty meant simply the imperfection of human knowledge runs into an immediate problem, however, because Knight devoted a considerable amount of space to investigations of probability theory (Knight 1916a, chapter 6; and 1921a, chapter VII) and of the available means by which individuals and businesses could protect themselves against some of the consequences of their imperfect knowledge (Knight 1916a, chapter 8; 1921a, chapters VIII and IX). The assimilation of these "risks" into the market framework through the development of insurance markets and the organizational structure of firms implied that competition could still work perfectly, even in environments characterized by imperfect knowledge, if the consequences of that imperfect knowledge could be translated in some fashion into the cost structure of a firm. But there remained for Knight those uncertainties that could not be assimilated into the market framework. These "true" uncertainties, as Knight often referred to them, gave rise to profit because they could not be accounted for in an enterprise's cost structure and, hence, called forth entrepreneurial activity.[5]

But what did Knight believe prevented true uncertainties from being assimilated into the market? The key to answering that question lies in Knight's recognition of the effect that imperfect knowledge has on people's expectations. "In business as in other departments of life, men *act on what they think*; and here as elsewhere it is necessary constantly and carefully to take account of the undisputed but frequently overlooked truth that men *do not know everything*" (Knight 1916a: 175, italics in original; also see 1921a: 199). Perfect knowledge is directly related to perfect competition for Knight, because he believed the market could only allocate resources efficiently when the expectations of individuals were based upon certain knowledge of the outcomes of all their possible plans. "For perfectly rational behavior it is necessary for each individual to know that he does possess perfect knowledge and that all other individuals are similarly equipped" (Knight 1916a: 175). Uncertainty upset the ideal efficiency of the market because it rendered the expectations of individuals less than perfect. The market's inability to assimilate uncertainties, therefore, had something to do with the individual's ability to form perfect expectations.

It is at this point that Knight pulled one of his most important moves, because he linked his description of the limitations of the individual's ability to form expectations that have some degree of certainty to his theory of the limitations of theoretical reasoning in general (compare chapters I and VII in Knight 1921a). Intelligent action, either on the part of the individual seeking the maximum benefit from his or her choices, or the social inquirer seeking to provide guidance to social choices, requires knowledge of all the potential outcomes of the range of possible actions. In either case, Knight argued, knowledge emerges from the analysis of previous experience through the processes of measurement and classification. Knowledge fails to function as an instrument for intelligent action, however, when there are aspects of our experience that cannot be adequately measured or classified. True uncertainties were to be distinguished, Knight claimed, by the fact that "there is *no valid basis of any kind* for classifying them" (Knight 1921a: 225, italics in original). The presence of these uncertainties significantly reduces the prospects of success for rational action at either the individual or social level. Yet, paradoxically, they open the door for entrepreneurial action at the same time.

Knight's identification of an individual's formation of expectations with theoretical reasoning forces us to modify substantially the claim that his central concern was the operation of the market as a system (i.e. the claim advanced in LeRoy and Singell 1987). Knight's claim that the efficiency of market outcomes depends, at least in part, on the certainty of knowledge implied for him that a systemic analysis of the market could never be entirely divorced from a characterization of the processes by which individual agents reason and form expectations. Knight, therefore, could not accept the "givenness" of expectations, and consistently wove his discussion of the nature of "human knowledge and conduct and the like" (LeRoy and Singell 1987: 402) into his discussion of the market as if they were one and the same – which, for him, they were. Many economists today would consider this interdependence of Knight's analysis of market and individual behavior to be methodologically ambiguous. It is important to realize, however, that out of this ambiguous mixture appeared what was arguably the book's most important theoretical question; i.e. What are the systemic effects of the actions of individuals operating within an environment characterized by uncertainty?

Another way of identifying the importance of Knight's identification of expectation formation with theoretical reasoning is to note that its acceptance would have required economists to recognize the *creativity* of an individual's estimates or subjective judgments. True uncertainty does not leave the individual impotent; rather, it provides the occasion for the individual to draw upon their past experience in a creative fashion in order to form the best and wisest judgment they can. The best way to examine the importance that Knight attached to the treatment of the individual as a creative, purposeful subject is within in the context of his use of probability theory.

Knight's use of probability theory in *Risk, Uncertainty, and Profit*

Most contemporary interpreters of Knight's theory of uncertainty approach it either from the perspective of someone who accepts modern subjective probability theory and wants to consider how Knight's probability theory can be assimilated into it or from the perspective of someone who rejects modern subjective probability theory (probably on Shacklean grounds) and wants to consider how Knight's probability theory differs from it.[6] Neither of these perspectives, however, take adequate notice of Knight's own interests in connection with probability theory. The need to take Knight's own interests into account takes on even more force when one realizes that he gave it a full and careful treatment at a time when most other social scientists either avoided it or were antagonistic to it (see Ménard 1987; and Morgan 1990). It would not be for at least another decade, and in the case of subjective probability theory, at least another three decades, that probability theory would again play as prominent a role in economic analysis as Knight assigned it in *RUP*.

In order to show why Knight made such extensive use of probability theory, I need to connect the comments he made in *RUP* on the relation between knowledge and experience with those he had made on the same topic several years earlier. In a student essay for Professor Ernest Albee, a neo-Hegelian who taught the course on "Empiricism and Rationalism" that Knight took while still a graduate student in philosophy at Cornell, Knight identified clearly the instrumentalist view of knowledge toward which he pointed in *RUP*. The paper, entitled "Causality and Substance," described the central problem of human thought as "that of making experience intelligible, or as intelligible as possible. Knowledge is in and of and for human experience" (Knight 1913: 1). To the extent that the data of experience are unchanging, experience is capable of being completely knowable. It is change that renders the sequence of, or causal relations among, instances in our experience complex and mysterious. Thus, "it is primarily the world of change which furnishes us our intellectual problem" (Knight 1913: 6).

"Causality and Substance" was written in the midst of Knight's battles with the neo-Hegelian idealists who dominated the Cornell philosophy department, and it reflected the nature of that particular debate. *RUP* preserved much of the essay's argument, but recast it in terms of the broader social debate by extending the essay's instrumentalist theme and clarifying more carefully the nature of the intellectual problem change presented. The key problem, Knight argued, is not simply change (see Knight 1921a: 37–8, and chapter V), but whether the sequential relations of instances in our experience are sufficiently stable to allow representation within the context of a deterministic model. Accepting the fact that change rendered much of our experience unstable, and, hence, unknowable within the confines of a strictly deterministic model, Knight then asked if our experience was sufficiently random to allow representation within the context of a probabilistic model. If it was, then the risk of various possible outcomes could still be measured, classified, and known, even though the actual outcome was not known. From the standpoint of intelligent action, there was no real difference between a world of complete determination and a world of complete randomness. In either case, future outcomes are knowable, in the sense that they can be measured and classified. Hence they can be translated into costs today (see Knight 1921a: 212–13). The real problem for critical intelligence lay with those aspects of change that were not completely random; in particular, with changes that were determined by immeasurable things like human intentionality.

> If there is real indeterminateness, and if the ultimate seat of it is in the activities of the human (or perhaps organic) machine, there is in a sense an opening of the door to a conception of freedom in conduct. And when we consider the mystery of the role of consciousness in behavior and the repugnance which is felt by common sense to the epiphenomenal theory, we fell justified in further contending for at least the possibility that "mind" may in some inscrutable way originate action.
>
> (Knight 1921a: 221)

Thus, Knight's claim that one could not ignore the subjective judgments of individuals in the explanation of human action ultimately led him to explain uncertainty in terms of the dynamic indeterminacy those judgments created.

The claim that *RUP* was not intended as an attack on the entire scope of the objectivist program in social science, and the claim that Knight saw the ultimate source of uncertainty in human experience to lie in the creative power of subjective judgments, appear to be incompatible. In fact, they are – but that does not necessarily mean that Knight's book is incoherent. Rather, it simply points back to the therapeutic purpose that lay behind it. Knight set out to convince his fellow social scientists that traditional economic theory was useful and should have a place in the analysis of the workings of the present system; but that its usefulness was limited, like all theoretical reasoning, by its idealizing conditions. At the heart of those conditions lay a problem Knight had already encountered; namely the tension between the need for stability in human experience required for analysis and prediction, and the recognition of human free will demanded by moral philosophy. From the tension between the two emerged the therapeutic richness of *RUP*. But what Knight did not completely see at this point was that his subjectivism and indeterminism placed him squarely at odds with the objectivist program. At the time, he thought he could hold the two in balance; by the early 1920s, he realized that he could no longer identify himself as closely with objectivism (see his letter to Viner 1925e). Eventually, of course, he separated from them almost entirely.

Social aspects of uncertainty

The tension between Knight's general support for the objectivists' reformulation of the languages of American social discourse and the subjectivism inherent in his theory of uncertainty was reflected in another tension that emerged from his reflections on uncertainty. This second tension involved the relation between uncertainty and the prospects for social reform that Knight developed in the last chapter of *RUP*, entitled "Social Aspects of Uncertainty and Profit." This often-overlooked chapter was added during the process of revision and reflected Knight's concern to show more explicitly the connection between his theory of profit and the larger social debate over society's organization and control.

In the last chapter of *RUP*, Knight attempted to assess the significance of his investigations of human conduct in the presence of uncertainty for the reconstruction of society, especially in relation to the prospects for the substitution of public control for the private ownership of industry. Two themes were emphasized. First, Knight argued that the substitution of public for private control would be possible *if* society could overcome the difficulties that he had earlier described as inherent in the relation between owner and manager (in chapter X). Social progress would be furthered if public control could be organized in such as way as to lead managers to "*feel*" that they were working for themselves and were being judged solely on the basis of their capacity to perform the job well; it would be arrested if managers felt like bureaucrats, "doing things for other people." The key to succeeding at this, Knight argued, lay in convincing managers that they were already social functionaries. The manager, Knight said,

> *is really a social functionary now*. Private property is a social institution; society has the unquestionable right to change or abolish it at will, and will maintain the institution only so long as property-owners serve the social interest better than some other form of social agency promises to do. ...
>
> The suggestion that inevitably comes to mind is that a democratic economic order might conceivably appeal as effectively to the same fundamental motives [as those to which private enterprise appeals]. What is necessary is a development of political machinery and of political intelligence in the democracy itself to a point where men in responsible positions would actually feel their tenure secure and dependent only on their success in filling the position well. ... The essential problem is wisely to select such responsible officials and promote them strictly on a basis of what they accomplish, to give them a "free hand" to make or mar their own careers. This is the lesson that must be learned before the democratization of industry will become a practical possibility. If we substitute for business competition, bad as it is, the game of political demagoguery as conventionally played, with rotation in office and "to the victors belong the spoils" as its main principles, the consequences can only be disastrous.
>
> (Knight 1921a: 359–61, italics in original)

The other side of this chapter, however, fits less well with Knight's reformist concerns. Throughout the chapter, he emphasized the ongoing nature of social organization and the resulting adaptation of the existing structures of society to the uncertainties of human experience. Most reform proposals fail, Knight argued, because they do not adequately examine the nature of the present system, and hence do not see where changes would be progressive, and where they would not. The chapter concludes along this cautious line with these words:

> The ultimate difficulties of any arbitrary, artificial, moral, or rational reconstruction of society center around the problem of social continuity. ... The existing order, with the institutions of the private family and private property (in self as well as goods), inheritance and bequest and parental responsibility, affords one way for securing more or less tolerable results in grappling with this problem. They are not ideal, nor even good; but candid consideration of the difficulties of radical transformation, especially in view of our ignorance and disagreement as to what we want, suggests caution and humility in dealing with reconstruction proposals.
>
> (Knight 1921a: 374-5)

Conclusion

The tension that Knight sustains in the final chapter between his desire for social reconstruction and his growing appreciation for the manner in which organizations respond to reconstructive "experiments" in ways that undermine the experiments' goals provides a good conclusion to his book because it brings together the paradoxes that *RUP* contains. Knight intended the book as a contribution to reform-oriented social science; his conclusion was a warning against expecting too much from mere changes in the structure of social organization. He wanted to defend the role of theoretical reasoning in social science; most of his book was concerned to show its limitations. He saw himself participating with the objectivists in the reformulation of American social discourse through the language of social efficiency and control; his uncertainty theory emphasized the subjectivity of human experience and the necessity of wise (as opposed to rational) judgments. He was concerned about the social fragmentation that occurred from the market mode of social organization; his analysis emphasized the way in which rational agents will respond to uncertainty by introducing non-market organizational forms into the market if they are given the freedom to choose. A confused book? Perhaps. A paradoxical book? Certainly. But in its paradoxes lie its therapeutic strength.

4   The Economist and the Entrepreneur

Modernist impulses in *Risk, Uncertainty, and Profit*

> *The culture of modernism springs from the unsettling but liberating experience of uncertainty.*
>
> (Kloppenberg 1998: 82)

> But now, spurred on by its powerful illusion, science is rushing irresistibly to its own limits, where the optimism essential to logic collapses. For the periphery of the circle of science has an infinite number of points, and while it is as yet impossible to tell how the circle could ever be fully measured, the noble, gifted man, even before the mid-course of his life, inevitably reaches that peripheral boundary, where he finds himself staring into the ineffable. If he sees here, to his dismay, how logic twists around itself and finally bites itself in the tail, there dawns a new form of knowledge, tragic knowledge, which needs art as both protection and remedy, if we are to bear it.
>
> (Nietzsche 1993: 74)

Economic theorists generally consider *RUP* a classic statement of the theoretical core of neoclassical economics and a precursor to several of the most important twentieth-century developments in economics (including decision theory, the theory of imperfect competition, and market-failure-based theories of the firm). Beyond that, interpretations diverge significantly. History of economic thought textbooks generally focus on the first half of the book – which George Stigler (1971: ix) identified as "a condensed restatement of the theory of value ... crowded with advances over the existing literature." Recent interpretations, however, have turned attention to the second half of *RUP,* where Knight explains "the crucial importance of uncertainty, and its inevitable consequence, ignorance, in transforming an economic system from a beehive into a conscious social process with error, conflict, innovation, and endless spans and varieties of change" (Stigler 1971: x).

Unfortunately, proponents of these recent interpretations have had a remarkably difficult time defining Knight's notion of uncertainty and agreeing on its effects on the enterprise economy. Recognizing that the notion of uncertainty in *RUP* reflects Knight's concern for the consequences of human action within an open-ended universe in which knowledge is limited (see Boudreaux and Holcombe 1989; Emmett 1989; Fontaine 1999; Foss 1993; and Langlois and Cosgel 1993), interpreters have rejected the traditional interpretation of the risk/uncertainty distinction (based on the measurability of probabilities). Knight scholars remain divided on how best to reconstruct Knightian uncertainty in a manner relevant to contemporary economic theory, however. For example, among recent interpretations, uncertainty is defined variously as (1) the potential for the decision-maker to face multiple subjective probability distributions (Bewley 1989); (2) instances which are uninsurable (LeRoy and Singell 1987); (3) the circumstances which render classification difficult (Langlois and Cosgel 1993); (4) the computational complexity of problems where information is partial (Norman and Shimer 1994); (5) the inverse of the reliability associated with information about a situation (Schmidt 1996); or (6) situations in which neither a priori nor statistical probabilities can be determined (Runde 1988).

The interpretation of *RUP* offered here does not attempt a definitive reconstruction of Knight's notion of uncertainty in terms accessible to contemporary economic theory; in fact, I tend toward the view that the creation of alternative reconstructions is to be encouraged (see Emmett 1997b). Rather, the interpretative perspective taken here examines *RUP* in the light of the historical and cultural movement that we call *modernism*. Yet this interpretation suggests why *RUP* remains unsolved by modern economists – why it is (in the words of one reviewer of this article) "an itch that neoclassicals [and others] just must keep scratching." For the modern economist, bent on pursuing the science of economics to its limits, *RUP* presents a cognitive tragedy: in an open-ended universe, "the essential evil of uncertainty" (Knight 1921a: 347) is the impossibility of complete knowledge. Confronted with the ineffable, and dismayed that our best efforts at rational action and intelligent control are brought to grief, there may perchance dawn in the economist a new form of knowledge – tragic knowledge – that accepts the limits imposed by uncertainty.

Readers will undoubtedly protest at this point that, while the Economist may be a tragic figure in *RUP*, the Entrepreneur certainly is not. Tragic knowledge, after all, requires art as its solace and remedy. Despite Knight's doubts about human cognitive abilities in the face of uncertainty, one senses in *RUP* that the limitations of our knowledge present as much an occasion for responsible action as the frustration of rational expectations, the creation of a game as much as the breakdown of a mechanism, the opportunity for profit as much as an obstacle to economic knowledge. If the Economist in *RUP* is constrained and frustrated by the unsettling experience of uncertainty, then surely the Entrepreneur is liberated.

Knight does not let us off that easily, however. The uncertainty that frustrates the Economist also plagues the Entrepreneur. Provided with the opportunity to take responsibility and create something new (and possibly reap profits in the meantime), the Entrepreneur ends up creating an organization that is fractured by the principal agent problem. Entrepreneurial success depends upon a unified organization responsibly directed by the entrepreneur, but the creation of such an organization requires critical judgment on the part of the entrepreneur regarding the capacities and character of potential managers – characteristics about which the entrepreneur cannot be certain. Like a modernist work of art or literature, in which the quest for a unified aesthetic expression is fragmented by its own quest for unification, in *RUP* the unity of the entrepreneur's creation is fragmented in the process of creation. In the end, Knight finds no more solace in art than in science. Hence, Knight presents us with an *entrepreneurial tragedy* to accompany the cognitive one.

The Economist and the Entrepreneur

The Economist and the Entrepreneur: the former is certainly more familiar to the modern economist than the latter. Knight's method of "analysis and abstraction" – isolating assumptions and constructing a model which specifies the relations between variables, and then examining the implications of changes in key assumptions for one's theoretical conclusions (Knight 1921a: 3, 15–18) – is the defining characteristic of the Economist and a central part of modern economic method. And economists are far more comfortable with Marshall's dictum *natura non facit saltum* [echoed in Knight's remarks about change (ibid.: 141–73)] than with any suggestion of radical discontinuity and subjectivity. If nature makes no sudden leaps, then surely we can come to know its processes. If resources are given and preferences are "enduring and stable" (ibid.: 53), then prediction is possible, and intelligence can guide social policy.

The Entrepreneur and the Economist: Knight's Entrepreneur does not appear frequently in modern economics.[1] After all, how much room can be there for a character who must not only decide how to accomplish a goal efficiently, but also choose which goal to pursue (Knight 1921a: 52, 225), who exercises critical judgment in the face of the radical uncertainty that frustrates economic rationality (ibid.: 211–12, 241–2), and whose business activity looks more like a game than a calculated reconciliation of means with given ends (ibid.: 53–4)? Yet the Entrepreneur's creation – the organization – *is* a prominent feature of contemporary, post-Coasian economics. Under the conditions of uncertainty, economists recognize that some forms of social organization succeed and others fail. The principal agent problem has become central to explaining the evolution of social organization in the context of an open-ended world. And Knight's argument that the existing form of social organization should be evaluated in terms of its costs relative to actual alternatives rather than its distance from the ideal of perfect competition (ibid.: 347–9) is by now a familiar feature of the economics literature.

The Economist and the Entrepreneur: in a larger picture, are not these two characters Knight creates for us representatives of common responses to the problem of modernity? On the one side, we have the cognitive response: the individual who, faced with the loss of certainty, nevertheless reaffirms our quest for knowledge as the only way to face the future. And on the other side, we have the aesthetic response: the individual who sees in the possible discontinuities of the future the opportunity to write a new story, create a new morality, see with a new perspective, or (why not?) make a profit. The two impulses are not usually found in the same work: the entrepreneur is as absent from modernist social science (especially economics) as the economist is from modernist literature. Yet in *RUP* they are both present. In his response to the anxieties of modernity, Knight holds in tension our desire to know and the subjectivity of our knowledge, and offsets our desire to predict in order to control the future with the necessity of voluntary action to create a future. In order to understand the tension that Knight creates and what it implies for his response to the problem of modernity, we need to discuss the cognitive and aesthetic responses more carefully, and look at their presence in *RUP.* Those tasks will occupy our attention in the next two sections of the article.

The Entrepreneur and the Economist: the presence of both modernist impulses in *RUP* provides it with a quality seldom found in other works of twentieth-century social science. In an earlier treatment of *RUP* (Emmett 1989), I identified this quality as *therapeutic* or *edifying* in the sense that Richard Rorty (1979) uses those terms in reference to the work of the Nietzsche, John Dewey, and Martin Heidegger. But if the tragic elements of both the Economist and the Entrepreneur are present in *RUP,* a less optimistic term seems appropriate. Hence, I will borrow the term *agnostic modernism* from Dorothy Ross (1994b: 9) because it carries the implication that Knight is not ultimately committed to either modernist response. The combination of doubt and hope produced by Knight's agnosticism in the face of modernity lends the book its unique quality. Suggesting that *RUP* is characteristic of agnostic modernism also allows me to consider recent arguments regarding Knight's relation to postmodernism (McCloskey 1998; Hands 1996). Rather than identify the pluralist aspects of Knight's work as postmodern moments, I conclude that he was thoroughly modernistic. The agnostic quality of Knight's modernism has attracted postmodernists to his work, however.

Modernism

Historians of economics have recently become familiar with the term *modernism* through the work of D. N. McCloskey (1998, 1994) and others (see Klamer 1993 and the various authors in Lavoie 1991 and Samuels 1990). In the main, "modernist" economics has been identified with the highly formalized, mathematically sophisticated tradition epitomized by the work of Paul Samuelson and Kenneth Arrow or the equally formal but more empirically oriented tradition epitomized by the work of Stigler and Milton Friedman. Despite their differences, both modernist economic traditions share a commitment to the advancement of economics as a scientific enterprise. In keeping with their Enlightenment roots, modernists claim that the ability to identify economics as a science distinguishes it from historical, humanistic, hermeneutic, policy-making, or artistic endeavors. The modernists' methodological trouble, of course, is defining a science which escapes the epistemological traps identified by late-nineteenth- and twentieth-century philosophy of science. Hence the introduction of the term *modernism* within the history of economics has paralleled the call for a postmodern economics in which the quest to distinguish "scientific" economics from other human endeavors is dropped, and a thousand methodological flowers are allowed to bloom.

Among intellectual historians, the term *modernism* has a broader, and often less pejorative, range of meaning than that common to the history of economic thought literature (Ross 1994a). First identified with *fin de siècle* French literary artists, the term has come to refer to various strategies employed across the arts, humanities, and social sciences in response to the problem of modernity. If *modernity* refers to the social order that emerged from the conflux of liberal democratic and nationalistic ideologies, capitalist economic processes, and the authority of science, then the problem of modernity is the uncertainty created within that social order by the unsettling recognition of the subjectivity of knowledge and the necessity of voluntary action (see Hollinger 1994; Kloppenberg 1986; Kolb 1986; and Ross 1994b). Victorian science had promised to reduce the problem of human action (deciding what to do and how to do it) to a problem of knowledge, for which science could provide solutions. As the objective certainty that science promised became elusive, and the old moral verities lost their appeal, modernists were cast adrift, seemingly without a rudder to master the unsettled sea (metaphor from Lippman 1914).

Intellectual historians have identified two major responses to the problem of modernity. The first response, which we have already seen in the "modernist" economics literature, is the reaffirmation of our quest for knowledge as the best means of confronting the modern world's uncertainty. The central characteristics of *cognitive modernism* (Ross 1994b) are captured in David Hollinger's (1994) archetype of the "Knower" (see table 4.1).[2] Whether positivists or progressivists, institutionalists or marginalists, Knowers celebrated a culture organized around (and by) the human cognitive capacity. Despite society's loss of the Victorian era's certainty of science's boundless potential, scholars from Dewey to Friedman, from Charles Beard to Karl Popper, expected to reconstitute the enterprise of liberal society through the steady accumulation of scientific knowledge.[3] When George Lundberg asked, *Can Science Save Us?* (1947), the numerous scholars who populated the growing number of social science departments at colleges and universities across North America and Europe responded with, Nothing is certain, but science is the best hope we have.

The quest for more scientific knowledge is not the only modernist response to the uncertainty of modern life, however. Ask literary scholars or philosophers for directions to their modernist literature, and you are likely to be pointed toward the

Table 4.1

The Knower	The Artificer
Finding	Making
Referential	Generative
Demystifying	Myth-constructing
Authenticating	Contriving
Interdependent	Self-sufficient
Intersubjective	Intrasubjective
Suspicious of moral commitments	Makes its own morality
Uniformitarian	Discontinuity-affirming

Source: (Hollinger 1994: 30)

work of Nietzsche, Eliot, Kafka, Sartre, Joyce, Dostoevsky, Bergson, the James brothers, Yeats, or Kierkegaard. *Aesthetic modernism,* as Ross (1994b) designates it, rebelled against the modern world created by the conflux of the economic forces of capitalism, the ideological attraction of liberalism and nationalism, and the intellectual power of science. Rather than depend on our ability to know, aesthetic modernists looked to creative artists, who acted in the face of the radical discontinuities and uncertainty of modern life by writing their own myths, creating their own morality, or painting their own perspectives on the canvas of life. Aesthetic modernism has been a common modernist theme in the humanities and arts (see Kolb 1986, and Singal 1991), and occasionally appears in the human sciences (see Hughes 1961 and Kloppenberg 1986). Hollinger identifies the "Artificer" as the archetype for the aesthetic response (see table 4.1) – echoing Oscar Wilde's remark that "The first duty of life is to be as artificial as possible" (Wilde 1969: 433).

These polar responses to the fundamental problem of modernity are not complete opposites, of course. Cognitive modernists frequently tell us that only more knowledge will enable us to break from the confines of tradition and history, to create afresh, to boldly go where no-one has gone before. And creative artists who seek to express their own perspective end up creating art which only those with expertise in the arts can appreciate ("art for art's sake" provides an aesthetic parallel to the formalism of modernist economics – see Klamer 1993).

Underlying both responses is a common commitment to create unity in the presence of the fragmenting forces of modernity. Cognitive modernism depends upon the universal, and hence impersonal, appeal of scientific knowledge to combat fragmentation (reread the introduction to Friedman's [1953] methodological essay – there is the Knower's central appeal) Aesthetic modernism, on the other hand, embraces the personal, expecting that a unitary self can be created and sustained (Taylor 1989). Thus, despite the differences between cognitive and aesthetic modernism, the Knower and the Artificer provide important reference points for modernism because "so many ... define the dilemmas and opportunities of modern culture so extensively in the terms of these two personae" (Hollinger 1994: 36).

Modernist impulses in *Risk, Uncertainty, and Profit*

The modernist archetypes of the Knower and the Artificer appear in *RUP* in the personae of the Economist and the Entrepreneur (see Table 4.2). We will begin our investigation of *RUP's* modernist impulses with a look at the Economist.

The Economist as Knower

"Knowing" pervades *RUP.* Consider, as a starting point, the justification Knight provides in his preface for undertaking a theoretical study such as his own:

> The "practical" justification for the study of general economics is a belief in the possibility of improving the quality of human life through changes in the form of organization of want-satisfying activity. More specifically,

Table 4.2

The Economist	The Entrepreneur
Abstracting and analyzing	Producing
Predictive	Generative
Demystifying	Myth-constructing
Mechanism	Game
Interdependent	Responsible direction
Market exchange	Internal organization
Intersubjective	Intrasubjective
De gustibus non est disputandum	Exercise critical judgment
Natura non facit saltum	Discontinuity-affirming

most projects of social betterment involve the substitution of some more con-sciously social or political form of control for private property and individual freedom of contract. The assumption underlying such studies as the present is that changes of this character will offer greater prospect of producing real improvement if they are carried out in the light of a clear understanding of the nature and tendencies of the system which it is proposed to modify or dis-place. The essay [*RUP*], therefore, endeavors to isolate and define the essen-tial characteristics of free enterprise as a system or method of securing and directing cooperative effort in a social group. As a necessary condition of success in this endeavor it is assumed that the description and explanation of phenomena must be radically separated from all questions of defense or criticism of the system under examination.

(Knight 1921a: xi-xii).

While Knight goes on to say that the "net result" of his study "is probably to emphasize the inherent defects of free enterprise" (Knight 1921a: xii), the impor-tant point here is threefold: knowledge is essential to discussions of social organi-zation and betterment; science provides the key to unlocking that knowledge; and science and social criticism are separable activities.

The isolation and definition of "the essential characteristics of free enterprise as a system" proceeds, as Knight shows in chapter 1, according to the rules and conven-tions of static analysis, which are integral to science. "The method of economics is simply that of any field of inquiry where analysis is in any degree applicable. ... It is the scientific method" (ibid.: 8). Later, he explains further what he means:

The aim of science is to predict the future for the purpose of making our con-duct intelligent [Knight cites Dewey at this point]. Intelligence predicts ... through analysis, by isolating the different forces or tendencies in a situation and studying the character and effects of each separately. Static method and reasoning are therefore coextensive. ... *Thought,* in the scientific sense, and *analysis,* are the *same thing.*

(Knight 1921a: 16–17)

The Economist's contribution to public discussion about social organization, therefore, is based on the scientific status of economic knowledge. "A sharp and clear conception" of economic knowledge, Knight says in the preface, is necessary to determine what can reasonably be expected of a form of economic organization and whether any social reform "offers sufficient chance for improvement to justify experimentation" (Knight 1921a: xii; see also 9–16). Social criticism, on the other hand, is closer in form to aesthetics (see the conclusion of Knight 1922).

The important role that the Economist as Knower plays in *RUP* is also evident in the structure of Knight's argument. In the first half of *RUP* – Knight's treatment of the theory of perfect competition – the Economist is fully in control. Economic agents always make choices that maximize their welfare, and economic theorists are able to isolate, abstract, and analyze the resulting patterns of exchange correctly *(homo economicus* and the Economist are, after all, merely the Knower in different guises). Perfect knowledge, which Knight repeatedly reminds us is the source of social efficiency, is ensured by the central feature of the world of perfect competition – the stability of all its underlying conditions: "We have, then, our dogma which is the presupposition of knowledge ... : that the world is made up of *things,* which, *under the same circumstances*, always *behave in the same way*" (Knight 1921a: 204; emphasis in original). Stability is the key to both perfect individual choice and perfect competition because it enables the economic agent and the Economist to know the eventual outcomes of the entire range of possible actions (see *RUP* chapters 1 and 7). The efficiency of perfect competition simply reinforces the point – the Economist as Knower is essential to society.

Of course, that is only half the book, but Knight's next step is a continuation of the process of analysis described above as the scientific method: remove a key assumption and analyze its effects. The Economist still appears to be in control, if only for the moment. Knight begins chapter 7 by indicating that he will remove the assumption of perfect knowledge on the part of individual economic agents.[4] As we have seen, however, knowledge depends upon stability, and a significant amount of space in the rest of the book is devoted to a discussion of change and the uncertainty it may create. Knowledge flounders on the uncertainty created by the subjectivity of our responses to change: "The essence of the situation is action according to *opinion*," based on partial knowledge (Knight 1921a: 199). For the Economist, the link Knight forged in the first half of *RUP* between the assumption of perfect knowledge and the Economist's theoretical knowledge now becomes a constraining chain. Instability renders knowledge imperfect: individual agents' opinions and beliefs are open to error and incompleteness, and economic theory is similarly incomplete and susceptible to error. Both the economic agent and the Economist are left exposed to the unsettling experience of uncertainty.

Understandably distressed by Knight's suggestion that the quest for knowledge may not be able to solve modernity's problem, the Economist nevertheless musters the strength for one last major speech (chapters. 7 and 8). The reassurance offered in the speech comes from the separation of risk from uncertainty. Knight's distinction between risk and uncertainty has occasioned many interpretations, of course, but here we want to focus on how the distinction relates to the Economist as Knower.

In order to do that, we will reorganize Knight's argument slightly and compare the conditions present in a risky universe with those in a certain universe (the assumptions of perfect competition). This approach is opposed to the conventional attempt to distinguish risk from the conditions present in an uncertain universe.

In the deterministic world of perfect competition, stability allows the classification of instances and the construction of laws that regulate the relations among instances. Remove that stability, and the cognitive and predictive abilities of economic agents and the Economist are frustrated. These are, of course, the conditions that Knight sets for uncertainty. But suppose we take instability to the extreme and ask what conditions would be in a universe completely opposite to the stable, deterministic ideal of perfect competition. What would happen in a random universe? Is not the opposite of a deterministic world one in which everything happens according to chance? What hope would the Economist have there?

The Economist's final speech surprises us with an answer to these questions which provides a comforting thought for Knowers: the Knower can be as much at home in a random universe as in the deterministic universe of perfect competition. Randomness obviously prevents us from knowing what outcome will occur, but it does not prevent us from knowing the probability of alternative outcomes. Stability returns, not in the form of deterministic laws, but in the laws of probability analysis which enable us to group or consolidate instances and hence predict.[5] From the standpoint of intelligent action, there is no real difference between deterministic and random worlds (Knight 1921a: 219–20). In either case, future outcomes are knowable in some form. Or, to put it in economic terms, because insurance enables the consolidation of random instances and the conversion of all potential values into costs, a random universe is as profitless as a deterministic one. Even in a random world, then, the Economist as Knower is essential.

Nevertheless, the interlude provided by the Economist's speech offering the comfort of insurance against risk rather than the instability of uncertainty is like a cool drink offered to a prisoner chained in the sun. Eventually, the heat returns – and with a vengeance. Human action, Knight tells us, is neither determinate nor random. The uncertainty created by the dilemmas and contradictions of subjective knowledge and voluntary action in an open-ended universe means that neither scientific nor probability analysis will provide the knowledge of individual action or social consequences that the Economist craves:

> If there is real indeterminateness, and if the ultimate seat of it is in the activities of the human (or perhaps organic) machine, there is in a sense an opening of the door to a conception of freedom in conduct. And when we consider the mystery of the role of consciousness in behavior and the repugnance which is felt by common sense to the epiphenomenal theory, we feel justified in further contending for at least the possibility that "mind" may in some inscrutable way originate action.
>
> (Knight 1921a: 221)

The Economist as Knower loses importance in an open-ended universe, for two reasons. First, because instability renders prediction impotent, individuals must act on the basis of their best guess or estimate of what will happen. Although estimates may be expressed in probabilistic language, the process of judgment or intuition behind them bears little resemblance to the method of scientific analysis Knight described in the first chapter of *RUP* (Knight 1921a: 210–11, 223–7).[6] *Thought,* in the scientific sense, and *common sense* are two different things.

Second, the Economist's importance in the modern world is reduced because uncertainty changes the nature of the problem of human action. Economic reasoning is instrumental, but in a changing world, the decision about what goal to pursue may be as important as the decision about how to accomplish it. "With uncertainty present, doing things, the actual execution of activity, becomes in a real sense a secondary part of life; the primary problem or function is deciding what to do and how to do it" (Knight 1921a: 268). The problem of human action shifts from instrumental rationality to critical judgment, from efficiency to evaluation. The uncertainty created by change leaves the character of our future self open. We become free to experiment and explore various goals and values. What we want, Knight says at one point, "is not so much to get things that [we] want as it is to have interesting experiences" (ibid.: 53–4; see also Knight 1922).

With the introduction of true uncertainty, then, the Economist loses control and is forced to admit that the quest for knowledge through science cannot solve the problem of modernity:

> It is a world of change in which we live, and a world of uncertainty. We live only by knowing *something* about the future; while the problems of life, or of conduct at least, arise from the fact that we know so little
>
> (Knight 1921a: 199).

But I would be remiss to suggest that Knight entirely abandons the cognitive response to modernity. The role the Economist plays in *RUP* is important to Knight because it holds out the hope of unified knowledge untouched by the fragmentaton of modern life. Regardless of the severity of its limitations, within the realm created by its boundaries, scientific economics provides knowledge which can be depended upon. Separating that realm from the uncertainty of reality becomes the first scientific task:[7] "It is imperative that the contrast between these simplified assumptions and the complex facts of life be made as conspicuous and as familiar as has been done in mechanics" (Knight 1921a: 11). And Knight holds out the hope that the separation of science from life required for a unified body of scientific knowledge may provide at least a means for reducing the uncertainties of life (see Knight 1921a: 313). Because the tendencies isolated for study in the idealized world of perfect competition are present to some degree in the midst of the complexities of actual human action, studying economics is not a worthless task:

> The makers and users of economic analysis have in general still to be made to see that deductions from theory are necessary, not because literally true – that

in the strict sense they are useful *because not* literally true – but only if they bear a certain relation to literal truth and if all who work with them constantly bear in mind what that relation is.

(Knight 1921a: 14–15)

Assuming the mantle of the Economist for a moment, Knight argues that even though uncertainty reduces its predictive power, economic knowledge can take us a long way toward understanding the world we live in. To say that the problem of human action in an uncertain world requires more than knowledge is not to deny that the latter has a significant role to play in the problem's solution.

The Entrepreneur as Artificer

Despite Knight's defense of the Economist, the problem of human action in the modern world is larger than the problem of knowledge, and the cognitive response to the uncertainties of modernity is inadequate. "Living is an art," Knight (1933c, 4; originally written in 1925) tells students in the text he wrote shortly after *RUP*, "and art is more than a matter of scientific technique, and the richness and value of life are largely bound up in the 'more'". Knight's discussion of the boundaries and limits of human cognitive capabilities in the face of uncertainty, therefore, serves to make room for his introduction of the second character in *RUP*: the Entrepreneur.

The Entrepreneur's entrance occurs in chapter 9, immediately prior to the following passage:

When uncertainty is present and the task of deciding what to do and how to do it takes the ascendancy over that of execution, the internal organization of the productive groups is no longer a matter of indifference or a mechanical detail.

(Knight 1921a: 268)

Initially, the Entrepreneur's activity shares a close resemblance to the Economist's: the Entrepreneur forecasts consumer preferences and directs the production of goods that will satisfy those preferences. Both of these appear to be functions with which the Economist would also be comfortable. The differences between the two characters, however, soon become evident.

"The essence of enterprise is the specialization of the function of *responsible direction* of economic life, the neglected feature of which is the inseparability of these *two* elements, *responsibility* and *control*" (Knight 1921a: 271). In the presence of uncertainty, production is undertaken in anticipation of future consumer wants. Because resources are committed to production which may not be purchased, someone has to take responsibility for the liability. In exchange for assuming that responsibility, the Entrepreneur assumes control of the productive process and receives whatever profit is to be made.

All of this is familiar, of course, but Knight takes the familiar and reveals its underlying form in new perspective. Responsible direction transforms the enterpriser from *homo economicus,* rationally calculating the efficient balance of costs and values, into the Entrepreneur, a creative person whose generative powers call into being an entity which is a reflection of the Entrepreneur's own self. By assuming responsibility, the Entrepreneur decides what is worth doing and commits resources in light of that decision. In taking control, the Entrepreneur exercises critical judgment regarding the capacities and characters of the other people involved in the productive process. Responsible direction and the creation of an internal organization, therefore, are aesthetic (rather than cognitive) actions.

Unfortunately, perhaps, the Entrepreneur as Artificer is not allowed to bask in the limelight of center stage for very long (or perhaps there is simply not much to say about aesthetic expression in a monograph intended for economists?). By the beginning of chapter 10, uncertainty has begun to constrain the Entrepreneur in the same way it affects the Economist. Because the implications of uncertainty are most evident on the "control" side of the Entrepreneur's activities, we will start there.

Entrepreneurial success inevitably leads to the creation of a production process large enough to require supervision beyond that which the Entrepreneur can provide. The hiring of managers, however, confronts the Entrepreneur with a new problem: there is no way of knowing (in the scientific sense used earlier in *RUP)* who will make a good manager, and, to make matters worse, managers often assume a portion of the entrepreneurial function – which is by definition (for Knight) not subject to analysis. The Entrepreneur, therefore, must judge the capacities and character of potential managers and form an opinion upon which a hiring decision can be made (Knight 1921a: 291–4). Judgments and opinions can be in error, and hence entrepreneurial success is endangered.

> Under organized dealings with our environment, attention and interest shift from the errors in men's opinions of things to the errors in their opinions of men. Organized control of nature in a real sense depends less on the possibility of knowing nature than it does on the possibility of knowing the accuracy of other men's knowledge of nature, and their powers of using that knowledge.
>
> (Knight 1921a: 292–3)

Of course, there is a way around this problem: the Entrepreneur could hire someone who has a proven record of success as a manager. The higher salary paid to an experienced manager should be recoverable in increased sales and productive efficiency. Yet this solution, attractive as it is, ultimately brings with it the undoing of the Entrepreneur.

The capacity to convert good judgment into a salary suggests two things. First, it allows the reentrance of the Knower into the problem of social organization, this time in the form of the manager (chapter 10 is subtitled "The Salaried Manager"). If good judgment can be taught, if it is something one can learn, then it can be analyzed and others can acquire it. If it can be acquired in the market, then it becomes a cost, and profit disappears. Like risk, then, perhaps uncertainty also can be consolidated through the creation of an organization (Knight links risk and uncertainty in this way throughout the last several chapters). But when aesthetic expression through the creation of a productive process falls into the hands of managers, the creative act becomes mechanical, routinized, and a product of instrumental reasoning. (Can you hear the Economist laughing offstage?)

Second, the existence of the highly salaried manager calls into question the Entrepreneur's own capacity. What is it that makes the Entrepreneur successful? If it is continued good judgment, is the Entrepreneur's return not a form of wages or rent? If entrepreneurial success is merely the assumption of financial responsibility, is the Entrepreneur's income not a form of interest (see Chapters 10 and 11)? Can the Entrepreneur take any credit for profit, or is it sheer luck?

> Profit arises out of the inherent, absolute unpredictability of things, out of the sheer brute fact that the results of human activity cannot be anticipated. ... The receipt of profit in a particular case may be argued to be the result of superior judgment. But it is judgment of judgment, especially one's own judgment, and in an individual case there is no way of telling good judgment from good luck, and a succession of cases sufficient to evaluate the judgment or determine its probable value transforms the profit into a wage.
>
> (Knight 1921a: 311)

In the end, then, the Entrepreneur is no better off than the Economist. Success cannot be attributed to any action on the Entrepreneur's part, and continued success converts the Entrepreneur into a salaried manager. The aesthetic response to modernity, therefore, fares no better against uncertainty than the cognitive response. What it leaves behind is an organization, not an aesthetic creation.[8]

The Economist and the Entrepreneur? Agnostic modernism in *Risk, Uncertainty, and Profit*

The presence of both the Economist and the Entrepreneur provides *RUP* with a quality that is unique among the major texts of modernist economics. On the one side, we have Knight's defense of the Economist as Knower within the boundaries of theoretical economics. On the other side, we have Knight's presentation of the Entrepreneur, the creative, generative individual willing to assume responsibility in expectation of profit. Unfortunately for the Economist, Knight's defense simultaneously raises grave doubts about the attempt to depend on our quest for knowledge as a solution to the problem of modernity. Yet the Entrepreneur fares no better. The Entrepreneur's creation becomes an organization: "The typical form of business unit in the world today is the modern corporation" (Knight 1921a: 291). Neither the Economist nor the Entrepreneur can produce unity in the midst of uncertainty.

Cognitive doubt and the hope for better knowledge; the joy of aesthetic expression and the anxiety of a fragmented creation. If neither modernist response is adequate, what other option remains?

Knight's inability to affirm either modernist impulse completely has led some recent commentators to suggest that his work is a precursor to postmodernism.

The lack of commitment to scientific economics, the pluralistic vision of human action (see Hammond 1991; Hands 1996; and Kasper 1993), the introduction of the Entrepreneur – are these not all postmodern moments in Knight's work? If he is not a convinced modernist, is Knight a postmodernist?

In the economics literature, the postmodern turn is often portrayed as a rejection of the modernist attempt to construct a scientific economics separate from other human endeavors, and as an embrace of what economics (even as a science) shares with other human activities, particularly artistic creation. Defining postmodernism in opposition to modernism, however, belies the connection between postmodernism and aesthetic modernism which is suggested by this description of the postmodern turn. If postmodernism is "the aesthetic metacritique of 'truth,' wherein 'the work of art,' or 'text,' or 'language' is seen as establishing the grounds for truth's possibility" (Megill 1985: 33), what is the difference between it and aesthetic modernism?

Allan Megill's (1985) portrayal of postmodernism can help us here. Rather than seeing postmodernism as a complete rejection of modernism, perhaps it is better to see it as a different form of aesthetic response to the crisis of modernity. As I suggested earlier, aesthetic modernists found in the uncertainty of modern life the freedom to create a unitary self in the midst of social fragmentation and alienation. Megill argues that postmodernism shares with aesthetic modernism its concerns about the impact of subjective knowledge and alienation from the social order of modernity, and its aesthetic response. In terms we have been using throughout this article, "the parts of modernism against which postmodernism is the most sharply defined would seem to have less to do with the Artificer than with the Knower" (Hollinger 1994: 45). Where aesthetic modernism defined itself (in part) in opposition to scientific knowledge and sought an aesthetic "balance of crisis and restraint" (Megill 1985: 324) in the face of the unsettling experience of uncertainty, however, postmodernism defies any attempt to separate scientific knowledge from other human endeavors and seeks no balance between fragmentation and the desire for order. The postmodernist has given up the struggle against uncertainty – neither science nor art can provide a unified vision by which to live – and confronts it instead with irony. Quoting Wilde, Megill identifies the ironic position taken in the postmodern turn as "an indecision about the meanings or relations of things … matched with a willingness to live with uncertainty, to tolerate, and, in some cases, to welcome a world seen as random and multiple, even, at times, absurd" (Megill 1985: 322). The dawn of tragic knowledge becomes the occasion for celebration, at which art may be asked, not for solace, but to serve as master of ceremonies.

Three things are striking about this description of the difference between aesthetic modernism and postmodernism in relation to Knight's work. First, unlike the postmodernist, Knight makes every effort to separate science from art. The balance that Knight sustains between knowledge and judgment, or freedom and organization, is part of the aesthetic modernism he attempts to introduce into the cognitivist conversation of economists. The balance depends upon the maintenance of the gulf between science and art, however: only if it is present can there be hope for unity in the midst of the fragmentation of modern life. For Knight, the dawn of tragic knowledge needs art as its protection and remedy if we are to bear the unsettling experience. Unfortunately, the entrepreneurial tragedy undermines art's protection and suggests (at least to a postmodernist) that there may be no point to the separation, but for Knight the effort must still be made.

Second, Knight has not given up on the struggle against uncertainty. The loss of certainty *is* the modern problem, and the struggle to overcome it dominates *RUP.* The Economist's and the Entrepreneur's best efforts will ultimately turn to naught, of course, but the effort is still worthwhile. Our knowledge is fragmented, but if we isolate and analyze each piece, perhaps we can give everything its proper place (with due respect for its limitations, of course). For every entrepreneurial dream that becomes an institution, a new opportunity may be created. Yet, at every turn, for every response, uncertainty remains: "We have examined this dogma and been forced to the conclusion that whatever we find it pleasant to assume for philosophic purposes, the logic of our *conduct* assumes real indeterminateness, real change, discontinuity" (Knight 1921a: 314).

Finally, there is no hint of irony in Knight's response to the problem of modernity. His introduction of aesthetic modernism is not an ironic turn, but a serious effort to force the Economist to recognize that the problem of human action in the modern world cannot be reduced to a scientific exercise. *We* may see the parallel failure of the Entrepreneur as ironic, but for Knight the fragmented result of both the Economist's and the Entrepreneur's best efforts is cause for lamentation. Unable to return to a world of certainty, yet unwilling to despair in the face of uncertainty, Knight cannot escape his struggle with uncertainty. And yet, he perseveres.

The balance of hope and anxiety, doubt and perseverance found in *RUP* suggests a connection between Knight's work and the work of several scholars (chiefly William James, Sigmund Freud, and Max Weber) who are described by Ross (1994b: 9) as agnostic modernists. In a manner similar to Knight's, these social scientists and philosophers introduce elements of aesthetic modernism into traditions that were otherwise exemplars of cognitive modernism (see Hughes 1961; Kloppenberg 1986; and Rieff 1961). Their "balanced suspension [of] the provisional order and the inherent disorder of modern life" (Ross 1994b: 11), and critical engagement with the cognitive modernism that dominated their respective disciplines, marks their agnosticism. Unwilling to reduce the problem of modernity to the quest for knowledge, yet unable to accept completely the aesthete's joyful rejection of cognitivism, the agnostics remain modernists, but without options. Science and art, the Knower and the Artificer, the Economist and the Entrepreneur: the agnostics still use modernist oppositions in their response to the dilemmas and contradictions of uncertainty. Yet they cannot bring themselves to affirm either option fully. Tragic knowledge needs art as its protection and remedy, but somehow art provides little consolation for the agnostic modernist – the dual tragedies of the Economist and the Entrepreneur, the Knower and the Artificer. In the end it is the "gift of [their] 'negative capability,' the ability to hold contrary beliefs, and to give them artistic expression" (Joravsky 1994: 127) which distinguishes their work. The "negative capability" of Knight's agnostic modernism is also the gift which gives *RUP* its unique and enduring place in modernist economics.

5 Frank Knight's dissent from Progressive social science

Dissent is more than disagreement

Does dissent mean anything other than disagreement with a dominant paradigm of scientific discourse? Including Frank Knight in the roster of dissenting economists must assume that it does. To see why, consider the following.

Knight wrote at a time (the interwar period) when American economic thought was not dominated by one paradigm. Instead, it was characterized by the conflux of several methods and theories. Marginalism occupied an important position, but not until the end of the interwar period did neoclassical economics begin to dominate in America.

Second, the rise of neoclassical economics during the interwar period is, in no small part, directly attributable to Knight. In fact, many consider Knight the quintessential American twentieth-century neoclassical economist. *RUP* defined neoclassical economics and ensured its acceptance. His subsequent articles clarified some of the most difficult problem areas in economics, especially cost theory (Knight 1921c), the notion of social cost in welfare theory (Knight 1924b), and capital theory (Knight 1933b, 1934a, 1935d, and 1936b). For these contributions, Knight was awarded the Francis A. Walker medal by the American Economic Association in 1957.

But perhaps more important, as a professor at the University of Chicago from 1928 until the 1950s, Knight occupied a unique position among American economists. As "the dominant intellectual influence" (American Economic Association 1973: 1048; also see Patinkin 1973) in the Economics Department at Chicago, which was "the intellectual center of American academic life, especially in the ... social sciences" (Purcell 1973: 3; also see Bulmer 1984: 211–14), Knight defined what graduate schools in economics taught. The Chicago School, which emerged during Knight's tenure at the University of Chicago, has played an important role in North American economics ever since (Reder 1982; Samuels 1976).

Third, Knight was an economist who wrote extensively about philosophical issues – especially the relation between economics and ethics (Knight 1922 and 1923a), economic methodology (Knight 1924a and 1940a), and the dilemmas of liberalism (Knight 1947a, 1947b, 1948, 1951c and 1960a). Contemporary economists often consider this work ancillary to his scientific contributions. LeRoy and Singell

(1987: 402) complain about having to wade through "extended Austrian-style disquisitions on the foundations of human knowledge and conduct and the like" in *RUP*, but Knight regarded this as part of his work as a social scientist. At the root of his work lies the question of what it means to be a social scientist.

For Knight, social inquiry was not science, but an art involving the application of critical judgment. He confronted an ideology giving unique authority to science and appointing social scientists as the guardians of public discourse about social problems. In dissenting from this ideology, Knight challenged the authority of science within social inquiry and the public role of the social scientist. To understand his dissent, therefore, we have to approach it from the standpoint of his disaffection with giving social science a special social status. If we focus only on his agreement or disagreement with economic theory we shall miss Knight's dissent.

A paradigmatic case of dissent – eighteenth-century English dissent[1]

Before turning to examine Knight's dissent from the dominant ideological framework of his time, a better understanding of the notion of dissent used here can be gained by looking at what has come to be the paradigmatic example of dissent, namely English dissent during the eighteenth century. The eighteenth-century English Dissenters found themselves walled in by a social and political ideology, grounded in the authority of Trinitarian doctrine, which legitimated the dominant institutions of public life (Church, King, and Parliament), and circumscribed the boundaries of acceptable public discourse. The Dissenters' problem was to find an intellectual strategy by which the hegemony of that ideology could be cracked.

> Doctrinally, the problem for the disaffected within a Christian-monarchical polity was precisely that of rejecting Trinitarian orthodoxy, the intellectual underpinning of Church, King, and Parliament. It could not be ignored or disregarded; the difficulty was to find an intellectual strategy which would permit escape from a political theology whose theoretical power and widespread reception walled in the dissident.
>
> (Clark 1985: 277)

In order to create space in the realm of public discourse for themselves, the Dissenters had to break down the authoritative, ideological position that Trinitarian doctrine held in English social thought. To do this, the Dissenters developed a twofold attack. First, they attacked the Trinitarian foundation of Church doctrine, attempting to weaken that doctrine's role within the Church (for example, the Feathers Tavern Petition demanded that Anglican clergy no longer be required to subscribe to the Thirty Nine Articles). Second, the Dissenters attacked the established position of the Church in English society, attempting to weaken the political power the Church of England wielded (see Clark 1985: 258–76).

> The radical critique was aimed mostly against what society saw as its fundamental political ideology: Trinitarian Christianity, as interpreted by the

Church of England. Consequently, the main impetus of attack was against the Church's established status, and against its official commitment to the key articles of its creed.

(Clark 1985: 278)

Drawing together my observations about Knight and English Dissent, we can say that dissent needs to be located, not in the context of economic discourse, but rather in the general intellectual framework where social science discourse is set. In that context, dissent emerges from disaffection with the underlying social and political ideology. The dissenter searches for an intellectual strategy that can successfully confront an ideology that legitimates certain social institutions, circumscribes the boundaries of social discourse, and elevates certain groups to the status of guardians of that social discourse. The social and political power of the dominant ideology, I shall argue, comes from widespread acceptance of its response to what society perceives as the fundamental social question.

Knight's dissent, therefore, must be located within an ideological context. He sought to break the boundaries of acceptable social discourse, and he attacked the social and political status certain institutions and groups had achieved because of that ideology. Underlying our analysis of Knight's dissent will be recognition of the fact that the power of the dissenter's voice as dissent, and not just disagreement, lies in the extent to which the dissenter engages the dominant ideology at its deepest level. Only when dissent challenges the widely accepted solutions to the most fundamental problems of society will the dissenter's voice be understood as a significant threat to dominant social and political power.

The orthodoxy of Progressive social science

To understand Knight as a dissenter is to see him disaffected by the social and political ideology of Progressive social science, an orthodoxy that increasingly came to depend upon science to help it address society's most fundamental problems. The ideological power of Progressivism evaporated at the end of World War I under the onslaught of social pluralism through immigration, the ongoing naturalistic attack on religion, and the failure of President Woodrow Wilson's foreign policy. But the dream remained of solving the "social question" (a common Progressive era term for the set of dilemmas posed by the intersection of scarcity and inequality) in a manner that allowed Americans to recognize their interdependence and exercise their collective responsibility for society. To replace the religious moralism that motivated previous generations to action, American intellectuals turned to the one certainty that weathered the storms of the late nineteenth and early twentieth centuries – science. Combining the notions of social cohesion, interdependence and social responsibility, with the "noble dream" of scientific objectivity, social scientists in the interwar years created a powerful new progressive framework for social discourse. At the centre of that framework stood a new solution to America's "social question": scarcity and economic inequality would be requited by economic progress guided by social control. Social scientists, claiming the authority of science, offered their expertise to assist in directing that process.

The new Progressive ideological framework, which we shall call "the language of social control" (following Rodgers 1982: 126), emphasized the need to apply scientific intelligence to the problems of social action. Despite a lingering debate over exactly what science was, and what a science of society was (see Ross 1991; M.C. Smith 1994), for most Americans there was little doubt about what science could do. New advances in the control of nature had emerged from the scientific study of the natural order; social scientists argued that similar advances in the control of society could be expected from a scientific study of the social order. The demise of American Protestantism as the prominent language of social discourse left the ship of democracy adrift in a sea of uncertainty. Who better to control the ship and lead it to safe harbor than the masters of the scientific method (imagery adapted from Lippmann 1914)?

The new language of social control did not immediately dominate social discourse; revolutions in social ideology are not the gestalt switches Thomas Kuhn described scientific revolutions to be. The old ideological frameworks of American Protestantism and classical liberalism lost their prominence slowly, and continued to shape social discourse long after they had lost their dominant position. Nevertheless, it is fair to say that the interwar period marked the crucial transition period. Before the end of the Great War, despite the inroads made by the social reformers, the place of prominence still belonged to the older ideologies. By the time the Great Depression began in the early 1930s, the new language of social control gained prominence, as well as the social sciences and the professions (management, social work, psychiatry) that depended upon them.

Frank Knight's dissent

Knight dissented from the emerging orthodoxy of scientific social control. He viewed this belief in progress through science as dangerous. Also, the language of social control legitimized social science in ways that circumscribed public discourse. To attack the rising ideology, Knight needed to simultaneously undermine the authority of science and broaden the boundaries of public discourse. The strategy he adopted incorporated both of these elements. First, he attacked the quest to make social inquiry more scientific, in order to weaken the authoritative position science held within the social sciences. Second, Knight attacked the role of the social sciences within American society, in order to weaken their position as authorities. We next examine these two strategies.

Science and its limits in social inquiry

Knight's virulent response to positivist methodology in economics is well known (Knight 1940a), and has previously been the focus of methodological commentary on his work (see Hammond 1991). Less well known is that Knight's infamous review of T.W. Hutchison's book in 1940 came after two decades of debate with other social scientists regarding the role of science in social inquiry.

The debate began for Knight in *RUP*, where he argued that economic theory was a necessary part of social inquiry because it used the scientific method of abstraction and analysis, but that the presence of uncertainty, which frustrated analysis, severely limited the applicability of scientific economics to the real problems of society. The latter half of *RUP* is an argument for a more institutional and historical approach to the problems of economic life. After publishing *RUP*, Knight moved the debate over science in social inquiry along two different lines.

First, he extended the argument of *RUP*. In subsequent articles and book reviews, Knight put forward several alternative formulations of the argument that economic theory was scientific, but partial, in its treatment of social and economic life; and therefore economics had a limited range of applicability. One place where he struggled to express the tension between the power of scientific theorizing and its limitations was his capital theory debate with the Austrians, especially Hayek (Emmett 1997a). While we usually characterize the debate in terms of the conception of capital as a permanent fund or a non-permanent collection of temporal goods, the debate also involved competing conceptions of the scientific nature and role of equilibrium theory. Hayek's intertemporal equilibrium model (Hayek 1936) was developed to demonstrate the pure logic of choice (independent of past historical events, and achievable by a dictator with the scientific expertise of an economist). Equilibrium was always possible because all contingencies were known. Because the logic of decision-making was a theoretical construct, Hayek simultaneously severed the world of theory from the real world and provided a theory accounting for future changes. In the context of the real world, however, with all its partially-known contingencies, Hayek's theoretical construct could only point out that market participants would more readily respond to change than central planners, and therefore markets had a tendency to move towards equilibrium.

Knight refused to sever the world of theory from reality. He insisted that capital decisions were historical events (Knight 1930a, 1933b, 1935a, 1936b). Explaining those events required understanding static equilibrium theory (which would illuminate the essential characteristics of choice), and understanding the historical and cultural evolution of the values, tastes, resources, and technology (the givens of economic theory) that decision-makers have available at the moment of choice. Because the effects of changes after the moment of choice were uncertain, and the evolution of the "givens" of economic theory was a historical process, economic theory had little to say outside the context of the moment of choice. Knight (1936a, 1936b) therefore dismissed dynamic equilibrium theory in favor of historical or institutional analysis for explaining economic change. Furthermore, Knight (1936b: 463) argued that the uncertainty of potential changes, and the dependence of capital decisions on their institutional context, provided powerful reasons to reject the notion that there was any necessary movement towards equilibrium in a market or collectivist system.

Similar arguments regarding the role of scientific economics appear in Knight's writings on economics and economic methodology. A proper understanding of neoclassical value theory is essential to explaining human conduct because it illuminates important choices facing the decision-maker. But it cannot predict choice in a scientific sense, both because of uncertainty and because the theory ignores the historical evolution of the institutional context within which a decision-maker operates. The theorist articulates the theoretical core of economics as carefully as possible, and the historian interprets the evolution of the institutional context. The applied economist has a responsibility to assist the decision-maker in judging the relevance of history and theory to particular decisions (Knight 1924a: 35; 1930b: 8–11; 1951b). Decision-making (that is, life itself) was ultimately an art, not a science.

The second line of argument that Knight used to develop his dissent from the ideology of scientific social control takes us closer to the heart of our concerns here. In several places (most importantly in Knight 1922) he argued that if one considered human action to be a scientific problem, economics was the only science of society; but since human action was ultimately not a scientific problem, scientific economics had little place in social inquiry. Economics had to be supplemented by an ethical theory of value. In order to understand the import of this line of argument, we need to backtrack slightly and look more closely at the assumed relationship between science and value in the new ideology of social control.

Social scientists operating within the language of social control wanted to create a scientific basis for social inquiry that would provide society with the means to realize the traditional values of American democracy. This implied that the social sciences were primarily concerned with the relation between a set of possible means (alternative forms of social organization, as well as potential modifications to the existing social arrangements) and a given set of ends (traditional American liberal values).

Wolfe placed this means–end relation at the centre of his argument for an economics modeled after the natural sciences. He argued that, because the economic system was a set of means organized around given ends, scientific analysis of the available means was only possible within the context of social agreement on what ends the system would seek to achieve. Wolfe rejected appeals to an absolute system of ethics as the foundation upon which agreement on social values could be built. Instead, he argued that because human conduct was socially determined, scientific analysis could uncover human values in the same way that it could discover the correct means to fulfill those values (Wolfe 1924: 473–82). Like other social scientists of his time, Wolfe assumed that the scientific study of values would affirm America's traditional democratic values.

Knight took up the argument about the means–end relation that Wolfe and others used to defend the role of social science in achieving America's common values. If the scientific point of view assumes that the central problem of life is using available means to given ends, Knight argued, then economics is the science of life, because economics studies the social consequences of the effort by members of society to satisfy their given preferences efficiently. The realm of economics, therefore, covered every aspect of human activity – from individuals economizing within budget constraints, to the organizing activities of firms (which Knight explored in *RUP*) and to the institutions of liberal democracy.

In so far as the means are viewed as given, as data, then all activity is economic. The question of the effectiveness of the adaptation of means is the only question to be asked regarding conduct, and economics is the one and all-inclusive science of conduct. ... The assumption that wants or ends are data reduces life to economics.

(Knight 1922: 51)

Despite the imperialistic tone of this passage, Knight did not argue that economics was the science of society in order to assert the supremacy of economics over the other social sciences. Rather, his argument was designed to emphasize the tension between the need for a science of society (economics) and its inherent limitations. The scientific view makes choice an economic problem. But human choices, he argued, are more than economic problems. They are also moral (and possibly even spiritual) problems.

The problem of life is to utilize resources "economically," to make them go as far as possible in the production of desired results. The general theory of economics is therefore simply the rationale of life. ... how far life is rational, how far its problems reduce to the form of using given means to achieve given ends. Now this, we shall contend, is not very far; the scientific view of life is a limited and partial view; *life is at bottom an exploration in the field of values, an attempt to discover values, rather than on the basis of knowledge of them to produce and enjoy them to the greatest possible extent.* We strive to "know ourselves," to find out our real wants, more than to get what we want. This fact sets a first and most sweeping limitation to the conception of economics as a science.

(Knight 1924a: 1; emphasis added)

Reducing life to economics was merely a prelude to asking, "Is life all economics or does this view require supplementing by an ethical view of value?" (Knight 1922: 51). Knight answered that an ethical theory of value was needed in addition to an economic theory of value.

Before we consider the realm of values, we might examine the impact that Knight's attempts to limit the range of scientific economics had upon economics. Ironically, the argument that economics was scientific, but that its applicability was limited and it needed supplementing with an ethical theory of value, laid the groundwork for two developments in American economics that Knight resisted. On the one hand, Knight's isolation of the scientific core of economic theory from economic policy, or institutional and historical study, became dominant as mathematical formalism took over economics after World War II. Jettisoning the last vestiges of progressive interest in social reform, many economists sought to analyze the structure of the economy through abstract mathematics (echoing Knight's description of economics in the first chapter of *RUP*). Knight assisted this process by severing theoretical considerations from historical or policy considerations; yet he resisted the effort to circumscribe the economist's role as social scientist by the formal boundaries of economic theory (Knight 1947b, 1956a, 1960a). On the other hand, it took only one small (and fundamental) change in assumptions to reject Knight's call for an ethical theory of value to supplement the universal presence of economics in human life (and thereby lead to the Chicago School of Economics). That change was due to Stigler and Becker (1977), who argued that, as scientists, economists had to take values and preferences as given. If values could not be criticized, all life becomes economic, and economics could emerge as the only science of human conduct and society. In an ironic twist, Knight's dissent from the use of science to undergird the ideology of his day prepared the way for a social science that depends even more heavily on the authority of science for ideological power.

Value and the role of social science in a liberal democracy

The second strand of Knight's dissent from the ideology of scientific social control was his attack on the role that ideology assigned to social scientists as the guardians of public discourse on social problems. In order to understand this argument, we need to look first at his understanding of the nature of a democratic society.

For Knight, the essence of democracy was a social conversation (he used the word "discussion") among all members of society about what wants and values we should have, or the kind of people we want to become. Coordinating our wants and values with the resources available was a technical problem, best solved by the price system. Just as scientific economics does not encompass all of life, so too the market does not encompass all of human conduct.

For Knight, the actual practice of democracy was only distantly related to its ideal. During the early 1930s, he argued that the ideal of government by discussion was debased by the lack of any real desire for intelligent judgment among the general public. But when discussion was trivialized, the door was open for groups with powerful voices and agendas – like some social scientists – to manipulate the discussion to their own advantage.

For democracy as discussion to work, Knight argued, people had to talk about their wants and values, and do so in a manner that was cooperative rather than conflictual or competitive. They had to decide it was more important to work together to discover the truth, than to insist upon the correctness of their own ideas and beliefs. Discussion, Knight said, "is a co-operative quest of an impersonally, 'objectively' right (or best) solution of an impersonal problem. It cannot be an attempt to 'sell' a solution already reached, or it is not discussion" (Knight 1933a: xxxiii). Two things prevented modern democracy from being a true discussion.

The first is aptly summarized in Knight's "First Law of Talk: cheaper talk drives out of circulation that which is less cheap" (Knight 1991: 64). In a free society, as in a free market, there is no guarantee that people will actually want to improve the quality of their wants and values. Rather, it is likely that exactly the opposite will occur; freedom to pursue our own interests and form our own opinions will reduce our conversation to the lowest common denominator, the basest interests and the cheapest talk. Thus, paradoxically, the freedom that democracy allows as part of the search for the best values handicaps that search by allowing the propagation of cheap tastes.

The second thing that Knight thought hindered democracy as discussion was a tendency to turn discussion into debate. In actual practice, social discussion became "a contest for personal aggrandizement" (Knight 1933a: xxxv). Here Knight blamed those whom he believed ought to know better – economists and other social scientists. In their enthusiasm to apply the scientific method to the practical problems of social life, they failed to recognize that the method of science was inappropriate to social discussion. The difference between these two types of activity, Knight argued, could not be greater – where social discussion required the generation of new ideas, the scientific method tested ideas that were already held; where social discussion drew people into a cooperative quest for better values, the scientific method focused attention on the conflict between competing theories; where social discussion required conversation, the scientific method encouraged debate. Knight's "Second Law of Talk" made the point in a characteristic fashion:

> The more intelligent people are, the more certain they are to disagree on matters of social principle and policy, and the more acute will be the disagreement. The more intelligent they are, the more finely they discriminate and the more importance they attach to fine discriminations, and the more completely their entire mental activity runs into the borderland region of doubt.
>
> (Knight 1991: 68)

By carrying the scientific method over into social discussion, social scientists reduced the latter to debate and competition. The inevitable result would be social "conflict, and finally chaos and tyranny" (Knight 1933a: xxxiv). The irony, of course, was that the tyranny would be exercised by the "protectors" of American values and "objective" observers of American life – social scientists and professionals.

Conclusion

Knight's dissent during the interwar period involved a twofold strategy. On the one side, he tried to isolate economic theory from criticism by describing it as scientific. On the other side, he wanted social discourse to be an open discussion in which members of society explored together what the true, the good, and the beautiful could mean in the modern world. The desire to keep social discourse open-ended led Knight to protest the emerging dominance of the language of social control, which granted social scientists special privileges in public discussion. Because the privileged position of economists and other social scientists depends on their scientific authority, Knight sought to de-legitimize that authority, both within the realm of social inquiry and in social discourse. In the realm of social inquiry, Knight argued that the scientific part of economics was limited in its range of applicability, or that, despite the relevance of economic analysis to every aspect of life, social inquiry must be supplemented by an ethical analysis of values. Either way, Knight claimed, economists had no special status in social discourse. Unfortunately, Knight was not optimistic about the ability of society to resist the language of social control, and he despaired about the prospects for a post-liberal society dominated by the tyranny of expertise. In the end (that is, after the interwar period) his dissent was soured by his cynicism.

6 "What is truth" in capital theory?

Five stories relevant to the evaluation of Frank Knight's contributions to the capital controversy

> I am absolutely convinced that such theories are completely wrong, but – what is truth!
>
> (Knight 1933d; speaking of Austrian capital theory)

At the conclusion of "Economic Theory and Nationalism," Frank H. Knight called for the scientific community of economists to eschew self-promotion and institutional allegiances, avoid public displays of dissension among themselves, and devote themselves exclusively to the self-sacrificial vocation of truth-seeking. Only a unified search for better economic knowledge, guided by the criteria of the scientific method operating in a context in which other interests such as public esteem and power were held apart, offered hope for liberal society in a beleaguered world (Knight 1935b).

Standard histories of the interwar years of "high theory," written in the "absolutist" tradition of historiography in economics, sometimes imply that economists actually heeded Knight's call: the development of economic theory is told as a progressive process, efficiently guided (with only a few unfortunate disruptions) by the criteria of scientific truth-seeking. Despite the texts we use in classes, however, many historians of economics today recognize that a multiplicity of stories about "progress" can be told about the interwar period. The unity and progress of economic science is also being questioned on other grounds. For one thing, the recent challenge to "methodology" (the identification of a unified set of scientific criteria for truth-seeking) has undermined the possibility of defining "progress" in any meaningful way, and suggests that historians need to look closely at the particular criteria operating in specific situations, whether or not these criteria correspond to current notions of "proper" scientific method. For another, recognition of the role of institutional allegiances, personal biographies, public debate, cultural "mindsets," and the like in scientific communities suggests that interests other than truth-seeking are not held apart. Scientific practice, like all human activity, is a tissue of paradox in which interests conflict and competing criteria of evaluation are employed. We do not live "by truth alone," and our historical accounts of scientific communities cannot artificially assume that we do.

In what follows, some of these recent insights are reflected back on the study of Knight's work during the 1930s – the decade of Knight's controversy with the

Austrians over the theory of capital. At the center of the study are five interrelated stories about the themes that occupied Knight's attention during the 1930s. In the interplay among these five stories, we will see several things: that theoretical debate can reflect differences in scientific criteria; that the justification of theoretical arguments is informed by a variety of concerns; and that the line between personal biography and scientific pursuit becomes blurred. Taken together, the close intertwining of the five stories of Knight's work makes it impossible to separate scientific activity from other activities: at what point is Knight qua economist separable from Knight qua social philosopher or Knight qua educator or even Knight qua spouse/ex-spouse and father?

Theme 1: Personal crisis

Knight's appointment to the University of Chicago in 1927 was accompanied by his divorce and deteriorating health. Most of the story of the family separation remains hidden in family letters, but the *Daily Iowan* reported that Knight wanted "congenial and more intellectual companionship" and freedom from family responsibilities. In a subsequent letter to his mentor, Frederick Kershner, Knight said: "I may say that there was no violent or acute special occasion for the step. ... Whatever 'fault' there was was on my side, [but] it is not clear to me how far one is to blame for being what one is" (Knight 1929). Minerva Knight and their four children stayed in Iowa City, where she continued to work and study at the University of Iowa. Frank Knight provided financial assistance to the household throughout the 1930s (apparently more than the courts of the time would have required), until the children went on to their university studies.

The related details of Knight's relationship with Ethel Verry are better known. A student in one of Knight's first classes upon his return to Chicago, she was for years the director of the Chicago Child Care Society. They were married in September 1929 and spent six months during 1930 in Europe on a Guggenheim Foundation fellowship (Knight visited Vienna during this trip).

Shortly after moving to Chicago in 1928, Knight began to experience serious health problems. Health complaints are common in his letters to both family and friends during the late 1920s and early 1930s, and he apparently considered taking disability leave from the University in 1928. While the intensity of the pains he experienced eventually diminished, he never fully recovered his health; in letters to friends throughout the rest of his life he complained of tiredness and either being overworked or not being able to work for health reasons.

Behind this sketchy story lies an emotional and financial crisis that we know little about. While the increase in real income Knight experienced over the decade of the 1930s (because of President Robert Hutchins's promise of stable faculty salaries) ensured that he could continue to support two households, providing support to Minerva Knight's household undoubtedly constrained his ability to support his own new, and growing, family (Frank and Ethel had two children, born in 1933 and 1936). In what ways did his abandonment of his family parallel his abandonment of liberalism? Was his decision the search for better conversation, an exercise of free choice in personal relations, or an act of force and coercion – the epitome of what he believed the demise of liberalism had brought us to? To what extent were Knight's health problems the result of, or an addition to, the chaos of his personal life? And are we to "discount" Knight's aggressive response to the Austrians and nihilistic comments about the state of economics and liberal democracy as the remarks of an emotionally, financially, and physically stricken man?

Theme 2: Historical and institutional economics

> You may or may not have heard echoes of the fact that I have become more or less involved in controversy in economic theory, the theory of capital and inter-est in particular. I came to Chicago expecting ... "institutionalism" to be my main field of work. But Viner went to Geneva two different years, leaving me the main course in theory. ... The controversy referred to grew especially out of my growing realization that the treatment of capital and productive factors generally in this material and in all my previous teaching is simply "wrong." A year ago I started in seriously to re-work this material, but found myself wrestling with unsolved problems over virtually the whole field of traditional theory. Really, I haven't made very much headway with the whole project, except for getting some of my ideas more or less straightened out, but chiefly finding out how muddled they (and those of the elite in the field generally) really are.
>
> (Knight 1936d)

When Frank Knight returned to the University of Chicago in 1927, he did not intend to assume the mantle of theorist. Indeed, he had no need to – Chicago was already blessed with one of the best theorists of Knight's generation, Jacob Viner. Knight's role was to complement Viner's instruction in theory with courses in the history of economic thought, economics and social policy, and historical or institutional economics. The latter, in particular, was an emerging area of inter-est for Knight, and one toward which he intended to direct the majority of his attention.

"But Viner went to Geneva," and once Knight began a reevaluation of modern economics, he found it difficult to stop. Furthermore, in the course of teaching the history of economic thought, he realized that many of the difficulties he saw in contemporary economics were related to "errors" inherited from classical economics. Chief among these were the ongoing adherence to utilitarianism, which led marginalism to focus on "subjective" utility evaluations rather than "objective" alternative cost evaluations (Knight 1935e), and the vestiges of the classical notion that production was the creation of commodities rather than a stream of services (see Knight 1935c).

Knight's reevaluation of value and distribution theory also led him to revisit his treatment of the nature and limitations of equilibrium price analysis. In his earlier writings on economic method (especially Knight 1921a and 1924a), he had identified economic theory as an exercise of abstraction and analysis: abstraction in the sense that economics studied a constructed realm that bore little resemblance to the real world, but which, if the process of abstraction was successful, iso-lated the underlying, unchanging forms of reality; and analysis in the sense that, once isolated, the underlying forms could be examined within the context of the constructed realm in terms of both their individual impact and their interaction. The central purpose of the scientific discipline of abstraction and analysis was the pursuit of truth – understood in "definitional" rather than "empirical" terms. "Good" theories were like "good" definitions: if the elements that polluted analy-sis were successfully stripped away, then the theory was true – it correctly captured the meaning of the particular aspect of human experience under consideration. Economics was "scientific," therefore, because it followed the discipline of abstraction and analysis, not because of its "empirical" content. Whether the truths of economic theory were applicable to the particularities of the "real" world was not ultimately the concern of the economist qua theoretical scientist. The art of application (judging how the truths of economics and other social sciences were relevant to an immediate situation) was the task of economic policy makers and, more importantly, of every citizen.

Knight's notion of economic theory as a process of abstraction and analysis was associated with his early advocacy of the method of successive approximations. However, in his reworking of equilibrium theory during the early 1930s, Knight weakened the relationship between abstraction and approximation. Despite occa-sional references to the usefulness of the approach (for example, Knight 1944a: 28), in practice Knight abandoned the method in favor of a clear dichotomy between the abstractions of economic theory and the study of the changing insti-tutional structure of capitalist society. No process of successive approximation would enable us to move from the abstract realm characterized by the absence of uncertainty to the conditions of real life, in which change brought uncertainty; instead, the two realms required different types of investigation.

The transition from the method of successive approximation to the clear divi-sion between different realms is found in Knight's attempts to articulate the differ-ence between the "static" analysis of equilibrium price theory and the need for a new "dynamic" analysis. Knight argued that any changes in the conditions of the economy that displayed an underlying stability would fit within traditional "static" analysis, but that most changes did not display such stability because they were the result of free choices made by human beings. The nonmechanistic nature of those changes would frustrate any attempt at a "dynamic" science – abstraction and analysis did not work in the realm of change. Because theorizing was the process of abstraction and analysis, "static" equilibrium price analysis, therefore, was all that economic science could offer. Unfortunately, the reality of change and the uncertainty it created meant that the time horizon for the predictions of any static analysis was extremely short. The study of the economy in a changing world required supplementing theory with an examination of the evolution of the econ-omy's underlying conditions – changes in its wants, resources, and technology; the distribution of resource ownership and monetary conditions; and the politi-cal, legal, and moral system (Knight 1930a: 172–4). Central to that examination would be a historical study of the institutional structures by which the underlying economic conditions were created and continually reshaped. For that historical examination, equilibrium analysis was practically irrelevant.

> Our general conclusion must be that in the field of economic progress the notion of tendency toward equilibrium is definitely inapplicable to particular elements of growth and, with reference to progress as a unitary process or system of interconnected changes, is of such limited and partial application as to be misleading rather than useful. This view is emphasized by reference to the phenomena covered by the loose term "institution." All speculative glimpses at trends in connection with price theory relate to a "competitive" or "capitalistic" economic system. But all the human interests and traits involved in this type of economic life are subject to historical change. Moreover, no society is or could be entirely and purely competitive. The roles of the state, of law, and of moral constraint are always important and that of other forms of organization such as voluntary co-operation may be so. Business life in the strictest sense never conforms closely to the theoretical behavior of an economic man. Always history is being made; opinions, attitudes, and institutions change, and there is evolution in the nature of capitalism. In fact evolution toward other organization forms as the dominant type begins before capitalism reaches its apogee. Such social evolution is rather beyond the province of the economic theorist, but it is pertinent to call attention to the utter inapplicability to such changes, i.e., to history in the large, of the notion of tendency toward a price equilibrium.
>
> (Knight 1930a: 184)

Three things mitigated against Knight's efforts to develop an alternative institutionalism, however. The first was his own fault: he usually spent so much time preparing the ground for his examination of the evolution of the institutions of modern society that he seldom ended up with much time or word-space to examine their evolution. Hence, despite the fact that he was the translator for the first of Max Weber's works to appear in English (Weber 1927), that he reviewed numerous books by historicists and institutionalists, and that he developed a course on institutionalism (Economics 305: Economics from an Institutional Standpoint – first taught in the summer quarter of 1932), his institutionalist work appears preliminary.

The second and third mitigating factors relate to the changing context of American social science during the 1930s and early 1940s. On the one hand, the emergence of national socialism and communism in Europe in the midst of capitalism's worst depression cast a long shadow over any discussion of the evolution of the market. Some of Knight's best institutional analysis, therefore, took place in the context of a comparative study of the institutional structures of capitalism and socialism (for example, in Knight 1940b and 1939a). On the other hand, the type of economic study Knight envisioned became increasingly rare among economists as the discipline became more formal and mathematical in its orientation (his institutionalist work was labeled "social philosophy", obviously outside the realm of economics). Ironically, Knight's radical separation of economic theory from any form of historical analysis, and his focus on theory in both his economic and historical work, helped to contribute to the discipline's emerging ahistorical orientation (Ross 1991: 427) – a result he personally was unhappy with.

Theme 3: Capital, time, and the interest rate

> In the large, I think I understand what the drift of [your response] is, and it serves to emphasize the fundamental problem in my mind these days, which is the question whether there is any profit in the discussion of fundamental issues in economics. … In this connection, I recall the observation in your letter, that systematic exposition rather than the meeting of specific questions is the way to "advance knowledge." I am strongly convinced of the opposite.
>
> (Knight 1934e)

Knight's capital theory contributions consist of a string of conversations with other theorists in which his own reworking of the relevance of equilibrium price analysis to the problem of capital is intertwined with his questions for other approaches to the same issues. This combination has caused some problems for commentators because it does not fit the "standard" model of scientific argumentation, which calls for theorists to set out their own approach in comprehensive and systematic fashion. Fritz Machlup, for instance, indirectly called on Knight to stop asking questions and systematically set out his own theoretical position for comparison and criticism in his rejoinder to Knight (Machlup 1935b). Nicholas Kaldor was less gracious when he described Knight's persistent questioning of the Austrian position as akin to the launching of a military offensive and remarked that Knight's arguments were "frequently clothed in paradoxical sentences which are intended to challenge the mind but without a sufficient indication of where to turn in order to uncover those mental processes which must have led up to them" (Kaldor 1937: 201, 202–3).

For Knight, however, conversations and questions were an integral part of his own theoretical work, which was an ongoing process with an incomplete product. If theorizing is like the creation of a good definition, then asking questions of other treatments of the topics that point toward polluted elements in their analysis – rather than the systematic modeling – was essential to the scientific task. Of course, there was a need to pause occasionally and assess what the definition/ theory now looked like. But in Knight's case, the guiding principle in that assessment was not "Which theory best corresponds to empirical reality?", but "Have we correctly defined what marginal theory has to tell us, and are we aware of the limitations that the process of abstraction and analysis place upon us?" The result has been that those searching for a new theoretical position in Knight's capital theory articles have found his approach "very difficult to understand and, also, either apparently or really, contradictory" (Lutz 1967: 104).

A case in point is Knight's conversation about capital with the Austrians. Knight took the opportunity provided by the call for a contribution to *the festschrift* for

Gustav Cassel to examine the "Jevons-Bohm-Bawerk-Wicksell" capital theory in light of his reformulated opposition to the "classical" theory of production. His contribution (Knight 1933b) was constructed around the definition of terms such as production, wealth, income, value, and capital. For each of these terms, Knight's goal was to strip away extraneous meanings that prevented economic theorists from correctly characterizing these notions. In the process, however, Knight also sought to reveal the limitations of equilibrium theory by identifying the difference between their meaning in a stationary economy and their meaning in a dynamic economy. Capital proved to be the central term in relation to the time dimension of a dynamic economy, and its proper definition both falsified the Bohm-Bawerk theory and identified the need for an alternative (but yet here unspecified) method for examining capitalistic production.

In the two initial articles aimed at identifying the extraneous elements that polluted the Austrian theory of capital, Knight (1933b, 1934a) focused his attention on two questions: What is meant by the period of production? Why must one relate the quantity of capital to a period of production, however defined? Knight believed that a properly defined theory of interest removed the need for the concept of a period of production by basing the interest rate on the relation between the marginal productivity of capital and the momentary supply of capital (moving beyond the moment would, as indicated already, require an historical, rather than an equilibrium, analysis). Bohm-Bawerk's theory, on the other hand, required the notion of a period of production because it related the interest rate to one's willingness to abstain from using a specific quantity of potential capital for consumption purposes: one would want to know minimally the average length of time one's funds might be tied up. But, Knight argued, the definition of a period of production provided in Austrian theory depended on elements of classical economics that conflicted with the basic facts of economic production recognized by modern economic theory. In order to convince Knight, therefore, the Austrians would have to redefine the period of production in a manner consistent with a marginalist capital theory that was freed from these classical errors.

Knight's attack on the foundations of the Austrian theory of capital required a response, and both Machlup (1935a, 1935b) and Friedrich von Hayek (1936) took up the task. While Machlup sought to defend Austrian theory against Knight's attack, however, Hayek's engagement with Knight formed a part of his own reformulation of capital theory. In the Knight–Hayek debate, then, we will see two theorists reworking their understanding of equilibrium theorizing and arriving at different points. Are they simply talking past each other, or are their different formulations the result of the application of different criteria of evaluation?

The Knight–Hayek debate is particularly interesting because of the correspondence that exists between the two men during this time (in the Frank H. Knight Papers, Box 60, Folders 10–11, Special Collections Research Center, University of Chicago Library), the similarity in their concerns as theorists, our knowledge of the fundamental shift in Hayek's own thinking that occurred during the 1930s, and the relation of Hayek's theoretical innovations to the postwar emergence of a dominant neo-Walrasian mode of theorizing. Like Knight, Hayek in the mid

1930s sought to make sense of the relevance of equilibrium theorizing for a world characterized by change and the presence of collectivist institutional structures. Part of Hayek's response assigned a role to knowledge in relation to individual choice reminiscent of *RUP*'s treatment of imperfect knowledge and entrepreneurial choices – in the real world, human action is contingent on our expectations of others' actions; hence, uncertainty is systemic and creates the potential for systematic misinterpretation of market signals. The systematic misunderstandings of price signals imply that equilibrium will not be achieved; nevertheless, because entrepreneurs are free to respond quickly, the market process naturally has a tendency toward equilibrium. In contrast, the slowness of bureaucratic response in a centrally planned economy would create economic havoc from even the smallest errors (Hayek 1937).

To show why equilibrium would not be achieved in the contingent world, the nature of the errors that could be made and their consequences, and why the differences between entrepreneurial and bureaucratic responses were important, Hayek (like Knight) adopted a notion of theorizing that departed from the common method of successive approximation. Furthermore, Hayek successfully redefined capital theory in terms that did not depend on the classical tripartite division of the factors of production – one of Knight's main requirements. Nevertheless, Hayek's development of a pure logic of intertemporal equilibrium (Hayek 1936, 1941) was still unacceptable to Knight, although it is difficult to provide a clear and consistent account of the reasons for their disagreement. One is left with the unsettling impression that, while they are obviously talking past each other at one level, the issues that continue to divide them are real but entangled in a multitude of other concerns, especially their respective evaluations of the prospects for liberal society.

The debate began with Hayek's first attempt to restate Austrian capital theory in a form that would not be susceptible to the type of criticism Knight raised (Hayek 1934). Knight apparently initiated discussion of their differences in correspondence shortly after that article, but he became increasingly disillusioned about the chances for agreement over the course of their correspondence. Eventually Knight published his criticism of Hayek, reiterating the questions he had asked Machlup, the necessity of defining capital as a perpetual fund, and his frustration with the Austrian's unwillingness (as he saw it) to provide a satisfactory answer to his argument about the symmetrical relation among the factors of production (Knight 1935d). The correspondence continued until shortly after Hayek's response, in which he clearly breaks with the Bohm-Bawerk theoretical framework. Knight's final letters indicate that, although he recognized Hayek's new direction, there were still significant outstanding issues at stake between them; issues that, for Knight, emerged from Hayek's refusal to accept the notion of a perpetual fund of capital. Resorting back to publication, Knight concludes his side of the debate with another reassessment of capital theory, once again emphasizing the importance of the perpetual fund (Knight 1936b).

Because the notion of a perpetual fund of capital appears as the key theoretical point of contention between Hayek and Knight, we can use their disagreement on this notion to explicate their different understandings of equilibrium theorizing. In his response to Knight's critique, Hayek agreed with Knight that the Jevons-Bohm-Bawerk theory was "responsible for much of the confusion which exists on the subject" (Hayek 1936: 200), but he went on to say:

> But Professor Knight, instead of directing his attack against what is undoubtedly wrong or misleading in the traditional statement of this theory, and trying to put a more appropriate treatment of the time element in its place, seems to me to fall back on the much more serious and dangerous error of its opponents of forty years ago. In the place of at least an attempt of analysis of the real phenomena, he evades the problems by the introduction of a pseudo-concept, devoid of content and meaning, which threatens to shroud the whole problem in a mist of words. ...
>
> This basic mistake – if the substitution of a meaningless statement for the solution of a problem can be called a mistake – is the idea of capital as a fund which maintains itself automatically, and that, in consequence, once an amount of capital has been brought into existence the necessity of reproducing it presents no economic problem. According to Professor Knight "all capital is normally conceptually, perpetual," "its replacement has to be taken for granted as a technological detail," and in consequence "there is no production process of determinate length, other than zero or 'all history'," but "in the only sense of timing in terms of which economic analysis is possible, *production and consumption are simultaneous.*" ...
>
> Against this I do indeed hold that ... all the problems which are commonly discussed under the general heading of "capital" do arise out of the fact that part of the productive equipment is non-permanent and has to be deliberately replaced on economic grounds, and that there is no meaning in speaking of capital as something permanent which exists apart from the essentially impermanent capital goods of which it consists.
>
> (Hayek 1936: 200–204; emphasis in original)

Hayek's own response to the nonpermanence of capital goods was the construction of an intertemporal equilibrium theory in which individual capital goods were assigned different prices at different times and places. The problem of valuation was resolved in Hayek's model by the logical relations among the intertemporal own rates of return of current nonpermanent production goods (each good's own rate of return being a relation between time preference and productivity, and therefore unrelated to past events). According to Hayek, the trade-offs among time-discounts, the duration of individual capital goods, and their productivity help us understand the nature of exchange over time when the existing capital goods need to be maintained or replaced and new capital goods created. If the trade-offs are known, then a dictator with control over all resources could construct a perfect intertemporal plan of action – Hayek's intertemporal equilibrium is a purely logical construct. The imperfections and contingencies of entrepreneurial plans in the real world, however, cause the actual course of a market economy to depart from the flawless coordination of the perfectly planned economy.

In contrast, Knight's approach asks us to consider the output of the economy to be like a choral music production (Knight 1934a). The choir's act of producing the music we enjoy is simultaneous with our act of consumption. Production is the creation of a stream of enjoyable services; consumption is the enjoyment of the stream of services – although we often distinguish between them, the two processes occur at the same moment. In fact, the value of the services is entirely determined at the moment of production/consumption: there is no value produced or consumed prior to, or after, the choir's performance. Of course, economic activity is a continuous process of production/consumption without interruption – a never-ending song. Investment is the diversion of a portion of the endless stream of consumption services into increasing our capacity to produce more services. Under the normal assumptions of perfect competition, once capital has been added to the economy, nothing can destroy it except the discontinuation of the stream of production/consumption. Because modern society has accumulated over its history an enormous set of productive capacities, the addition or loss of a small amount of capital will not effect the overall flow of consumption services. Only a major dissolution of the institutions that sustain the stream of capitalistic production/consumption could interrupt or end its flow; an event that lies outside of economics because economic theory takes the institutional structure of society as given. Thus, capital is perpetual, although its value (the interest rate) is always determined at the moment of production/consumption.

Despite the obvious differences in their theoretical frameworks, Hayek and Knight share several key things. First, they both abandon the method of successive approximation in favor of a sharp division between the constructed realm of theory and the contingent world of lived experience. For Hayek, the theoretical realm is completely separate from reality, yet modeled as a process of dated goods existing through time. For Knight, theory captures one element of our lived experience at the moment and has no relevance beyond the allocative aspect of that moment. Second, for both authors, the difference between the realm of theory and the realm of lived experience is primarily based on the presence of uncertainty in the real world. Third, both men share a rejection of the Bohm-Bawerk theory of capital. Hayek moves to an intertemporal microeconomic theory, while Knight continues to treat society's output in the aggregate, although it would be better to say that he treats society's output as a nondivisible whole. Yet neither Knight nor Hayek is willing to accept the other's reformulation of capital theory. Knight thinks Hayek is perpetuating the classical error of treating output as definable commodities rather than a stream of services, and Hayek labels Knight's perpetual fund a "mythology."

Fourth, behind both men's reconstructions of capital theory lie their concerns for the state of liberal society. Hayek's intertemporal equilibrium construct allows him to identify the key ingredient to understanding the difference between capitalism and socialism as the contingent nature of individual decisions about nonpermanent capital goods. Knight's emphasis on the relevance of equilibrium theorizing for the moment only allows him to focus attention on the historical evolution of capitalist and socialist institutions and their comparative impact on society's wants, resources, and technologies. If there is a significant difference in their social outlook, it is that Hayek believes market processes tend toward equilibrium, while Knight cannot hold out that promise. Hayek's intertemporal equilibrium theory shows what equilibrium over time would look like if achievable; Knight increasingly refuses to model equilibrium over time because change in the presence of uncertainty would not only create a moving equilibrium, but would alter the institutional structure that equilibrium theorizing takes as given.

These themes in Knight's theoretical framework provide the backdrop for his reassessment of capital theory in a two-part article at the end of the Austrian controversy (Knight 1936b). Similar in nature to the two articles that preceded his debate with the Austrians, the follow-up article reiterates Knight's central issue – the limits of equilibrium theorizing in relation to economic life (Knight 1936b: 612). Continuing to insist that static equilibrium models could capture the maximization problem, but increasingly reluctant to draw implications of equilibrium analysis apart from the immediate moment of exchange, Knight included a diagrammatic presentation of the supply and demand for capital, but claims that there was "no grounds for drawing a supply curve for capital" (ibid.: 463), effectively reducing the supply curve to a point (ibid.: 628) and vitiating any attempt to apply equilibrium price theory to the determination of capital and the interest rate over time. "There is absolutely no presumption," he concluded, "that actual changes in historic time will tend to establish equilibrium" (ibid.: 463). Finally, in his insistence that economic theory does not need to treat the possibility of a "decadent" society in which significant disinvestment occurs, he identified the relationship between his understanding of equilibrium theorizing and the massive realignment of the institutional structure of society that would occur in a "decadent" society – nothing less than the creation of humans who no longer have an interest in getting ahead (1936b: 457–58).

Theme 4: Modern education

Knight's tenure as professor of economics at the University of Chicago (fall 1927 to spring 1951) overlapped almost exactly with the tenure of one of the university's most famous and controversial presidents, Robert M. Hutchins (1929 to December 1950). During the years of Hutchins's presidency, the University stood at the forefront of educational reform in the United States. In the graduate faculties around which the University was built, these years saw increased specialization and academization accompanied by interdisciplinary dialogue and initiatives (such as the creation of the Committee on Social Thought, of which Knight and Hutchins were founding members). Whatever the successes of earlier years (and they were many), these were the years that enshrined the University as one of the premier research universities in the world in the social and natural sciences. At the undergraduate level, the creation in 1930 of Hutchins's New College Program, initially as a two-year program of general education intended to be followed by specialized study in a discipline and then (in 1942) as a four-year general education degree program, provided a paradigm of undergraduate education that is still a model for colleges and universities across North America (McNeill 1991: 41–71; Dzuback 1991: 109–228).

The successes were enmeshed in controversy, however. The controversy took several forms, but at its core lay the following question: Does American society need its higher educational system shaped by the modern methods and knowledge of the sciences (both natural and social) or by the classical methods and knowledge of the liberal arts, especially philosophy? The dispute took on new intensity as the depression deepened, the threat of war emerged in Europe, and the Chicago university community realized that America's economic, social, and political structures were in crisis. The future of the American dream, and therefore all of Western civilization, was at stake, and it was just as important for the "battle" to be won on the educational front as in Europe and Asia.

The chief proponents of the classical liberal arts were Hutchins and Mortimer Adler, who Hutchins brought with him from Yale Law School. While Hutchins worked to create a general education program that gave its place of prominence to the Western tradition of philosophical thought rooted in the "great books," Adler provoked Chicago's scientists in both public and private debate with his doubts about the truth claims of science. Adler's provocations reached a peak in the 1933–4 academic year when he debated physiologist Anton Carlson before an overflow crowd in Mandel Hall (McNeill 1991: 58–9). During the same year, he held a year-long seminar in the division of social sciences in which he castigated the division's members for their failure to understand and accept the Aristotelian underpinnings of a proper, unified social theory. Later, on the eve of America's entrance into the war, Adler declared in a public lecture at a conference in New York that America's greatest danger lay not in the external threat of Nazism in Hitler's Germany, but in the internal threat posed by its atheist professors (Adler 1940).

Knight was a key opponent of the Hutchins–Adler educational program. His friend and colleague Harry Gideonese was appointed to the College in 1931 to participate in designing and teaching the new, year-long Introductory General Course in the Study of Contemporary Society. In consultation with Knight and other members of the division of social sciences (the graduate faculty), Gideonese and his College colleagues created a course that had as its operating principle not the elucidation of timeless truth available in the "great books," but "the notion that human beings had accumulated amazing knowledge and skill across the centuries by using the power of reason to overcome irrational impulses and institutional stupidity" (McNeill 1991: 55) – including those of traditions such as Judeo-Christianity and Aristotelianism. The section of the course that introduced the students to economics was anchored by a set of introductory economics material that Knight had first developed in 1924–5 while still at the University of Iowa (eventually published as Knight 1933c).

Knight was also the author of an influential defense of modern thought against the charge of "anti-intellectualism." The article was rejected by the pro-Adler campus newspaper the *Daily Maroon*, but was eventually published in the university's alumni magazine (Knight 1934c). More important, it was given a place of prominence in the reading packet for Gideonese's general social sciences course throughout the 1930s.

Yet Knight's defense of modern thought was not necessarily a defense of his scientific colleagues. For years he had been resisting the objectivist or naturalistic tendencies of American social scientists, and although he joined them now in opposing a greater threat – the moralistic approach to social problems that characterized the new medievalism of Hutchins and Alder – he retained his skepticism about their project of recreating American liberalism under the authority of science (see Knight 1932). Indeed, while he was responding to Adler's attack on the professors, he also launched a scathing attack on T. W. Hutchison's introduction of logical positivism into economics (Knight 1940a). Thus, we have the anomaly of Knight siding with the positivists and pragmatists in defense of educational reforms that bring the insights of modern natural and social scientific knowledge to bear on the problems of society but, at the same time, decrying the impact of that knowledge on society. Unfortunately, in an era when positivism offered the certainty of science in place of the rejected authorities of religion and the classical liberal arts, and pragmatism was the chief intellectual option for Americans struggling to live with uncertainty, Knight's unwillingness to seek common ground with either party marginalized him even from those who might have become his allies.

Theme 5: The dilemmas of liberalism

Knight's faith in liberalism was fundamentally shaken by his disputes with other economists and social scientists, the beginning of the Depression, his interchanges with those he described as "new medievalists" and "positivists," and the political changes of the early 1930s in the United States and other industrial countries. Six days before the 1932 election in the United States, Knight gave a talk for a group of students on the University of Chicago campus entitled "The Case for Communism: From the Standpoint of an Ex-liberal" (Knight 1991).

While the title of the talk may have been a joke, its central theme – the self-contradictory nature of liberalism – showed up in several other essays and lectures. One of the ways that Knight found to express this theme emerged from his concern for the relation between theorizing and truth seeking. As a liberal committed to the right of individuals to seek knowledge independently of the constraints of any tradition (religious or otherwise), Knight valued both the pursuit of truth and the right of individuals to hold different views. Unfortunately (from Knight's perspective), the fact that truth is only one among many values in the liberal framework forces those pursuing truth to compete for resources with those pursuing other values, and eventually even to compete with each other. This competition interferes with the pursuit of truth because it turns the free discussion that marks the joint production of truth into a debate in which the participants seek to assert the primacy of their own positions at the expense of others. The self-contradictory nature of liberalism is exposed, Knight argued, when its greatest achievement – the freeing of truth seeking from the shackles of tradition – is reduced to the search for applause or the quest after control of the coercive power of the state. Because ultimately the quest for power and applause cannot be reconciled with the quest for truth, liberal society will eventually have to either give up democracy or replace the quest for truth with the manipulation of public opinion (see Knight 1936c). In the 1930s, Knight believed that society was in the process of doing both of these things simultaneously, and hence that liberalism was in its death throes.

Conclusion

The introduction to this article closed with a question: At what point is Knight qua economist separable from any other aspect of Knight's life? Fives stories have been told here to suggest that no separation exists, and that an account of his scientific practices will need to examine the interplay between his work as a theoretical economist, his social philosophy, his interest in modern education, and his personal life in order to be complete. Despite his quasi-religious call to the intellectual "priesthood," Frank Knight did not live "by truth alone."

I wish to push the issue somewhat further, however. If human activity is a tissue of paradox, ought we to expect that the interplay of these themes in Knight's activities flow seamlessly together? Most of the stories ended with a puzzle: How can Knight claim to be interested in a historical study of economics when his theoretical work occupies so much of his attention? Why was he not able to articulate a theory of capital that was at least consistent? What are we to make of the way he marginalized himself among social scientists and social philosophers with regard to modern educational reform and the prospects for liberal democracy? Can we form a consistent whole if we put the themes together? If not, will gathering more stories of Knight's life during the 1930s "solve" the puzzles and provide a unified story? Or is the story of each theme a mirror of the fragmentation of the others – each raising more questions than it solves?

More important, should we expect order and unity in the stories? The requirements of academic publication necessitate the construction of a linear account that puts each element in its place, but is that not just the "tyranny of science" all over again? Perhaps the conjunction of seemingly disparate elements can reveal the truth. But, then, what is truth?

7 Maximizers versus good sports

Frank Knight's curious understanding of exchange behavior

> The Economic Man neither competes nor higgles … he treats other human beings as if they were slot machines.
>
> (Knight 1939a: 18)

The notion of "economic man,"[1] central to neoclassical economics was a troubling one for many late nineteenth- and early twentieth-century American economists. Despite the emergence of marginalism as a theoretical tool during the 1870s, an established neoclassical tradition did not appear in the United States until well into the 1920s, after the publication of *RUP*.[2] In between, criticisms of neo-classicism – in particular, criticisms of the assumption that markets are actually peopled by individuals who can realistically be characterized as rational utility-maximizers – seem to mark American economic thought (the contributions of the later J. B. Clark and A. T. Hadley aside). Thorstein Veblen's work is the best known of these criticisms, but the ruminations of the early J. B. Clark and others who sought an ethical economics, and the development of an institutionalist tradition in the work of John Commons and Clarence Ayres, cannot be overlooked (see Morgan 1994 and Rutherford 1994b).

At first glance, Knight's contributions to the debate over economic man appear straightforward. Called the "philosopher of the counterrevolution" (Breit and Ransom 1982: 193), Knight spearheaded a newly emerging American neoclassicism, paying attention, in particular, to providing a defense for the neoclassical assumption of rational, utility-maximizing individuals that was consistent with economics' status as a science. But first appearances can be deceiving, and in Knight's case they definitely are, for his "defense" of the maximizing assumption simultaneously entailed a delineation of the weaknesses of any social analysis based on that assumption – weaknesses based in part on many of the points raised by the critics. Furthermore, these weaknesses, in his view, set sweeping limitations on the social usefulness of any "scientific" economics.[3] His discussion of economic rationality, therefore, is characterized by the tension he sustains between a strong statement of the scientific validity of the neoclassical maximizing assumption and an equally strong statement of the assumption's inadequacy, both empirically and ethically, as a description of actual exchange behavior.

One of Knight's favorite ways of sustaining the tension between the strengths of an economic science and its limited range of applicability was by contrasting the neoclassical metaphor of the market as a mechanical maximization process with the metaphor of the market as a *game*. In contrast with Veblen, who spoke of the interplay between rivals in the market as a game of prowess and predation exhibiting the arrested moral development of capitalist society (see especially Veblen 1899, 1904), Knight used the notion of gaming behavior in the market to highlight the exploratory and essentially moral nature of exchange behavior. As we shall see, for Knight the fact that the market as a form of social organization enabled playful behavior had both positive and negative effects on society.

Knight first introduced the metaphor of the market as a game in the revised version of his dissertation, published in 1921 as *RUP*.[4] The notion reappeared in essays he wrote throughout the 1920s and 1930s (most prominently Knight 1923a, 1935b), and in many of his later critiques of market society (e.g. Knight 1956a, 1960a; and several essays in 1947a). In contrast with the neoclassical metaphor of the rational economic man, a character whose actions epitomize mechanical maximization, Knight's description of the market as a game introduced the metaphor of the "good sport," a character whose actions cannot be described in purely maximizing language and, therefore, invokes moral categories. While the object of the game may be to win, good sports are distinguished from other players by the moral quality of their play, which balances the personal interest in winning the game with the social interest in continuing it.

> Unless people are more interested in having the game go on than they are in winning it, no game is possible. And the social interest … is precisely the interest in keeping up the game, preventing it from deteriorating, and beyond that in making it a still better game.
>
> (Knight 1935b: 302)

If the moral quality of play is sacrificed for the sake of winning, something essential is lost from the game itself.

The contrast Knight draws between *maximizers* and *good sports* presents us with a paradoxical tension in his work. Here we have someone who has had a formative influence on the neoclassical tradition in the United States, criticizing the tradition's description of exchange behavior by attacking its strongest assumption. Does this tension between participation in, and criticism of, the neoclassical tradition represent an inconsistency in Knight's work? Is it, perhaps, as James Buchanan has suggested, a "methodological ambiguity" (Buchanan 1987: 74) that Knight never resolved, but which, nonetheless, increases his appeal to us? Or does Knight refuse to resolve the tension for a particular reason?

The answers to these questions provided in the following pages will center, in the end, on Knight's attempt to strengthen the neoclassical tradition by limiting its range of application. The tension in his work is neither an inconsistency nor an ambiguity, but a strategy he employed for a particular reason. Paradox is essential to his work, because ultimately he was less interested in mapping out the territory that economic theory explained well, than in exploring the uncharted, and often disputed, regions where economics came into contact with other ways of thinking about social organization. To ensure that those uncharted regions were not simply claimed by economists for their own before society could discuss the competing claims and reach consensus, he set very narrow boundaries for "scientific" economics.[5]

Before we describe the strategy Knight employed, and examine the role that he gave the notion of the market as a game, however, we need to look first at his understanding of economics as a science and the role he assigned the maximizing assumption within the theoretical core of neoclassical economics.

Transactors as maximizers

> ... There is a science of economics, a true, and even exact science, which reaches laws as universal as those of mathematics and mechanics. The greatest need for the development of economics as a growing body of thought and practice is an adequate appreciation of the meaning, and the limitations, of this body of accurate premises and rigorously established conclusions.
>
> (Knight 1924a: 28)

Knight's understanding of economics' claim to be a science, and of the role that the maximizing assumption plays in establishing that claim, constitute one of the distinguishing features of his framework. For Knight, economic theory studies the abstract, idealized world of perfect competition, in which rational individuals with perfect knowledge efficiently satisfy their preferences through exchanges in markets that work perfectly. The theorist's task as a scientist is to isolate the assumptions about human behavior and the market that ensure that such exchanges are reduced to a purely mechanical process. Only when those assumptions are well specified can the theorist determine the critical distance between the perfect markets of economic theory and the imperfect markets of actual human practice.[6]

According to Knight, the central assumption for a scientific economics was the maximizing assumption: the notion that the individuals engaging in exchange relations are rational, utility-maximizing agents. Placed second in most of his lists of the central assumptions of economic theory (behind a general statement regarding the nature of market society), the maximizing assumption was central to his formulation of neoclassical economics for three reasons. First, it identified the nature of human activity in the market as the deliberate, knowledgeable, and calculated accommodation of known means to given ends. Second, it distinguished the morally neutral notion of economic rationality from the morally charged nature of social discussion about what is "good" in human action. Finally, as he formulated it, the maximizing assumption explicitly connected maximization with the assumption of perfect knowledge – a connection which was fertile theoretical ground for Knight himself (see Knight 1921a) and many others. All three of these reasons for the centrality of the maximizing assumption to the neoclassical tradition can be seen in his statement of the assumption in *RUP*:

> We assume that the members of society act with complete "rationality." By this we do not mean that they are to be "as angels, knowing good from evil";

we assume ordinary human motives ...; but they are supposed to "know what they want" and to seek it "intelligently." Their behavior, that is, is all "conduct" as we have previously defined the term [i.e., efficient adaptation of known means to given ends]; all their acts take place in response to real, conscious, and stable and consistent motives, dispositions, or desires; nothing is capricious or experimental, everything deliberate. They are supposed to know absolutely the consequences of their acts when they are performed, and to perform them in the light of the consequences.

(Knight 1921a: 76–7)

The theoretical conclusions Knight draws from the maximizing assumption need not detain us here, for they are familiar to anyone schooled in neoclassical economics. There are, however, a couple of unique features of his formulation of the maximizing assumption that deserve special mention. The first, which has already been mentioned, is the special relation he draws between the maximizing assumption and the assumption of perfect knowledge. With the exception of his discussion of risk in *RUP* (see below), he tends to conflate the two assumptions: people maximize want-satisfaction through actions based upon complete knowledge of the consequences. "In acts looking to the future," he tells us, "intelligent action requires perfect foreknowledge" (Knight 1935b: 283). The question we might ask is: Why did he think it necessary to conflate the two assumptions?

The answer will emerge from a look at the other unique feature of Knight's formulation of the maximizing assumption, namely his belief that, properly formulated, the assumption enables economic exchange to be reduced to an impersonal, mechanical process.

The social organization dealt with in economic theory is best pictured as a number of Crusoes interacting through the markets exclusively. To the economic individual, exchange is a detail in production, a mode of using private resources to realize private ends. The "second party" has a shadowy existence, as a detail in the individual's use of his own resources to satisfy his own wants. It is the market, the exchange opportunity, which is functionally real, not the other human beings; these are not even means to action. The relation is neither one of cooperation nor one of mutual exploitation, but is completely non-moral, non-human.

(Knight 1935b: 282)

Conceptualized in this fashion, economic exchange is simply a "mechanical sequence" of want-satisfaction (Knight 1935b: 280; see also 1923a: 69). Blessed with perfect foresight, the individuals in the perfectly competitive economy know what equilibrium prices are and can proceed automatically to fulfill their wants and desires within the constraints of their resources. There is no competition, higgling, cooperation, rivalry, or any other kind of human interaction between the two parties to an exchange in the neoclassical model. The market, which provides the context for want-satisfaction to be fulfilled, is what is real to each person; the individuals with whom exchange occurs are mere details – they "might as well be "vending machines" (Knight 1960a: 73). "The Economic Man," Knight says, "neither competes nor higgles … he treats other human beings as if they were slot machines" (Knight 1939a: 18; see also 1923a, 1935b, 1930a).

Reduction of all exchange relations to mechanical processes brings us full circle and illustrates the close relation for Knight between the maximizing assumption and the scientific status of economics. If people can maximize perfectly, exchange is reduced to a mechanical process and economics can claim to be a scientific study of social organization. "The statement that economics describes the way the economic order works," Knight tells us, "refers to its working as a mechanism; *that is the meaning of being scientific*'" (Knight 1960a: 72, emphasis added). From this perspective, then, "the first question in regard to scientific economics is this question of how far life is rational, how far its problems reduce to the form of using given means to achieve given ends" (Knight 1924a: 1).

Knight's criticism of the maximizing assumption

Given his participation in the neoclassical tradition and the significance he attached to the maximizing assumption, unsuspecting readers of Knight's writing may be surprised when they discover passages in which he rejects the maximizing assumption as a valid guide to either personal action or the understanding of human action – and the reader *will* encounter them, because they appear over and over again.

For example, one finds a criticism of the maximizing assumption in *RUP*, where Knight suggests that uncertainty is the fundamental context of many (perhaps most) economic activities, and that, when uncertainty is present, the judgment required for good behavior departs from the rational calculation required for maximization. For him, the essential differences between certainty, risk, and uncertainty are related to the limits of human knowledge, and hence the potential for maximization. In a *certain* universe, all outcomes are known perfectly, and maximization is guaranteed. In a *risky* universe, the probability of all outcomes can be known perfectly, and maximization is also guaranteed. Hence maximization works equally well in a fully determined, or a fully stochastic, universe. Maximization is rendered sterile by *uncertainty,* however, which exists whenever we lack any objective basis – either deterministic or stochastic – upon which to base our knowledge of the consequences of possible actions:

> It is a world of change in which we live, and a world of uncertainty. We live only by knowing *something* about the future; while the problems of life, or of conduct at least, arise from the fact that we know so little.
>
> (Knight 1921a: 199)

When neither the outcomes of our actions nor their probabilities are known, wise choices must be characterized by *critical judgment* (a nonmechanistic notion for Knight), rather than maximization (Knight 1921a: 197–232).[7]

The criticism of the maximizing assumption first advanced in *RUP* is expanded upon in Knight's methodological and philosophical writings, where he argues that exchange behavior is fundamentally experimental – "an exploration in the field of values" (Knight 1924a: 1) in which individuals seek, through cooperation with others, to discover what they really want (e.g. Knight 1922, 1923a). In this literature, Knight's criticism focuses on the fundamental instability of preferences rather than the problem of imperfect knowledge. Human wants are unstable, he suggests, for three reasons. First, our actions are often impulsive: "a relatively unthinking and undetermined response to stimulus and suggestion" (Knight 1923a: 68). Second, because our wants are informed and shaped by the economic system itself (through advertising, for example, but also through education and social relations), the ends we pursue are not as independent as the maximizing assumption presumes (ibid.). Third, there is an inherent dynamism to human preferences that is related to the basic drive to improve: "The chief thing which the common-sense individual actually wants is not satisfactions for the wants he has, but more, and *better* wants" (Knight 1922: 42, emphasis in original). Unfortunately, deception and deceit in the marketplace often undermine our desire to improve, so that the wants we actually pursue do not lead us to become good people.

Knight's understanding of the instability of preferences and its moral implications are summarized in "The Ethics of Competition," his moral critique of the market system:

> [Even] the freest individual, the unencumbered male in the prime of life, is in no real sense an ultimate unit or social datum. He is in large measure a product of the economic system, which is a fundamental part of the cultural environment that has formed his desires and needs, given him whatever marketable productive capacities he has, and which largely controls his opportunities. Social organization through free contract implies that the contracting units know what they want and are guided by their desires, that is, that they are "perfectly rational," which would be equivalent to saying that they are accurate mechanisms of desire-satisfaction. In fact, human activity is largely impulsive, a relatively unthinking and undetermined response to stimulus and suggestion. Moreover, there is truth in the allegation that unregulated competition places a premium on deceit and corruption. … It is plainly contrary to fact to treat the individual as a *datum,* and it must be conceded that the lines along which a competitive economic order tends to form character are often far from being ethically ideal.
>
> (Knight 1923a: 68–9)

One way of summarizing Knight's criticisms of the maximizing assumption is to say that they focus our attention on the problems associated with the impersonal nature of a market operating under the maximizing assumption. This is not surprising, given discussion in the previous section, where we saw that the impersonal and mechanistic nature of exchange was central to his understanding of the role of the assumption in neoclassical theory. When people know what they want and how to get it, their exchanges become impersonal and the process by which they exchange becomes mechanical. The discipline that studies the mechanical process of exchange, therefore, can aspire to the scientific status given to classical mechanics. Knight's criticisms remind economists, however, that achieving the status of a science has a cost, because reference to the mechanical nature of the price system obscures as much as it reveals. And one of the things it obscures is that mechanical maximizers are neither human, nor do they interact with each other as humans: "The *view* of human behavior as a mechanical sequence … is *impossible* to human beings. … This is one of the main differences between the economic man and the real human being" (Knight 1935b: 280, 282, emphasis in original).

Because human action, for Knight, is ultimately a discussion about the kind of people we want to become, the impersonal nature of market exchange undermines our ability to become good people. Thus the answer to the "first" question of economic science – how far is life rational? – is "Not very far; the scientific view of life is a limited and partial view," and this "sets a first and most sweeping limitation to the conception of economics as a science" (Knight 1924a: 1).

The market as a game

The reader who peruses any significant amount of Knight's work will realize that his criticisms of the maximizing assumption are frequently accompanied by reference to the market as a *game*. He seems to have employed the notion of "playing," or "gaming," because it provided a particularly effective way of highlighting two aspects of his criticisms of neoclassicism. First, describing exchange behavior as playful gave him a way of suggesting that decision-making is as much a choice of ends as it is a choice of means. Two characterizations of this aspect of play can be found in his work, and they are not necessarily compatible. In *RUP* he began his first criticism of the notion of economic rationality with the statement, "Most human motives tend on scrutiny to assimilate themselves to the game spirit" (Knight 1921a: 53), where the concrete objective is a matter of accident and the primary purpose is simply to play.

> It is little matter, if any, what we set ourselves to do; it is imperative to have some objective in view, and we seize upon and set up for ourselves objectives more or less at random – getting an education, acquiring skill at some art, making money, or what-not. But once having set ourselves to achieve some goal it becomes an absolute value, weaving itself into and absorbing life itself. It is just as in a game where the concrete objective – capturing our opponents' pieces, carrying a ball across a mark, or whatever it may be – is a matter of accident, but to achieve it is for the moment the end and aim of being.
>
> (Knight 1921a: 53)

In his later philosophical work, however, Knight replaced the notion of an arbitrary selection of ends with a formulation of playful activity which fit more comfortably with his understanding of the explorative nature of human behavior. While it may be sufficient to allow the objective of the game to be simply a matter of accident for the purpose of pointing out the empirical inadequacy of the maximizing assumption, the arbitrariness that this implies did not provide him an adequate basis to argue that gaming behavior is explorative and experimental. In particular, it did not allow him to suggest that we keep trying different games until we find a *good* one. Some games call out the best in us; others leave us dissatisfied. The only way to discover the games we most enjoy and play the best is to experiment with different games.

But this, of course, raises the question of what constitutes a good game, which brings us to the second reason why Knight employed the notion of the market as a game, namely the opportunity it provided him to communicate the moral nature of all action: "The ethical character of competition is not decided by the fact that it stimulates a greater amount of activity; this merely raises the question of the ethical quality of what is done or of the motive itself" (Knight 1923a: 86).

Two things are important for Knight in regard to the connection between the notion of the market as a game and ethics. The first is the way in which playful behavior points toward the ethical and aesthetic aspect of explorative activity. If the choice of games is not simply a matter of accident, then that necessarily raises the question of the standards of value we use to judge games. For Knight, decisions regarding the norms by which we choose are one aspect of ethics and aesthetics: "The actual ranking of games would raise the same problems of value standards which beset the path to objectivity in all fields of artistic criticism" (Knight 1923a: 80).

What, then, constitutes a *good* game? Knight saw four elements as essential to any good game. First, it must involve some level of skill. Knight believed that while people like games of chance, most would agree "that games of skill are 'superior' to games of chance" (Knight 1923a: 80), because the outcome of a game of skill can be influenced by the effort one applies to it. Thus effort is the second element of a good game: it "must test the capacity of the players, and to do this it must compel them to exert effort" (ibid.: 79). At the same time, however, effort by itself (perhaps measured on some objective scale) is not sufficient to make a good game interesting; there must be some measure of uncertainty regarding the outcome: "The result must be unpredictable: if there is no element of luck in it there is no game" (ibid.: 79–80). Finally, there are the moral qualities that the good game calls out in those who play: "Some games are 'higher class' than others, depending presumably on the human qualities necessary to play them successfully and to enjoy them" (ibid.: 80).

How did Knight think the market rated as a game? If a good game calls out the best in people while balancing the elements of skill, effort, and luck, then, he argued, the market was probably *not* a good game, for four reasons. First, the outcome of the market game is not an accurate reflection of business skill:

> [The] differences in the capacity to play the business game are inordinately great from one person to another. But as the game is organized, the weak contestants are thrown into competition with the strong in one grand melee; there is no classification of the participants or distribution of the handicaps

such as is always recognized to be necessary to sportsmanship where unevenly matched contestants are to meet. In fact the situation is worse still; there are handicaps, but … they are distributed to the advantage of the strong rather than the weak.

(Knight 1923a: 80–1)

Second, while luck plays a large role in the market game, its effect compounds the problems associated with the differences in skill. Success in the first few rounds of the game (through skill, inheritance, or luck) confers a differential advantage upon the initial leader. Anyone may be eliminated after the first round, or may be "placed in a position where it is extraordinarily difficult to get back into the game" (Knight 1923a: 80). Hence the game, while fascinating for the leaders, reduces the participation of the rest to mechanical drudgery (ibid.: 83).

The third reason Knight provided in support of his argument that the market did not meet the requirements of a good game takes us to his second concern for the ethical quality of playful behavior: his concern for the impact of the market game on the formation of virtue, or good character. Even if the market did balance skill, effort, and luck in a pleasing proportion, it would still not rate as a good game, because it does not cultivate the highest human ideals or a "very high order of sportsmanship" (Knight 1923a: 81). Quoting John Ruskin, he pointed out that the winners in the market game are usually "industrious, resolute, proud, covetous, prompt, methodical, sensible, unimaginative, insensitive, and ignorant," while the game's losers include:

The entirely foolish, the entirely wise, the idle, the reckless, the humble, the thoughtful, the dull, the imaginative, the sensitive, the well-informed, the improvident, the irregularly and impulsively wicked, the clumsy knave, the open thief, the entirely merciful, just, and godly person.

(Knight 1923a: 82)

The moral qualities that the market developed, then, were not the kind of qualities that Knight believed were essential to the improvement of society. While they might foster winning, they did not encourage the kind of social cooperation that would keep the game going and keep it open to participation by all. In such a society, the "good sport" becomes a twisted reflection of the ideal player described earlier – separated from any notion of virtue or good character.

To "play the game" is the current version of accepting the universe, and protest is blasphemy; the Good Man has given place to the "good sport." In America particularly, where … the sporting view of life [has] reached [its] fullest development, there have come to be two sorts of virtue. The greater virtue is to win; and meticulous questions about the methods are not in the best form, provided the methods bring victory. The lesser virtue is to go out and die gracefully after having lost.

(Knight 1923a: 82–3)

Knight took the question of the moral qualities developed in the market a step further in his final criticism of the market as a game, asking whether "success in any sort of *contest,* as such, is a noble objective" (Knight 1923a: 82; emphasis in original). Contrasting "the predominance of the institution of sport" (ibid.: 90) and its spirit of rivalry in modern market societies with the pagan ethical ideal of perfect beauty and the Christian ethical ideal of spirituality, he concluded that we "search in vain for any really ethical basis of approval for competition as a basis for an ideal type of human relations, or as a motive to action" (ibid.: 89). Maybe even being a good sport is not enough to preserve society – a thought Knight returned to often in his work.

Maximizers versus good sports: Paradox as rhetorical strategy

In the previous sections, we have seen that Knight's criticisms of neo-classicism closely followed the key features of his formulation of the tradition's central assumption about human behavior – the maximizing assumption. We have also seen that he employed the notion of the market as a game as a means of drawing attention to the exploratory, non-mechanical nature of actual exchange behavior in contrast to the predetermined, mechanical nature of the exchange process in the world of perfect competition. What remains to be seen is why he refused to resolve the paradoxical tension between his participation in the neoclassical tradition and his rejection of the tradition's central assumption as a reliable guide to either human action or social inquiry.

To answer that question, we need to look briefly at the intellectual context in which he worked. As indicated in my opening remarks, the context in which most of the work considered here was written was the early twentieth-century debate over the relevance of economic theory to the most important social problems facing the United States. Marginalism, and the scientific status it apparently conveyed, had been essential to the establishment of an independent economics profession earlier (Church 1974; Ross 1991: 172–86). A full-blown body of neo-classical economic thought had not emerged in the United States, however, in part because of concern over neoclassicism's portrayal of people as lightning calculators of utility maximization (to use Veblen's phrase) and the concomitant rejection of laissez-faire economics, which neoclassicism was viewed as supporting. Early twentieth-century social scientists therefore often rejected neoclassical economics both as a theoretical framework and as a viable means of social control. They set out in search of new models of social inquiry which would place a greater degree of social control in the hands of social scientists and policy makers (see e.g. Barber 1985).

At least during the period in which most of his essays on the market as a game were written, Knight shared social scientists' dream of a social science that would enable the realization of liberal values within the context of modern society. He believed that many of the assumptions others made about human beings and the nature of society were mistaken, however, and that the means by which they pursued their goal were therefore flawed. In particular, he argued that the extension of the methods of the natural sciences into the social sciences was inappropriate, for both epistemological and ethical reasons, and that the increasing scientism of the social sciences was actually at odds with the liberal values social scientists sought to promote.

As I have argued in more detail elsewhere (Emmett 1991), the paradoxes and tensions in Knight's work emerge from his effort to delineate clearly the senses in which it was appropriate to speak of economics as science which had something to contribute to social policy-making in a liberal democracy. In contrast to most other social scientists of his time, he believed that the very things that made his discipline a science also rendered it inappropriate as a direct guide to democratic social action. The theoretical neoclassical tradition could not tell you what to do; but, if specified completely, it could sharpen the focus of those participating in the social discussion about what goals to pursue.

One of the ways Knight emphasized the limited range of the economist's vision was by limiting the "scientific" realm of economics to an area as small as possible, in order to highlight the nonscientific nature of social inquiry outside that small realm. In this context the paradox of the conflicting roles of the "maximizer" and the "good sport" in his understanding of exchange behavior makes more sense. Both sides of the paradox were essential to the tension he sought to sustain between economic theory and social practice in a liberal democracy. A sharply delineated characterization of the individuals who populate the world of perfect competition was needed to sustain the scientific nature of economic theory: for this, the metaphor of the mechanical maximizer worked well.

But science could only go so far in helping us to understand action in a liberal society. In the language of games, science played a role "only in connection with the interest of the individual in *winning* the game; it play[ed] none in having the game go on, still less in 'improving' it" (Knight 1935b: 301; emphasis in original). To talk about the explorative, experimental, and ultimately moral nature of the social interest in keeping the game going, Knight needed the metaphor of the good sport, the quality of whose actions would help prevent society from degenerating into a war of al against all. In his typical fashion, however, he suspected that in the end the market game would be incapable of creating more good sports, and would therefore undermine its own existence.

8   Frank Knight on the conflict of values in economic life

In his essay on Frank Knight in *The New Palgrave,* George Stigler (1987) suggested that there was a fundamental difference between the way Knight approached economics and the way most other twentieth-century economists have approached their discipline:

> For most present-day economists, the primary purpose of their study is to increase our knowledge of the workings of the enterprise and other economic systems. For Knight, the primary role of economic theory is rather different: it is to contribute to the understanding of how by consensus based upon rational discussion we can fashion [a] liberal society in which individual freedom is preserved and a satisfactory economic performance achieved. This vast social undertaking allows only a small role for the economist, and that role requires only a correct understanding of the central core of value theory.
>
> (Stigler 1987: 58)

Although in the course of this chapter we will see that there is at least one aspect of the basic orientation of Knight's work that is not captured by Stigler's remark, his identification of the centrality of the relation of economics to political life in Knight's work is a useful starting point because it highlights the two major themes of this chapter and points us toward the nature of their relation in Knight's work. The first theme is Knight's belief in the fundamental indivisibility of the intellectual and moral aspects of social problems. Knight was highly critical of the line of reasoning regarding the relation between the positive and normative that has become the conventional wisdom in twentieth-century economic thought, because of its implicit acceptance of the idea that there is widespread agreement regarding the goals of social policy, and hence that solutions for our social problems are to be found primarily in the improvement of our present social and economic knowledge.[1] Believing that disagreement over social policy changes within society emerged as much from disagreement over, and conflict among, the relevant values affected by the policy as from any disagreement over the facts regarding the policy's consequences, Knight continually emphasized the unity of the intellectual and moral aspects of social problems and the indivisibility of the positive and normative:

The social problem is not one of fact – except as values are also facts – nor is it one of means and end. It is a problem of values. And the content of social science must correspond with the problem of action in character and scope.

(Knight 1941a: 134).

The second theme highlighted by Stigler's remark is the important role that value theory played in Knight's thought, especially in terms of the relation of economic value theory to ethical or social value theory. The conventional wisdom regarding the relation between the positive and normative is built, in part, upon the assumption that the ethical commitments of individuals in society can be treated functionally as the correlates of the individuals' tastes and preferences because there is no rational means by which we can resolve conflict between the values of competing individuals. For values, as for tastes and preferences, economists assume that *de gustibus non est disputandum*. Following the methodological argument articulated most clearly by George Stigler and Gary Becker (1977) in an article bearing that Latin expression as its title, the conventional wisdom also tends to downplay the social significance of differences in values among the members of society, and changes in an individual's values over time, in favor of an emphasis upon the importance of differences, and changes, in our perceptions of the relative costs of various social policies. Knight, on the other hand, believed that all of our intentions had an inner, creative dynamism which made almost any choice, individual or social, a problem of ends as well as means. Social policy changes incite dispute, argued Knight, not only because they change the relative cost of achieving one's objectives – producing additional potential benefits for some at the expense of others, but also because they initiate institutional changes that shape the kind of people we are becoming, and therefore either support or undermine our differing conceptions of who we should be:

> The broad crucial task of free society is to reach agreement by discussion on the kind of civilization it is to create for the future; hence it must agree on the meaning of progress. … Discussion of … change must run in terms of general values or ideals. The politics of democracy cannot be a contest between individuals or interest groups in getting what they want at the cost of others. … One of the worst verbal confusions is using the same term, "value," for both subjective desires and ideals which, in seeking agreement, must be recognized as objectively valid, hence "cognitive." Social problems arise out of conflicts at either of the two levels, but they can be discussed only as differences in critical-intellectual judgment of norms. Mere assertion of opposed claims cannot tend toward agreement, but must intensify conflict.

> (Knight 1956b: 407)

The purpose of this chapter is to examine the way in which Knight developed his understanding of the inseparability of the intellectual and moral dimensions of social problems by investigating his approach to the conflict between social values and his insistence on the difficulty of achieving consensus over the ethical ideals for a liberal democracy. In order to show the relation between Knight's value theory and his understanding of social problems, I will begin by taking up the hint provided by Stigler when he said that Knight understood the role of the economist in social discourse to be circumscribed by economic value theory, and look first at Knight's discussion of the moral dimension of economizing problems.

The economizing problem as a moral problem

At the center of Knight's economic value theory was the same fundamental ambiguity in the word *value* that he berated as one of our worst verbal confusions in the comment, quoted above, regarding the nature of social problems. Early in his career as an economist, Knight explored the ambiguity of the term as it is used in economics in an important series of articles (see Knight 1922, 1923a, 1924a, 1925b, and 1935g; 1925a). In those articles, Knight argued that, if human preferences and ethical ideals are simply scientific data, "givens" to be accepted as static and unavailable for rational discussion and dispute, then economics *is* ethics, because the only possible evaluation of "given" interests is the one created by the coordinating mechanism itself. For a market society, this implies that price theory *is* value theory, because the pricing system provides the basic mechanism for the social coordination of individual interests. In Knight's own words:

> In so far as the ends are viewed as given, as data, then all activity is economic. The question of the effectiveness of the adaptation of means is the only question to be asked regarding conduct, and economics is the one and all-inclusive science of conduct. From this point of view the problem of life becomes simply the economic problem, how to employ the existing and available supplies of all sorts of resources, human and material, natural and artificial, in producing the maximum *amount* of *want-satisfaction,* including the provision of new resources for increased value production in so far as the present population finds itself actually desiring future progress. The assumption that wants or ends are data reduces life to economics, and raises again the question with which we started out, Is life all economics or does this view require supplementing by an ethical view of value?
>
> (Knight 1922: 51; emphasis in original).

Knight's subsequent insistence upon the possibility of evaluating wants, desires, and ethical ideals *outside* of society's coordinating mechanisms focused upon the limitations of the view that such interests could be taken as scientific data. In Knight's estimation, human intentionality has an inner, creative dynamism which makes our preferences and values unstable, immeasurable, and individually unique. Economic principles have only a limited scope of application to human conduct, because it is only within a very narrow range of human activity, if at all, that our interests can be taken as given.

Furthermore, the price system, which Knight believed to be the most effective mechanism for the coordination of competing "given" interests, would, in his estimation, quite likely prove to be an ineffective coordinator of competing "dynamic" interests, because it provided no standards by which to measure their moral progress: "The chief thing which the common-sense individual wants is not satisfactions for the wants which he has, but more, and *better* wants" (Knight 1922: 42; emphasis in original).

For Knight, therefore, the economizing problem itself was seldom simply a problem of means, for people want to know what constitutes "better wants," and hence there is a need for an independent, or non-price, evaluation of our personal interests. "It is," Knight said, "the higher goal of conduct to test and try these values (i.e. interests), to define and improve them, rather than to accept and 'satisfy' them" (Knight, 1922, p. 55). The job of ethics is to develop value standards which assist us in that task; standards which help us to exercise wise judgment without establishing absolute rules based upon values that are arbitrarily taken as absolute. Those ethical standards, Knight believed, would come closer to the standards by which we judge great literature and art than it would to those standards by which we evaluate scientific theories.[2]

The necessity of an independent ethics for the real world of dynamic interests implied two things for Knight. First, it implied that price and value theory could never be completely severed. Commenting once upon Gustav Cassel's repudiation of utilitarian value theory in favor of a pure exchange model in his Theoretische Socialoekonomie, Knight warned that:

> … the "repudiation of value theory" is very good, and the writer is altogether in favor of it – for the first stage in the discussion of economic problems. But should it not be kept in mind also that the ultimate object of economic theorizing is a criticism in ethical and human terms of the workings of the economic machine, and that a theory of value as well as price is indispensable?
>
> (Knight 1921d: 146).

Second, the necessity of an independent ethics implied for Knight that efficiency was not the chief criterion by which societies should judge coordination mechanisms; instead, they should be judged primarily in terms of the kind of wants and desires they create, and the character of the people they form. When Knight, in his justly famous essay, "The Ethics of Competition," turned the standards of two major ethical systems (Aristotelian and Christian) regarding the nature of our interests and the quality of our character on the market mechanism itself, he found it wanting:

> [Because] the social order largely forms as well as gratifies the wants of its members … it must be judged ethically rather by the wants which it generates, the type of character which it forms in its people, than by its efficiency in satisfying wants as they exist at any given time. … [T]he competitive system, viewed simply as a want-satisfying mechanism, falls far short of our highest ideals. To the theoretical tendencies of perfect competition must be opposed just as fundamental limitations and counter-tendencies, of which careful scrutiny discloses a rather lengthy list. Its standards of value for the

guidance of the use of resources in production are the prices of goods, which diverge widely from accepted ethical values; and if the existing order were more purely competitive, if social control were reduced in scope, it seems clear that the divergence would be enormously wider still. Moreover, untrammeled individualism would probably tend to lower standards progressively rather than to raise them. "Giving the public what it wants" usually means corrupting popular taste.

(Knight 1923a: 70, 74)

The really interesting thing about the two sides of Knight's economic value theory, however, is the fact that they are never clearly reconciled in his work. We have to remember that the man who wrote "Ethics and the Economic Interpretation" (Knight 1922) also wrote "Some Fallacies in the Interpretation of Social Cost" (Knight 1924b); that the man who said that price theory could never adequately encompass the realities of a world of dynamic intentionality was in no small measure responsible for the initiation of the "Chicago School" tradition of deliberately explaining actual human conduct solely in terms of price theory; and that the man who said that there was no ethical foundation upon which one could justify the market later turned the statement around to say that the market was a social institution which no ethical system had yet adequately comprehended (see Knight 1923a).

James Buchanan recently pointed out the perpetual presence of this tension between price and value theory in Knight's work in his rational reconstruction, along catallactic lines, of Knight's ethical critique of the capitalist order. After suggesting that Knight failed to recognize the possibility of separating price and value theory, and therefore underrated the ethical support for free markets, because he failed to escape completely the maximizing element of traditional economic theory, Buchanan concludes with the admission: "It is, of course, possible that it was precisely the methodological ambiguity that created the tension in Knight's analysis and that it is this tension that allows us to remain fascinated with his works" (Buchanan 1987: 74).

Despite his desire to resolve the tension within Knight's work by reeducating Knight in such a way as to convince him of the separability of price and value theory, Buchanan clearly recognizes that to do so would result in a vision of social and economic problems that is somehow smaller than Knight's own. The tension between the two concepts of value theory within Knight's work may frustrate the reader's desire for a coherent account of economics and its relation to ethics, but it also entices the reader to think more deeply about the problems of economic organization. Before moving from Knight's consideration of the economizing problem as a moral problem to his consideration of social problems as moral problems, we need to pause and consider the place that this type of tension had in Knight's thought.

The therapeutic orientation of Knight's work

Most economists familiar with Knight's work recognize that he often played a role which one author has described as that of a "Socratic gadfly" (Purcell 1973:

43) – seeking more to ask questions that explore the various limitations and constraints under which our ideas operate than to set out an improved system of ideas. His writings on economic and social philosophy, in particular, were marked by a question-oriented mode of thinking, which sought to edify by raising questions more than to construct by answering them. In the words of F.A. Hayek (1978: 51, n. 1), Knight was "a puzzler if there ever was one."

Despite widespread recognition of the "puzzling" or edifying quality of Knight's work, most interpreters are still tempted to distill out of his "Socratic" ruminations a clearly articulated philosophical doctrine on economics and society. Without denying that his work is shaped by certain philosophical commitments, I wish to suggest that it is nevertheless a major mistake to categorize his work by reference to those commitments. The inclination to discover a coherent system of ideas within a past thinker's work emerges from our desire to classify thinkers and place them within intellectual categories which serve our contemporary purposes. Although this is often useful, it must be recognized that it almost completely ignores the past thinker's own intentions as they were expressed in the interaction between the thinker's ideas and the audience to which they were addressed (see Pocock 1971: 3–41; Rorty 1984; Skinner 1969; and Wood 1979). For the purposes of interpreting Knight, such a perspective is almost fatal because a systematic exposition of his work will miss the main point, which is that his primary contribution to the development of a more coherent economic and social philosophy lay in the way in which he endeavored to show economists and other inquirers into human society their inability to encompass human experience within the confines of a single intellectual system, and the necessity of accepting the moral responsibility their intellectual limitations placed upon them. As Warner Wick said at Knight's memorial service, to speak of Knight as a philosopher is to say that he practiced philosophy:

> ... in its ancient character as an activity which has no end, and produces no authoritative doctrines, just because it reflects critically on the aims, interrelations, limitations, and inevitable distortions of all doctrines.
>
> (Wick 1973: 513)

Knight's work, then, is not some giant jigsaw puzzle, which, when finally put together, reveals a picture of a comprehensive system of thought about the economy or society; it is, rather, an assortment of ruminations that seek to destroy systems of thought because they are seen as inimical to the continued health of that great conversation we call human society.

In order to distinguish Knight's intentions from those of the great systematic thinkers on economic and social philosophy, I suggest that we describe his work as therapeutic in orientation. This term is borrowed from Rorty's recent description of the difference between modern philosophers such as Nietzsche, Dewey, Wittgenstein, and Heidegger, whose works are disturbing and paradoxical because they resist the effort to classify them according to traditional philosophical categories, and the great systematic thinkers of this century who provide cogently argued and systematically organized presentations of new approaches to the basic problems of philosophy (Rorty 1979: 5–6, 357–94). The works of these therapeutic thinkers, Rorty argues, are disturbing and paradoxical because they deliberately refuse to follow the generally accepted notions of what it means to do philosophy. By resisting reduction, classification, and institutionalization, they strive to keep us from interpreting their work as an incremental contribution to a progressive philosophical research program, and prevent us from reducing human conversation to scientific argument – *edification* rather than *construction* is their primary goal. By pointing out that the search for truth is merely one of many human projects (Knight added that the search for truth was subject to diminishing returns[3]), they speak of the conflicts which emerge between it and other human occupations and remind the philosopher and social scientist of the need for humility in the face of the creative complexity and novelty of human experience. And by offering stories, satires, and aphorisms in reaction to the prevailing currents of philosophical opinion, they parody the systematic philosopher's desire for sound logic and conclusive arguments and remind us of the need for the love of wisdom as well as knowledge. Knight himself captured the edifying message of the therapeutic philosophers when he said in his presidential address to the American Economic Association: "the right principle is to respect all the principles, take them fully into account, and then use *good judgment* as to how far to follow one or another in the case in hand" (Knight 1951b: 366; italics in original).

Recognition of the therapeutic orientation of Knight's work helps us to appreciate his personal refusal to specify any kind of resolution for the prioritization and coordination of competing dynamic interests, and hence to understand why he appeared to drop us off at exactly the point at which we should really begin. A more systematic thinker, of course, would try to guide us through the task of prioritizing and coordinating our ethical ideals with our economic interests, as the work of more recent thinkers as various as John Rawls, Amartya Sen, Robert Nozick, Hal Varian, and James Buchanan have done. Knight did not lead us through such an exercise because, ultimately, he believed that the quest for better interests was our responsibility and that the prioritization and coordination of interests required for that quest could only emerge from the actual *practice* of individuals and societies. His task was merely to bring us to the point where we recognized the moral nature of our practice and accepted the difficulty of fulfilling our responsibility. In turn, it was the need to fulfill that purpose that led Knight to expand his focus beyond the relation of the two sides of value theory in economics to their relation in the broader context of social practice. And it is to his therapeutic ruminations on that broader context that we now turn.

Social problems as moral problems

Like most social philosophers who follow in the tradition of classical liberalism, Knight saw democracy as the most compatible political partner for free markets, because the mechanisms of democratic political activity allowed for the coordination of individual interests in collective decisions in a manner similar to the coordination of individual choices by the market. Given the centrality of the tension between the two sides of value theory in his exploration of the market system, it is not surprising that the same tension emerged as a dominant theme in his exploration of liberal democracy.

One side of the tension in Knight's social thought was essentially contractarian and emerged from his recognition of the fact that, when our ethical ideals are taken up as interests, they play the same role within our collective decision-making as do our economic interests in our individual decision-making. Because interests conflict, their interaction within the context of collective choices requires a type of coordination similar to that provided by the market's coordination of tastes and preferences to ensure that the eventual outcomes are mutually beneficial, within the limits imposed by scarcity, for all participants. From this perspective, democratic action is simply a coordination mechanism (much like the market) for resolving the conflicting interests of freely associating individuals regarding collective choices, and the central political problem is the specification of an institutional structure for the coordination of interests that can resolve those conflicts efficiently. A good example of this side of Knight's social thought can be found in his critical review of two books by Michael Polanyi (Knight 1949). Despite his general agreement with Polanyi regarding the nature of scientific discussion and the organization of the quest for scientific truth, Knight takes Polanyi to task for trying to apply the model of freedom in scientific discussion to the problems raised by free discussion in democratic society. Social problems, Knight tells us, do not involve the search for truth, in any sense of that word comparable to its usage in science, rather, they involve the search for agreement among individuals who hold competing evaluations of the outcomes of policy changes. Better (i.e. more efficient) agreements may be reached through intelligent discussion of the issues involved, but even if unanimity is achieved, it could not be said that a "true" judgment had been made. The terms "true" and "false" are simply irrelevant to political decision-making. In the words of James Buchanan, Knight's criticisms of Polanyi emerge from a perspective which holds that: "Politics is the collective counterpart of individual choice and nothing more. ... [It] is the process through which the initial preferences [of individuals] are expressed, discussed, compromised, and, finally, resolved in some fashion" (Buchanan 1967: 306).

Despite the prominence that the contractarian side of Knight's social thought has reached through its extension in Buchanan's work, there was another theme in Knight's thought that, if we are to fully understand him, must be held in tension with the contractarian theme. This second theme emerges from the other side of his value theory – from the view that the creative dynamism of our intentions necessitates the development of a set of intersubjectively valid ethical standards.

On this second side of Knight's thought, values exist, not only as the subjective interests of individuals, but also as supra-individual expressions of our understanding of the common good for humanity. Put differently, our values reflect our corporate understanding of the kind of people we want to be. Furthermore, social institutions are not only coordination mechanisms, but embodiments of our values, albeit in imperfect ways. Social policy changes become problems for our

society because they initiate institutional changes that directly participate in form-
ing the kind of people we are becoming, and therefore support or undermine our
differing understandings of who we should be.

From this perspective, collective choices are similar to individual choices, not
because they both represent the resolution of conflict among various given interests, but rather because they both embody in human practice the quest for higher
ethical ideals. In a book review written early in his career, Knight described the
goal in the following terms:

> The larger problem is to arrange things so that people will find their lives
> interesting and will grow into such personalities that they can respect them-
> selves, admire others and enjoy their society, appreciate thought and beauty,
> and in general look upon creation and call it good.
>
> (Knight 1919a: 806)

Because actual social practice never realizes this goal, it can, in a sense, be
described as a lengthy conversation about nature of a good society, and the fact
that a specific conflict has been resolved is not as important as the fact that the conversation which that society represents has been continued and carried forward.[4]

The tension between values as the subjective interests of individuals and values as supra-individual ideals for the common good – or, to say the same thing in
a different way, the tension between democracy as a coordination mechanism and
democracy as a conversation – lies behind Knight's emphasis upon the conflicts
between freedom and justice, and freedom and order, within a liberal democratic
society. Knight generally identified freedom as the central value of a liberal society because, in keeping with the contractarian side of his thought, the absence
of coercion implied the rights of individuals to pursue their interests by making
changes, and to associate together with others for purposes of mutual betterment. Keeping within the boundaries of the contractarian side of his thought for
the moment, we can see that the need for an orderly process by which to make
changes that promote individual and group interests, and also ensure equality
of treatment among individuals, conflicts with, and places limitations upon, the
desire to maximize the freedom of the individual. Without agreement on constitutional principles to establish rules for the coordination of individual and
group interests, collective actions could only become the setting for social strife,
conflict, and chaos.

But there is more to Knight's discussion of the conflict among the values of
freedom, order, and justice than a call for constitutional rules to coordinate our
contractarian society, for social *practice* will always be pushing at the limits of
those constitutional rules from two different directions. On the one hand, the
imperfections and limitations of any particular constitutional rules will focus
social discussion on adaptations and changes to the rules that will make them
truer embodiments of the society's vision of the common good. The difficulty of
this task is, of course, compounded by the evolving nature of our understanding
of a just society; the central problem, Knight suggested, "is that of defining the

social good, or "justice" in the widest sense, by describing the social order which embodies the ideal in the highest degree" (Knight 1949: 281).

At the same time as our social practice requires us to reformulate our conceptions of the common good and reform our existing constitutional rules in an effort to promote progress toward those ideals, it also has a restraining effect upon progress because of the requirement to conserve the personal and institutional integrity found in the existing order of society. If social institutions are the embodiments of ethical ideals and significantly shape the kind of people we become, then, no matter how imperfectly they reflect their ideals, there is a need to conserve them for the sake of preserving our present personal and social character. Viewed from an institutional perspective, order is therefore the supreme value of society (Knight 1960b: 30), because, through the conservation of existing institutions, society strives to ensure that changes made in the name of freedom and justice will not undermine the existing character of our society and the gains already made.

Knight's own "conservatism" can be placed in perspective by these comments. Systematic thinkers and social reformers who desire progress on our major social problems find Knight's refusal to tackle the resolution of value conflicts frustrating, and often decide, after considering his willingness to let the tension among various values simply exist, that it represents a basic unwillingness to change the status quo.[5] This view seriously misreads Knight. His conservatism arises, not out of a love of tradition, but out of the almost paralyzing tension created by a strong belief in the need for social progress and an equally strong belief in the essential tragicness of human existence. Here was man who desperately desired a better world, but whose study of economics and society had brought him face-to-face with the terrible constraints that scarcity places upon us, and the fact that even our best-intentioned efforts fail to draw us closer to a better world. In a letter to none other than Richard Tawney, in 1939, Knight described the path along which his thoughts had taken him and the reluctance and disappointment he felt as a result:

> When I took up Economics as a career, I thought of it in terms of doing good in the world. But it seems as if the first step in any direct effort along this line is to choose between any high degree of accuracy and impartiality in dealing with the facts, and the possibility of cooperation with other people who declare themselves interested in social-economic betterment. It is certainly with reluctance and disappointment that I have felt myself forced to adopt a position of neutral, in most of the great discussions of issues currently going on – knowing that neutrality means being treated as an enemy by both sides, or escaping this fate only by being regarded as utterly insignificant, or being actually unheard of.

> (Knight 1939b)

The development of a therapeutic orientation seems to have been Knight's only defense against the reality of scarcity. The line of tension between the two sides of the conflict between freedom, justice, order, and other values runs throughout most of Knight's work after 1935, with almost no suggestions as to how the

tensions can be resolved. Once again, we find that Knight brings us to the essential
tension within the social discourse of a liberal society, without attempting to guide
us through it. With reluctance, he realized that it was only in actual social practice
that resolutions would be found, and that his role, as critic and philosopher, was
to bring us to realize the limitations of our values and accept the responsibility for
working out their resolution. As he often said: "(My) aim is merely to raise certain
questions, without attempting to give them final answers" (Knight 1930a: 149;
Knight 1960a: 121–2).

Section III

Interpreting Frank Knight and Chicago economics

9 Frank Knight, Max Weber, Chicago economics, and institutionalism

> [Max Weber is] one of the few men I have read for whom I still have some respect after reading them.
>
> (Knight 1936e)

Max Weber's approach to social scientific methodology and his comparative historical sociology were important resources that Knight drew upon in his efforts to create a social science that transcended the terms of the neoclassical–institutionalist debate during the 1920s and 1930s. An examination of the connection between Knight's reading of Weber's work and his effort to balance economic theory with a comparative economic history will enable us to understand better one of the central paradoxes regarding Knight's work: although Knight was the "dean of the opposition to institutionalism" (Yonay 1998: 144) and chief proponent of the scientific status of neoclassical theory during the interwar years, by the postwar period his work was relegated to the non-scientific realm of "social philosophy."

The paradox becomes clearer (although perhaps not resolved) when we provide a fuller account of the resources Knight drew upon in articulating the nature of a social science and the role within it of history, culture, and interpretation. *One* of those resources was the work of Weber. But the purpose here is not to append a new label – *Weberian* – to Knight's work, nor is it specifically to trace the "influence" of Weber on Knight or all the various connections between their work (for example, nothing will be said of the similarities in their treatment of entrepreneurship, for this see Brouwer 2002). Rather, an examination of how Knight drew upon Weber can broaden our understanding of the plurality of views present within American interwar economics and assist an investigation of the way some views were marginalized in the discipline as a new "scientific" economics emerged.

In order to assist the reader, let me state at the outset the perspective on Knight's work that has gradually percolated through my writings on Knight (see especially chapters 5 and 6 of this volume and Emmett 1999b), and that forms the background for this paper. First, labeling Knight as an "institutionalist," "neoclassicist," or "Austrian" is not particularly helpful once we accept the pluralistic context of the interwar period. (Nor is it necessary to find a new label for Knight, such as a "displaced" member of the Weber's German school of historical sociology – a suggestion made by Richard Wagner.) Rather than appending labels, our effort can be focused on understanding both how he used the resources at his disposal to make his point within specific debates among economists and social scientists, and how participation in those debates altered his viewpoint. Naturally, we cannot avoid some recognition of general differences between groups of economists, and want to associate individuals with the schools they articulate and defend. But when we say that Knight defended economic theory using an "ideal type" methodology, we are no more labeling him a "neoclassicist" or "Austrian" (see Yu 2002) than we are labeling him an "institutionalist" when we discuss his argument that a genetic (historical), rather than scientific, method is necessary to explain economic change (see Hodgson 2001).

Second, Knight's primary concern was the articulation of a *social science* (not only an *economics*) that could resolve the central tensions of modernity. One way of expressing those tensions is in the dual questions: how can scientific knowledge be employed for human betterment in a world of uncertainty where human action maintains its freedom and creativity? and at the same time, how can human action be free and creative when the modern institutions of science, industry, and culture constrain us and determine so much of what we do? Science and art, freedom and control, price and value, history and equilibrium, knowledge and judgment – these are the terms in which Knight attempted to work out his response to modernity. But Knight's articulation of a new social science changed over time, depending upon his perception of the key issues of the day and the resources he found useful. Weber drew his attention both because Weber saw the problems of modern social science in much the same terms that Knight did, (Kloppenberg 1986) and because Weber offered Knight a different way out of the intellectual morass of American social thought than that being followed by many of his contemporaries (Boyd 1997; Nopenney 1997).

The paralytic pluralism of interwar American economics

The context for Knight's reading of Weber was the impasse reached during the interwar period in American economics over the appropriate role for both economic theorizing and empirical or institutional study. Standard histories of American economics assume that the central story to be told is the doctrinal history of economic theory, and therefore marginalize elements of the story that may present a more pluralistic picture. American institutionalism, for example, is usually portrayed as a set of aberrant reactions to neoclassicism. But neoclassicism did *not* dominant American economics during the first half of the twentieth century: institutionalism and neoclassicism form "two parts of the same fascinating explanatory puzzle" (Rutherford 1997: 192; see also Goodwin 1973; Morgan and Rutherford 1998; Ross 1991; Rutherford 2003 and 2004; and Yonay 1998).

At the center of the struggle within economics during the interwar years was the question of what it meant to call economics a "science." Prior to World War I, the notion that economics was "scientific" had played a secondary (albeit increasingly active) role in legitimizing the social importance of economic knowledge. In the latter part of the 19th century, economic "orthodoxy" generally meant the tradition of "clerical laissez-faire" (May 1949: 14) that stretched back well before the Civil War and was almost inseparable from the traditions of Protestantism and classical liberalism in American moral philosophy. But during the Progressive era, a new moral perspective arose; one which emphasized social cohesion rather than individualism, and whose adherents, in the name of social unity and equality, challenged the moral authority of classical liberalism and re-fashioned American Protestantism in the manner of the Social Gospel (Rodgers 1982). By the end of the nineteenth century, most American social scientists, including many economists, thought economic orthodoxy irrelevant to the challenges of modern industrial society. The new social science they began to construct, however, depended only secondarily on "science" in the sense of the application of a rigorous, commonly accepted method. Rather, Progressivist social science rested primarily on the pragmatic assumption that liberal solutions were possible if adequate attention was spent studying a problem. Only as students of particular problems continued to disagree over solutions did that pragmatic assumption gradually come to require the reassurance that proper methods were being followed. By the early years of the twentieth century, methodological disputes had begun to occupy the attention of many social scientists: they began to identify disciplinary borders, and demarcate the first "schools" of thought within disciplines. When the Progressive era ended during World War I, "science" was sufficiently independent of Progressivism's disintegrating moral framework to emerge as the only (near-)certainty with which to confront modernity's ongoing challenges.

The social sciences, therefore, entered the interwar period with a new commitment to scientific practice, but with no common understanding of what that practice entailed. Vestiges of economic orthodoxy, historicism, pragmatism, marginalism, biological determinism, statistical inquiry, etc. co-existed uneasily with each other and with new approaches that emphasized the role of culture, urbanization, and institutions in the process of social change. In economics, the lack of a common understanding of what it meant to be a science is most often characterized as a debate between "institutionalists" and "neoclassicists," with a spillover into the debate regarding Keynesianism in the late 1930s and early 1940s. Yet the differences among economists of the period were plural, not dual, with the divisions among "neoclassicists," "institutionalists," or "Keynesians" often being as pronounced as those between the schools.

For Knight, the inability of American economists to reach agreement over the nature of their social science had paralyzed the discipline. His fear, voiced privately in numerous letters, and publicly in "The Case for Communism" (1991) and "Economic Theory and Nationalism" (1935b), was that the paralysis within the discipline would lead economists to appeal to the public in support for their various positions, thereby making public opinion the basis for scientific choice. "Such a contest," Knight argued, "must surely result in suicide for social science" (Knight 1935b: 350). He was on the lookout, therefore, for alternative viewpoints that might transcend the deadlock within the economics discipline (and, by extension, between neoclassicists and other social scientists). In particular, he needed resources that would support the argument he had already developed, namely that social scientists should reject the polarization of the theory *vs.* institutions debate and accept the necessity of pluralism.

Frank Knight and Max Weber

Although we do not know when Knight first encountered the work of Weber, it was probably before 1920. In the summer of 1913, upon graduation with a combined B.Sc. and M.A. (in German) from the University of Tennessee, Knight visited Germany, courtesy of his father, and returned with an armload of socialist and syndicalist pamphlets, and the desire to complete his studies in Europe. Maria Brouwer (2002: 85) suggests that Knight studied with Weber during this trip, but no evidence exists to defend that claim, and indeed it is unlikely that Weber was lecturing in 1913. Apart from attendance at several theological lectures by Wilhelm Hermann at the University of Marburg, the itinerary of the trip remains a mystery (Gonce 1996: 5). Both Richard Boyd (1996) and Alexander Ebner (2005) have suggested that Knight would have heard of Weber during the trip, given the interest in Weber's work among German philosophers and social scientists at the time. Surely the neo-Kantians at Marburg would have mentioned him during Knight's visit there?

If he did not encounter Weber's work during the 1913 trip, then he probably learned of Weber during his doctoral studies at Cornell after his return, in courses with Alvin Johnson and A.P. Usher (Nopenney 1997), or under Allyn Young's supervision of his dissertation (Boyd 1997). Usher is mentioned as providing some assistance with Knight's translation of Weber (Knight 1927: xvi), and Young claims credit for starting Knight on the translation in correspondence (Young 1927). The latest point at which Knight would have learned of Weber would be in 1917–19 at the University of Chicago, when he participated in an interdisciplinary study group on Thorstein Veblen's work (Neill 1972: 28).

Regardless of when his initial encounter with Weber's work occurred, we know that by the end of his tenure at the University of Iowa in the late 1920s, Knight had read extensively in the work of the German Historical School, including Weber (Nopenney 1997). In 1927, he published a translation of Weber's *Wirtschaftsgeschichte* (*General Economic History*) – the first book by Weber to appear in English. A survey of the German historical school followed the next year, in the guise of a review of the third volume of Werner Sombart's *Der moderne Kapitalismus* (Knight 1928). Knight's respect for Weber is apparent: Sombart is criticized for not following Weber, who, Knight says, is the "only one who really deals" with the origins of capitalism "from that angle which alone can yield an answer to such questions, that is, the angle of comparative history in the broad sense" (Knight 1928: 143). Knight's move to Chicago in 1928 intensified, rather than abated, his interest in Weber and comparative history, for reasons that will be explained below. Between 1929 and 1932, Knight wrote approximately 25 abstracts of books and articles by German historicists for *Social Science Abstracts*, a short-lived (four volumes, 1929–32) attempt to provide North American social scientists with access to the European literature.

The choice of *General Economic History* (1927, hereafter *GEH*) as the first posthumous English translation of Weber's work bears some comment. Given the methodological focus of Knight's critiques of institutionalism during the 1920s, one might have expected him to translate first some of the essays collected in *Gesammelte Aufsätze zur Wissenschaft-slehre*, first published in 1922, or *Wirtschaft und Gesellschaft*, also published in 1921–22. The fact that *GEH* was posthumously compiled from Weber's lecture notes also leads many scholars to categorize it as a lesser work. But *GEH* provided the only succinct mature formulation of Weber's comparative historical approach, which was Knight's primary interest. As Randall Collins has written, *GEH* provides:

> the most comprehensive general theory of the origins of capitalism … yet available … Weber's last theory is not the last word on the subject of the rise of capitalism, but if we are to surpass it, it is the high point from which we ought to build.
>
> (Collins 1980: 926–7)

Knight would have agreed with Collins, and translated the work in order to identify the foundation upon which he would build his own approach to social science.

Knight also continued to pursue the English translation of a greater portion of Weber's work. Shortly after the publication of *GEH*, he apparently began to plan a translation of the three-volume *Gesammelte Aufsätze zur Religionssoziologie*, which includes *Die protestantische Ethik und der Geist des Kapitalismus*, along with most of Weber's other writings on the sociology of religion. Through his colleague Paul Douglas, Knight was put in touch with Talcott Parsons, who also had plans for a translation (Parsons 1927). Although Knight felt strongly that a translation of the complete set of works was in order, Parsons shortly thereafter brought out *The Protestant Ethic and the Spirit of Capitalism* (1930). Knight and Parsons maintained a strong friendship throughout the 1930s (for an account of Parsons' side of the friendship, see Camic 1991 and Boyd 1997), although their intellectual differences gradually led them apart (their correspondence basically ended in 1940, with a few later letters spaced a decade apart, in 1950 and 1960/61). A recurring theme in the correspondence is both Parsons' and Knight's attempts to publish more of Weber's work. Knight had "Legal Sociology" ("Rechtssoziologie"), from *Wirtschaft und Gesellschaft*, and "Roscher and Knies and the Logical Problems of Historical National Economy" ("Roscher und Knies und die logischen Probleme der historischen Nationalökonomie") from *Gesammelte Aufsätze zur Wissenschaftslehre*, translated for potential publication, but nothing came of it (the translations are in the Knight Papers, University of Chicago Archives, Special Collections Research Center, University of Chicago Library). Parsons participated in the publication of other English translations of Weber's work, particularly the first volume of *Wirtschaft und Gesellschaft*, under the title *The Theory of Social and Economic Organization* (Parsons 1947). After the mid-1930s, Knight's participation in the translation of Weber's work ended. In fact, only a few scattered references to Weber occur in Knight's work after the 1930s. The conclusion of his active interest in Weber studies may account for the unusual comment that Knight made to Arthur Schweitzer in 1968: "There has been the work of one man whom I have greatly admired. If I were to start out again, I would build upon his ideas. I am referring of course to Max Weber" (Schweitzer 1975: 279). But, as we shall see, Knight's reading of Weber during the 1920s and 1930s had an impact on his work throughout the rest of his life.

Knight's comparative economic history

Some may find Knight's interest in Weber and comparative history during the 1930s surprising, given that in the same period he published many of his best known works in economic theory – especially his controversial string of articles criticizing Austrian capital theory. But Knight did not return to Chicago in 1928 to teach economic theory. During the 1920s he decided that he was not cut out to be a theorist – admitting to Jacob Viner that his only contribution to theory lay in asking questions and sharpening the definition of key terms (Knight 1925e). His reading of the German Historical School, therefore, marked a conscious career move – away from theory toward comparative economic history. At Chicago, this career shift was reflected in his teaching load and research interests. Throughout the 1930s, and well into the 1940s, courses in the history of economic thought, economics and social policy (eventually taught with philosopher Charner Perry), and historical and institutionalist economics dominate his teaching rotation. He was listed with John U. Nef as the department's teaching staff in economic history, and his research seminar in "Economic Institutions and their History" was devoted to reading Weber's work during the 1930s (Boyd 1997; Shils 1981; Stigler 1987: 56).

Economic theory, particularly theoretical controversy, sidetracked his new "life-work," however. He complained of this to Parsons:

> You may or may not have heard echoes of the fact that I have become more or less involved in controversy in economic theory, the theory of capital and interest in particular. I came to Chicago expecting … "institutionalism" to be my main field of work. But Viner went to Geneva two different years, leaving me the main course in theory. Even apart from that fact, I had intended all along to finish up the little book on theory that I started for Allyn Young's series about 1924 [NOTE: Knight refers here to a manuscript that builds upon the set of essays which eventually became *The Economic Organization* (1933c)]. Pressure in this direction was further increased when the people organizing the new general social science curriculum for the "College" here (freshman and sophomore years) decided to use the bulk of the material I had already put in shape and had been using in mimeographed form as auxiliary reading in my own classes. The controversy referred to grew especially out of my growing realization that the treatment of capital and productive factors generally in this material and in all my previous teaching is simply "wrong." A year ago I started in seriously to re-work this material, but found myself

wrestling with unsolved problems over virtually the whole field of traditional theory. Really, I haven't made very much headway with the whole project, except for getting some of my ideas more or less straightened out, but chiefly finding out how muddled they (and those of the élite in the field generally) really are. Now I am in quite a quandary as to what to do for a life work! A main difficulty is of course the fact that my capacity for work is so terribly limited. An ordinary university teaching program leaves me with little energy to do anything else, in spite of the fact that I make no pretense of doing the reading that I ought to do for my classes.

(Knight 1936d)

The "quandary" over his life-work escalated during the years prior to American involvement in the war, but did resolve itself as his involvement in theoretical debate diminished in the 1940s – his last "theory" articles are published during World War II.

But let us return to the first years of Knight's reappointment at Chicago before moving on to consider his work after the 1930s as part of his new social science. The focus on Knight's initiation of the capital controversy and the re-evaluation of cost theory which emerged from his "wrestling with unsolved problems over virtually the whole field of traditional theory" has drawn the attention of commentators on Knight's work away from his efforts at constructing a new social science during his early years in Chicago. It turns out that his reading of Weber had an important impact on those efforts.

One of the first articles Knight published after returning to Chicago was "Statik und Dynamik – zur Frage der Mechanischen Analogie in den Wirtshaftswissenschaften," which appeared for the first time in English five years later in *The Ethics of Competition* (Knight 1930a). The central claim of the article was that neoclassical economics was severely limited as a *social science* because the mechanical analogy, and in particular the notion of equilibrium, ignored the most important changes in economic life; those in the "givens" of theory – resources, knowledge, technology, and ends. Knight argued that these changes were unpredictable by any scientific method, but the processes involved could be understood through a study of the historical evolution of capitalist institutions:

Our general conclusion must be that in the field of economic progress the notion of tendency toward equilibrium is definitely inapplicable to particular elements of growth and, with reference to progress as a unitary process or system of interconnected changes, is of such limited and partial application as to be misleading rather than useful. This view is emphasized by reference to the phenomena covered by the loose term "institution." All speculative glimpses at trends in connection with price theory relate to a "competitive" or "capitalistic" economic system. But all the human interests and traits involved in this type of economic life are subject to historical change. Moreover, no society is or could be entirely and purely competitive. The roles of the state, of law, and of moral constraint are always important and that of other forms of organization such as voluntary co-operation may be so. Business life in the strictest sense never conforms closely to the theoretical behavior of an economic man. Always history is being made; opinions, attitudes, and institutions change, and there is evolution in the nature of capitalism. In fact evolution toward other organization forms as the dominant type begins before capitalism reaches its apogee. Such social evolution is rather beyond the province of the economic theorist, but it is pertinent to call attention to the utter inapplicability to such changes, i.e., to history in the large, of the notion of tendency toward a price equilibrium.

(Knight 1930a: 167–8)

At first glance, this familiar passage sounds quite similar to the methodological perspective Knight developed in *RUP* and in "The Limitations of Scientific Method in Economics" (1924a) which was his contribution to the volume of writings by the younger generation of institutionalists – a volume which figures prominently in almost every account of the interwar debates (Yonay 1998; Tugwell 1924). But it would be a mistake to interpret "Statik und Dynamik" this way. What has gone little noticed in accounts of Knight's methodology is the introduction in "Statik und Dynamik" of a different way of understanding the relation between neoclassical theorizing and the "real economy." In the earlier work, Knight specifically identified with the method of "successive approximation" common to economic analysis since at least the time of J.S. Mill: starting with the theory of perfect competition, theorists gradually relax assumptions to incorporate more features of the "real" economy into their analysis. "Statik und Dynamik," on the other hand, assumes a greater bifurcation between the theoretical world and the real world. The model of perfect competition here becomes one of Weber's "ideal types" – an analytical construct useful for scientific theorizing, but never realized in social life. The construction of "perfect competition" enables the economist to identify the central elements of economic life, but the study of how those elements change cannot be accomplished in theory. One must turn to history, where the process of change has no resemblance to an equilibrium process. The study of history, for Knight as for Weber, was the study of the pattern of relations created by the interaction of a wide variety of factors.

The difference between historical analysis built upon "ideal type" theorizing and the method of "successive approximation" is subtle, yet it had significant implications for the remainder of Knight's theoretical and methodological work. As I have argued elsewhere (Emmett 1997a), Knight's contribution to the capital theory controversies depends in part upon the history/theory division that is at the heart of Weber's methodology of social science. The same perspective underlies his rejection of a variety of developments in demand theory during the 1930s and 1940s (Knight 1944b). Later in his life, "ideal type" analysis becomes his default position in the small forays he made into discussions of labor economics (Knight 1951a). His most famous methodological essay, a vituperative attack on the positivism perceived in Terence Hutchison's *The Significance and Basic Postulates of Economic Theory*, is also a forceful defense of "ideal type" analysis and Weber's notion of *Verstehen* (Knight 1940a).

"Statik und Dynamik" may have first articulated the methodological basis for Knight's historical turn, but a more complete articulation was necessary. An initial attempt at a comparative history of capitalism was made in "The Development of Economic Institutions and Ideas," an unpublished essay prepared during the early 1930s for use in his course on "Economics from an Institutional Standpoint" and also circulated to a number of his friends. But Knight's most complete study of comparative economic history during the 1930s was "Economic Theory and Nationalism" (1935b), originally entitled "Nationalism and Economic Theory: an Essay in Institutional Economics." Knight compared three alternative institutional frameworks for economic life, and examined the role of social science in both interpreting and changing these frameworks.

"Economic Theory and Nationalism" begins with an examination of economics as an abstract or idealizing study, quite removed from historical changes.

> Economic theory is not a descriptive, or an explanatory, science of reality. Within wide limits, it can be said that historical changes do not affect economic theory at all. It deals with ideal concepts which are probably as universal for rational thought as those of ordinary geometry.
>
> (Knight 1935b: 277)

Comparing economics to medicine, Knight goes on to say that:

> a 'science' of human behavior, to be relevant to or practically significant, *must* describe *ideal* and not actual behavior, if it is addressed to free human beings expected to change their own behavior voluntarily as a result of the knowledge imparted.
>
> (Knight 1935b: 278; emphasis in original)

The ideal or abstract nature of economic theory implies that economics deals only with the "form" of human conduct, not its content:

> Economic theory takes men with (a) any wants whatever, (b) any resources whatever, and (c) any system of technology whatever, and develops principles of economic behavior. The validity of its 'laws' does not depend on the actual conditions or data, with respect to any of these three elementary phases of economic action.
>
> (Knight 1935b: 281).

To suggest that the idealized world of economic theory bears similarity with the real world is, for Knight, a mistake. Real people not only possess given wants, but want "resistance to be overcome in satisfying them" (Knight 1935b: 281). At any historical point, the resources provided have a history emerging from the complex interactions of a host of factors, as does the system of technology by which people adapt those resources to their preferences. Thus, history intrudes once we move outside the ideal type. But Knight argues that the unreality of economic theory involves more than the historicity of economic processes; real economic processes are also social. Economic theory's impersonal society is a "number of Crusoes interacting through the markets exclusively" (ibid.: 282). Human society, on the other hand, is personal: peopled with individuals who compete, emulate, manipulate, higgle, and bargain.

Yet the abstractions of economic theory do play a role in real society for Knight, because they provide ideals against which social actions in reality can be compared. To the extent that a society chooses to measure itself against its ideals *and change*, economics may be of social significance because it can point toward the changes that need to be made. Economic theory played such a role in nineteenth-century liberal society, because liberalism accepted individualism, and hence rejected proposals for change away from institutions that encouraged economic efficiency. Liberalism was also not the embodiment of economics' ideals, however; rather, those ideals stood in opposition to the ideals of the state which previously dominated European social thought (Knight 1935b: 285–8).

Any story of how real society has changed, therefore, must involve an interplay between social ideals such as those provided by economics, and institutional history. Viewing liberalism as the historical form of social organization that European and North American society was moving away from, Knight goes on in "Economic Theory and Nationalism" to compare liberalism with fascism (the form that he saw the world moving toward) and collectivism (an alternative which he saw as a form that would not be adopted). The essay ends with Knight's hope that liberalism could be maintained, but only if those who seek truth and those who seek change in social policy can work together; drawing upon both the study of ideal types and comparative institutional history.

Comparative analyses of institutional history continued to occupy Knight's attention during the 1940s and 1950s. Because essays like "Anthropology and Economics" (1941c), "Socialism: the Nature of the Problem" (1940b) and "The Sickness of Liberal Society" (1946), to name a few whose titles will provide obvious clues to readers of this paper, have traditionally been catalogued as "social philosophy" rather than comparative social science, the continuity of Knight's later work with his comparative historical turn in the late 1920s has been overlooked. The example of "Anthropology and Economics" is particularly interesting, because the comparison takes him some distance away from the familiar ground of the debate between capitalism and socialism and his own ruminations over the state of liberalism. A review of Melville Herskovits' *The Economic Life of Primitive Peoples*, this essay brings together Knight's appreciation for Weber's "ideal type" analysis with his interest in comparing forms of economic organization in different societies. Agreeing with Herskovits (and Weber) that a legitimate distinction between market and non-market societies exists, he nevertheless disagrees with Herskovits' conclusion that economists *qua* scientists should abandon their idealized study of market operation in favour of detailed studies of markets in specific cultural settings. If one reads this essay in isolation from his other essays of the 1940s, one is immediately reminded of "The Limitations of Scientific Method in Economics" (1924a) – his early attack on most brands of American institutionalism. Yet the other essays mentioned above reveal his own concern with the relation between culture and economic development. The review of Herskovits can then be seen less as a defense of neoclassicism than as a defense of "ideal type" analysis. In this sense, the reviews of Hutchison and Herskovits are simply flip sides of the same defense.

Finally, we can briefly examine one of the areas in which Knight's comparative approach most obviously touches on themes developed by Weber – the relation of religion and capitalism. In his review of Sombart, Knight summarized the literature regarding the Weber thesis, arguing that Lujo Brentano's argument about the relation between war and trade is more relevant to understanding the origins of capitalism than Weber's linkage with Protestantism. As any scholar familiar with Knight knows, the relation between religion and economic organization occupied his attention throughout his life. One of the most important of his reflections on the topic is his collaboration with Thornton Merriam in *The Economic Order and Religion* (1945). In preparation for his half of the book, Knight wrote, and re-wrote, a history of the relation between religion and economic organization which both assessed (negatively) the impact of religion on the history of liberalism, and expanded upon his critique of Weber's argument regarding the role of religion in economic development (various drafts exist in the Knight Papers; see Emmett 1999b and 1999c). Most of that history did not end up in the book (an abridged version of the history appears in Knight's first chapter). The core of his argument in this history and elsewhere is well-expressed in the minutes of a faculty seminar in "Economic Development and Cultural Change" on March 11, 1952:

> Mr. Knight urged that an examination of the origins of European capital-
> ism was relevant to a discussion of economic development, and in particu-
> lar called attention to Sombart's concept of the "spirit" of capitalism as the
> analytical essence of the problem. Contrasted with Weber's emphasis on
> the religious side of the problem, Mr. Knight believed that the change in the
> *Weltanschauung* of the Western world – the essence of which was ambition
> and curiosity, the acceptance of competitive, cumulative self-assertion as a
> worthy aspect of human personality – was the great cultural revolution of all
> history.
>
> (University of Chicago Research Center in Economic
> Development and Cultural Change 1952)

Because Knight interpreted religion as an opponent of ambition, curiosity, and self-assertion, his history emphasized the constraints that religion constantly placed on the *Geist des Kapitalismus*. Yet his disagreement with Weber is over the role of religion in the development of capitalism, not with the assumption that a compara-tive historical study of economic history would be relevant to the study of con-temporary economic development. Near the end of his life, Knight broadened his reflections on the historical relations of Christianity and market societies through comparison with the possible relation between the market and religion in cultures based on Eastern religious traditions, in "Philosophy and Social Institutions in the West" (Knight 1962).

The marginalization of institutionalism and comparative economic history

Despite Knight's ongoing work in comparative history, the immediate context in which he originally turned to Weber's work came to an end with the Second World War. As several recent histories of American economics make clear, the pluralism of the interwar years was resolved in the postwar period by the emergence of a new scientific standard for economics. Whether one describes the new standard as neoclassicism, the neoclassical synthesis, or mathematical economics, postwar economics possessed a unity that the discipline lacked during the interwar period. Most importantly for our purposes, the new standard redefined "economics" and "science" in ways that pushed most of the participants in the interwar debates to the margins of the economics discipline (Morgan and Rutherford 1998; Yonay 1998).

Knight's relation to this new standard is complicated. Partly through his efforts, Chicago economics came to represent one form of the new economics. While he did not play a role in the development of the workshops in which much of postwar Chicago economics was forged, Knight had been instrumental in defining the core requirements of graduate study during the 1930s and 1940s. He also continued to teach the mandatory Economics 301 ("Price and Distribution Theory") that elaborated the core of neoclassical theory throughout the 1940s and 1950s (he taught the course for the last time in the summer of 1956). Chicago's emphasis on theoretical competence and innovative application bred a school of economists who came to dominate American postwar economics (Emmett 1998b).

One could argue that the "ideal type" understanding of economic theory that Knight took from Weber helped keep the focus of his economic theory relatively narrow. If economic theory simply amplifies the assumptions:

> [T]hat every rational and competent mind knows (a) that some behavior involves the apportionment or allocation of means limited in supply among alternative modes of use in realizing ends; (b) that given modes of apportionment achieve in different "degrees" for any subject some general end which is a common denominator of comparison; and (c) that there is some one "ideal" apportionment which would achieve the general end in a "maximum" degree, conditioned by the quantity of means available to the subject and the terms of allocation presented by the facts of his given situation[…]
>
> (Knight 1940a: 383)

then the core of economics remains the theory of perfect competition. If all efforts to explain economic change through a scientific theory are doomed to failure (Knight 1930a), then most of the theoretical innovations of the postwar era were predetermined to be ineffective, and Knight's comparative historical approach was a necessary complement to the theoretical orientation of Chicago economics. Of course, few of his colleagues, even at Chicago, accepted Knight's perspective. Although he taught theory, comparative history continued to be the focus of Knight's own work for the remainder of his career. The themes sketched in the previous section were not secondary to his scientific work, but rather comprised the work he set out for himself as a social scientist. Inevitably, the narrowing of the disciplinary focus within economics, and Knight's continued work in comparative history, meant that Knight was gradually marginalized by the discipline. During the 1940s, economists labeled his work "social philosophy" (see the subtitle of Knight 1947a). The reader, of course, is supposed to recognize that "social philosophy" is not "economics," and therefore assume that the majority of Knight's work is addressed to some audience other than economists. Knight's own actions in the 1930s and 1940s provide support for this treatment of his work. He was cross-appointed in the Philosophy department at the University of Chicago in the early 1940s, and helped initiate the Committee on Social Thought, which provided an academic haven for those disenchanted with the entrenchment of disciplinary boundaries during the postwar era. Yet he retained the hope (albeit with some scepticism) that a social science capable of providing direction for intelligent social action could emerge that would integrate economic theory with the study of law and politics, the history of capitalist institutions, and ethical reflection (Knight 1960a).

10 Entrenching disciplinary competence

The role of general education and graduate study in Chicago economics

Central to the lore surrounding the University of Chicago's economics department is the story of its transition in the 1930s and 1940s from a "mixed bag" of proto-Chicago school types, institutionalists, and quantitative economists (Reder 1982: 361–2) to the unified research program that we call the "Chicago school." The story of this transition is sufficiently entrenched in the historical sensibilities of economists that most contemporary treatments simply equate Chicago economics with the school (Stein 1994) and therefore focus attention only on the ideological commitments, scientific theories, and policy/legal advice that form its unique approach to economics (Miller 1962; Bronfenbrenner 1962; Stigler 1962; Friedman 1974; Samuels 1976; Reder 1982, 1987; Schmidt and Rittaler 1989).

But other perspectives may reveal aspects of the story of Chicago economics that are obscured by the standard account. Suppose that instead of focusing attention on what is unique in the department's activities, we sought to focus attention on what is common. For example, what would we discover if we chose to examine the department's activities from the perspective of its curricular responsibilities? How might that perspective alter our usual account of Chicago economics during the period from the 1930s to the 1950s? And what would the altered account contribute to our understanding of the process by which American economics was transformed?

The results of my initial research on these questions are outlined in the next two sections. Two conclusions emerge. First, when Chicago economics is viewed from the perspective of its curricular responsibilities, the department's distinguishing characteristic over the period from the 1930s to the 1950s becomes the institutionalization of a *disciplinary self-critique*. Through its degree requirements, course material, comprehensive and preliminary examinations, research seminars, and the model of its faculty, Chicago economics enshrined the notion that a central feature of the work of a modern scientific economist was the use of the discipline's own methods to critique the work of other economists (including the "greats" of the past). Although this disciplinary self-critique has given Chicago economics its reputation for sharp criticism and narrowness of vision, its purpose was the single-minded pursuit of identifying and defining the proper zone of the discipline's competence. As the modern art critic Clement Greenberg (quoted in Klamer 1993: 241–2) has said: "The characteristic methods of a discipline [are employed] to criticize the discipline itself – not in order to subvert it, but to entrench it more firmly in its area of competence."

The second conclusion emerges from the first. Identifying the distinguishing characteristic of Chicago economics as the institutionalization of a disciplinary self-critique suggests that Chicago economics shared in the transformation described in the other essays in this volume. Rather than adopting an interpretive position that begins with the assumption that Chicago economics is unique and separate from the mainstream of American economics (e.g. through a focus on its monetary and industrial organization theorists), the interpretive position taken here allows us to view Chicago economics as part of a transformation that narrowed the boundaries of "legitimate" economics in the attempt to entrench it in its area of scientific competence.

The legacy of Progressive–Pragmatist education

To those familiar with the history of American higher education in the twentieth century, the decision to use the curricular responsibilities of a University of Chicago department as the lens through which to focus attention on its activities is obviously not accidental. The raging debates over educational reform that characterized the University during this period reflected ambiguities and uncertainties within American society with regard to how traditional values could best be recast in the context of a modern liberal democracy and what role higher education was to play in that reformulation. Furthermore, the pedagogical debates throughout the university were often intertwined with debates within (and sometimes between) disciplines regarding the scientific legitimacy of competing knowledge claims, the proper scope of the discipline's attention, and the relation between the discipline's knowledge and social discussion about policy issues.

Ostensibly, educational reform at the University of Chicago began in the early 1930s, after the installation of Robert Hutchins as the university's fifth president in 1929. In 1931, the New Plan for the College of the University of Chicago removed responsibility for general education from the divisions. From 1931 to 1942, the college provided a general education for all first- and second-year students, followed by two years of university education in a discipline supervised by a division. From 1942 to 1953, Chicago granted BAs on completion of the college (which was redesigned to admit students earlier, hence creating three to four years of general education). From 1942 on, then, all students entering economics were pursuing an advanced degree – the education of a specialist.

The reforms of the 1930s and 1940s, however, were predicated on a growing uneasiness regarding the appropriateness of the educational objectives inherited from the Progressive and Pragmatist movements at the turn of the century. Disturbed by the social impotence of individualism and traditional American Protestantism in an industrial capitalist society, Progressives had sought to restore order in the context of a free society. Lacking confidence in the all-encompassing certainties that traditionally undergirded American values, Progressives typically employed divide-and-conquer strategies that created boundaries between areas of human activity (work and home, science and art, urban and rural, civilization and wilderness, professional and amateur, biology and society) in order to develop mechanisms of control appropriate to each.

One of the divisions that Progressives pursued was the separation of disciplines within the academy. Traditional American higher education had emphasized the unity of knowledge undergirded by moral philosophy. Progressive education emphasized widening the circle of informed citizenry in order to eradicate ignorance. The task of spreading intelligence in a particular area of knowledge was increasingly entrusted to the "professionals" – academics who had studied the area intensively. Hence the separation of disciplines was closely related to the professionalization of the academy. Economic problems required the attention of a professional economist – someone who had taken the time to study the issues in depth. But we need to be careful here; studying a problem in depth does not necessarily depend on the acquisition of specialized knowledge or methods of inquiry. In the early twentieth century, professionalization created a new organizational context in which the search for economic knowledge took place, but the resulting separation of the disciplines took some time to generate knowledge claims based on the application of specialized methods (Geiger 1986: 27).

Distinguishing professionalization from specialized knowledge proves useful when examining educational reform in the Progressive Era. The central educational distinction for Progressives was between intelligence and ignorance. Although experts, such as professional economists, appeared during this period, their role emerged from their professional engagement in the task of creating informed citizens and overcoming the pressing problems of the day. Graduate education, therefore, was an extension of general education. If anything distinguished the two, it was the extra time that graduate education allowed for extensive examination of a particular problem. Looking back at graduate education during the Progressive Era from his vantage point in the mid-to late 1920s, the chair of the Chicago Economics Department, Leon C. Marshall, described it as a "continuation of senior college [work] … with little advance in method save for the thesis." Progressive era senior college work was identified by Marshall as consisting of "miscellaneous offerings in varying 'fields' or 'problems'" in economics (Marshall n.d.).

The Progressive era came to an end with the horrors of World War I, the frustrations of President Woodrow Wilson's foreign policy endeavors, and the recognition of the impassable void between public opinion and intelligence. The death of Progressivism intensified the problem of uncertainty by demolishing any lingering hopes that the divide-and-conquer strategy might eventually lead to some form of social order. But rather than developing an alternative strategy, social scientists directed their energy toward transforming the strategy in order to continue its domination, even without its millenarian hopes.

Among social scientists, the intensification of the divide-and-conquer strategy had several aspects. First, there was a gradual turn inward: Attention was directed away from the social questions and problems that had so preoccupied the Progressive era and toward questions circumscribed by the boundaries of the discipline.

For example, in the collection of essays that Rexford Tugwell edited, called *The Trend of Economics* (1924), contemporary economic issues are often identified as "larger problems" that lie outside (or above) the purview of the economist. More frequently, attention is focused on intradisciplinary controversies over appropriate methodologies.

Hand in glove with the inward turn was the practice of accepting criticism only from within the circle of those schooled in the discipline's methods. Although the lines between sociology, economics, political science, and history were still not secured in the 1920s, economists were less likely to take criticisms of their work by sociologists as seriously as they took criticisms from economists. And as methodological debate among American economists intensified during the 1920s, the circle of legitimate critics slowly shrank: legitimate criticisms became only those from within one's own methodological circle.

The interwar intensification of the divide-and-conquer strategy among social scientists also had an impact that histories of economic thought often overlook: It radically redefined social science education. Central to that revolution was the rapid demarcation of graduate education for disciplinary specialists from the demands of general education for an informed citizenry. Untethered from its stake in addressing present-day concerns, the education of the specialist gradually became focused on training in new methods and a self-referential disciplinary critique that would enable new Ph.D.'s to be better social scientists than their predecessors.

Marshall's previously mentioned memo chronicles a portion of this transformation as it occurred at the University of Chicago. By the mid-1920s, the principles of economics course had been moved to the first year, and second- and third-year students took introductory courses in various fields of economics, which Marshall identified as courses examining the various "functions" of economics rather than mere economic "problems." "Competent" senior students were admitted to "advanced work," in which the newest research methods were introduced. Graduate students continued this advanced study in their course work, although Marshall admitted that graduate education was still limited in terms of training students intensively in new methods and generating creative research. Marshall pointed the way toward what modernist education in economics was to become during the 1930s, however. What the Chicago department was working toward, he said, was a situation in which graduate students engage in only "creative" work using the newest methods. The new methods themselves were taught in university (as opposed to college) courses, which were available to competent senior undergraduate students who were considering graduate study. In his vision of graduate education at Chicago, then, Marshall encapsulated the radical transformation of social scientific education: a broadening of the economics education offered to develop informed citizens, coupled with a narrowing of the economics education offered in advanced and graduate work, the latter characterized by the acquisition and creative use of new methods (see Marshall's Papers in the University of Chicago Archives, Special Collections Research Center, University of Chicago Library).

Chicago economics and the "great debate" over general education

Chicago economics underwent a transformation during the period from 1930 to the mid-1950s that reflected its emerging focus on disciplinary self-critique. Integral to that transformation was the relation between Chicago's increasingly specialized research and its changing conception of economic education. In this section, we will examine the relation between Chicago economics and the changing conception of general education at the University of Chicago. The next section will examine the transformation of senior undergraduate and graduate education in the department.

The reform of general education at the University of Chicago had immediate impacts on the economics faculty. After 1931, and especially after 1942, departmental faculty had no responsibility for general education. Beginning in 1931, the college hired its own staff, who were assumed to be free from the research requirements of departmental staff in order to focus on general education: "The College is not an institution for research," its purpose rather is "to insure proper adjustment to [the] complex and changing environment" of modernity (E. H. Wilkins, quoted in Orlinsky 1992: 42).

But what type of education best ensured "proper adjustment" to modernity? That question gave rise to the "great debate," actually a set of debates over specific proposals for educational reform spread over a period of approximately 20 years.[1] President Hutchins (following Mortimer Adler) advocated a "great books" approach, but most faculty (in the college and in the divisions) advocated a continuation of the university's tradition of a Progressive-Pragmatist educational program that focused on showing how ignorance had been eradicated by the progress of science. The curricular reform emerging from these debates occupied the attention of many faculty members throughout the 1930s and 1940s and directly affected Chicago economics in three ways.

First, the development of the "General Course in the Social Sciences" reflected this debate and involved economists in both the college and the department. Harry Gideonese was hired in 1931 to help coordinate the new social science survey course, along with Louis Wirth (sociology) and Jerome Kerwith (political science). Under their guidance, the new course took a definite turn toward the "eradication of ignorance through the progress of science" direction. All the texts chosen were "classics" in the social sciences, but not the classics that Hutchins and Adler promoted in their "great books" course. Rather, the readings chosen were classics because they were *new* and represented the forefront of social scientific knowledge. In many cases, the new classics used the methods of a social scientific discipline to challenge conventional thinking; among the authors whose readings were included in the course syllabus in the 1930s were Max Weber, Bronislaw Malinowski, and Frank Knight (portions of *The Economic Organization*). Subsequent revisions of the syllabus during the 1940s and 1950s incorporated newer classics, frequently written by Chicago social scientists.

The students' background in the social science survey courses allowed the Economics Department to assume that incoming students were both well read in the classics of social science and familiar with Knight's introduction to economics prior to taking elementary economics. Departmental courses, even at the senior undergraduate level, could therefore focus on educating specialists. Students who had accepted the survey course's message regarding the eradication of ignorance through the progress of science were ready to move to the forefront of the scientific discipline.

Second, faculty members participated directly in the "great debate." With the exception of John Nef, the economics faculty stood against the Hutchins–Adler reform proposals. Knight's missive against Adler's neomedievalism is indicative of the economists' response. Asking the question "Is Modern Thought Anti-Intellectual?" (1934c) Knight answered in the negative and chastised his opponents for using education as the opportunity for advocacy rather than for the search for truth:

> Any education looking toward truth must place literally all possible empha-
> sis on the criticism and testing of individual ideas. ... It is simply a patent
> and unescapable fact that the immediate product of thinking is nearly always
> wrong and usually foolish. Yet so great is credulity that we see great numbers
> of persons open to influence by propaganda which, under the guise of human
> betterment, palpably looks toward making the promoters the rulers of society.
> This does not apply merely to any single small group. It is the nature of practi-
> cally all social reform propaganda. ... Neither society nor any group or class
> in it can be an intellectual community unless we begin with an overwhelming
> presumption against the soundness of any teaching whose promoters cannot
> place themselves above suspicion of motivation by other interests than love of
> truth and right. Between advocating and truth-seeking, meaning the quest of
> right answers to problems, there is a nearly *impassable* gulf.
>
> (Knight 1934c: 230–1)

Gideonese and his colleagues in the college immediately incorporated Knight's essay into the reading package for the General Course in the Social Sciences, where it remained until the syllabus was redesigned in the early 1940s. Knight and Henry Simons frequently commented on the campus debates in their classes, and Simons sometimes joined Gideonese for the weekly roundtable talks on the campus radio (hosted by Gideonese's college colleague Kerwith). Gideonese's running battle during the 1934–35 academic year with the Adlerite editor of the campus newspaper, the *Daily Maroon,* also won the support of Chicago econo-mists. When the editor refused to print Gideonese's responses to his editorials, Gideonese posted the responses outside his office door, where they found a ready audience of faculty and students.

Gideonese's campaign against Hutchins reached its high point in 1937 when he published *The Higher Learning in a Democracy: A Reply to President Hutchins' Critique of the American University* at the same time that he pursued the deanship of the college:

> "Books ... put in place of things." This is ... perhaps the final comment upon
> an educational proposal to substitute the classics of the Western world for

scientific training in our modern society. To have it come from the University of Chicago – which has always stressed the method of science since its birth – adds to the confusion of the higher learning in America.

(Gideonese 1937: 4, 23–4).

Needless to say, Gideonese did not become dean, and two years later Hutchins denied him tenure despite enthusiastic support from college and departmental faculty for his appointment (Dzuback 1991: 126–7, 181–2).[2]

Finally, the background of senior undergraduate and graduate students in general education produced a tension between disciplinary specialization and interdisciplinarity. One of the results of that tension was the creation of the Committee on Social Thought (CST) in the early 1940s. Two economists on opposite sides of the "great debate" were actively involved in the establishment of the CST – Nef and Knight – and the CST hosted Friedrich von Hayek during his stay at Chicago. The CST provided a graduate education option for those who did not want a specialist education and provided faculty who resisted specialization with a means of participating in graduate education. The CST option therefore had two unintended consequences: the creation of a cadre of specialists in interdisciplinarity who were well suited to teaching in the emerging general education programs of universities and liberal arts colleges, and increased specialization in the disciplines because graduate students and faculty who resisted specialization could always be redirected into the CST.

Graduate economics education: entrenching disciplinary competence

Over the period from 1930 to the mid-1950s, the structure of graduate education remained relatively stable, comprised of a sequence of intermediate courses in theory and what Marshall had described as "introductions to the graduate study of … ," followed by subfield survey courses and then research seminars. The new face of Chicago economics is seen, however, in the changing requirements, the altered focus of the various courses in the program, the changing role of the comprehensive and preliminary examinations, and the eventual appearance of workshops and research groups, the laboratories of modernist social science.[3]

The early 1930s continued the pattern described in Marshall's memo: building on the breadth of a general education to train specialists who were equipped to address fields of study that, although perhaps originally conceived as "problem areas," were emerging as "functional" areas or applied fields. Students faced relatively few specific requirements in their advanced degree programs, reflecting the Progressive era's legacy of assuming that general education prepared intelligent people to tackle the problems of society. From the mid-1930s to the mid-1940s, however, the structure of graduate education was gradually tightened through the introduction of a more regulated degree program. By 1945, there was little mention of the breadth of a student's general educational background, and the focus was on the structure of course work required in the department. Doctoral students, for example, were required to complete an intermediate or subfield survey course in at least 10 different fields of economics (required fields were economic theory, accounting, statistics, economic history, and money and banking; elective fields were corporate finance, labor and personnel administration, monopoly and public utilities, agricultural economics, government finance, and international economics) or related areas (only two of the 10 could be outside economics and were usually international relations, human development, or social thought); to select two of those fields, along with economic theory, as specializations; to write preliminary examinations in the fields of specialization (this usually required an additional three to five courses in each area of specialization); and to complete a thesis.[4]

The movement from flexible to structured advanced degree programs was accompanied by an altered focus within economics courses. During the early 1930s, the focus of most economics courses, apart from economic theory, was still largely problem oriented. This changed dramatically during the 1930s, however, as the courses underwent two simultaneous changes: the subfield survey courses became method-oriented rather than problem-oriented, and price theory came to play a dominant role in almost every subfield. The overarching presence of Knight, Jacob Viner, and Oskar Lange – the triumvirate who taught the core theory courses – certainly had something to do with the transformation, but equally important was the extension of a focus on methods into courses in public finance, monetary theory, agricultural economics, and statistics. Patinkin's comments on his experience in Simons's infamous senior undergraduate course in price theory are relevant to much of Chicago economics by the 1940s: "I learned the hard way ... that full understanding of the principles of economic analysis could be achieved only after sweating through their application to specific problems" (Patinkin 1981: 4). Thus, by the 1940s, Chicago economics courses focused on the application and extension of methods gained in the core areas of economic theory and statistics.

Two fields that are often thought to counteract the alteration in the focus of economics courses are economic history and history of economic thought. During this period at Chicago, however, this was not the case. History of economic thought was part of the economic theory core that all doctoral students had to take and was taught by Knight. From available accounts of the course and the lecture notes in Knight's papers in the University of Chicago Archives, it is clear that Knight's approach to the course is reasonably represented by his famous 1935 article, "The Ricardian Theory of Production and Distribution," (1935) which begins, "On the assumption that the primary interest in the 'ancients' in such a field as economics is to learn from their mistakes, the principal theme of this discussion will be the contrast between the 'classical' system and 'correct' views" (Knight 1935c: 237). By constructing a "classical" system of thought that could be separated from and contrasted with "correct" contemporary systems, Knightian history of economic thought trained students to critique economics from within in order to strengthen their hold on its contemporary competencies.[5]

Much the same can be said for economic history, although the story is a bit more complicated in that field. Under Nef, who was sympathetic to the neo-Thomism of Hutchins and Adler, economic history became the study of an economy set in a civilization separate from the unsettling problems of modernity. (See Cantor 1991 for an examination of how medievalists constructed an account of a unified society, which could be contrasted with the perceived fragmentation of modernity.) During the 1940s, Nef twice made an attempt to bring both Harold Innis and Earl Hamilton to Chicago, in part because Nef was gradually moving out of teaching economics in order to give more attention to his interdisciplinary responsibilities. Hamilton joined the faculty in 1947 and brought a different orientation to economic history than Nef's. Hamilton's attempt to construct a price history for Spain and Europe during the period of the influx of American treasure required the application of price theory. Unfortunately for Hamilton, Chicago economists in the 1950s were well versed in disciplinary self-critique, and several were quick to show that his well-intentioned point was not supported by a correct application of price theory (Kessel and Alchian 1960). Nevertheless, the controversy over Hamilton's work opened economic history to the application of economic theory, leading soon after to the initiation of quantitative history.

The revised structure of degree programs and the altered focus of course work in economics were reflected in the changed role of the department's comprehensive and preliminary examinations. Largely under the influence of Knight and Viner, with the participation of Simons, Lloyd Mints, and new department members such as Lange, examinations underwent significant change during the 1930s. Prior to the 1930s, examinations were primarily opportunities for students to exhibit what they had learned about a specific field. Although the questions on the examinations remained basically the same during the 1930s and 1940s, acceptable answers focused more on the candidate's ability to apply price theory.[6]

The changes in the degree structure, the alteration in the focus of courses, and the changes in legitimate examination answers reflect a fundamental shift from the 1930s to the late 1940s in Chicago economics. From the Progressive era, during which the University of Chicago was launched, through the early 1930s, a Chicago economist was an intelligent person dedicated to studying a particular set of problems and exercising a public responsibility to widen the realm of intelligence through teaching and researching. By the late 1940s, a Chicago economist was a person who possessed specialized methods for the acquisition of knowledge and the ability to discern between truth (knowledge that in principle was in accordance with the discipline's methods) and error. The Chicago economist's public responsibility now lay in acquiring new knowledge, training graduate students in the discipline's methods, and assisting the public in understanding the boundaries of the discipline's competence.

The most significant educational reform in the department after the initiation of more restrictive requirements for graduate degrees in the early 1940s was the introduction of workshops and research groups in the late 1940s and early 1950s. Collaborative research was a common feature of Chicago economics during the 1940s, and the notion that research groups could be the *loci* of collaborative research and the supervision of graduate students who were utilizing new research methods in their area of specialization was strengthened by the example of the Cowles Commission, which had moved to the University of Chicago in 1939 (Cowles Commission 1952; Hildreth 1986). During the late 1940s, several other research groups emerged, and in the early 1950s, the workshop model was explicitly adopted as the standard method for training Ph.D. students.

The educational rationale for the workshop model was provided in a memo to the department from H. Gregg Lewis (undated but probably from the late 1940s or early 1950s). Lewis, one of the departmental advisers of students, had been "discomforted for some time by the behef that graduate faculties of economics generally are neglecting their responsibilities for making economics an effective science and for training their students as scientific craftsmen" (Lewis n.d.). Citing Knight as a "shining example" of the economist as moral philosopher, Lewis chided his colleagues for thinking that they and most students had "the stuff that makes for good moral philosophers." While department members expend their energies primarily in that direction, "economics as a science languishes." Although no one solution would revive economics as a science, Lewis proposed a reorganization of graduate study in economics that would bring it closer to the model of scientific training in the natural sciences. Quoting Arthur Burns, who had first suggested the idea of laboratories in the social sciences, Lewis recommended that the Chicago department set up a system where each professor – whether of money and banking, business cycles, public finance, or what not – would have his own laboratory. He would have one or two assistants who would share responsibility for the laboratory, and other assistants as needed. The students (doctoral candidates) in a certain subject would get their training in the laboratory, by working on some project. The individual assignments would be of limited scope, but it would be the function of the professor in charge to see that they fit together. The projects would grow out of the research program of the laboratory and will be supervised closely. (Lewis n.d.)

The workshop model of Chicago economics began during the late 1940s, when several permanent research seminars were established in fields in which students could specialize as part of their doctoral programs: agricultural economics, labor, econometrics, and government finance. The Cowles Commission had been running seminars for several years before this, and they were integrated into the departmental offerings at this time. Perhaps the most famous of the first Chicago workshops was the one in money and banking that Milton Friedman organized in 1952. Shortly after its inception, it teamed up with the newly formed research group in economic development to create a social laboratory in Chile. Researchers-in-training were sent there to conduct experiments in monetary policy rules and the measurement of economic activity under the supervision of the department's senior researchers (Valdes 1995). In 1952–3, the Chicago department formally integrated graduate student participation in workshops and research groups into the doctoral program. By the mid-1950s, the department's research center sponsored workshops and research groups in money and banking (Phillip Cagan, Friedman); agricultural economics (Robert Gustafson, Dale Johnson, T. W. Schultz, George Tolley); public finance (Martin J. Bailey, Arnold Harberger); economic development (Hamilton, Harberger, Bert Hoselitz, Simon

Rottenberg, Schultz); labor economics and industrial relations (H. Gregg Lewis, Albert Rees, Rottenberg); and the economics of consumption (Margaret Reid).

When Burns originally suggested this model, he probably thought of the laboratories as extensions into graduate departments of the National Bureau of Economic Research model developed by Wesley Mitchell. At Chicago, however, theory and measurement existed in creative tension, and workshop discussions almost always focused on how well the analysis built on price theory (e.g., see Patinkin 1981: 15). The tension between theory and measurement in the workshops also strengthened the Chicago economics program's inculcation of disciplinary self-critique. The opportunity for graduate students and faculty to critique current research on an equal footing created an environment that, at its best, allowed for brilliant theoretical insights informing empirical studies and incisive critical exercises employing the discipline's basic principles and methods. Many of the classic articles of Chicago economics from the 1950s onwards emerged from and were refined by discussion in its workshops.

Conclusion

Within an institutional context that facilitated the radical demarcation of the education of the disciplinary specialist from the education of informed citizens, Chicago economics refined a disciplinary self-critique that entrenched a particular set of competencies, both theoretical and empirical, in its researchers and researchers-in-training (graduate students). If anything may be said to characterize Chicago economics, it is the intensity with which this disciplinary self-critique was carried out in a collaborative fashion. From the late 1930s to the 1950s, Chicago economics came to equate "good" economics with the construction of new "classics" – concise, clear, and elegant models that pushed the boundaries of form without abandoning the theoretical content of the discipline's mainstream.

11 *De gustibus* est *disputandum*

Frank Knight's reply to
George Stigler and Gary Becker's
"De gustibus non est disputandum"
with an introductory essay

Introductory essay

The essay that follows is obviously not Frank H. Knight's own response to Stigler and Becker's article; their article was published five years after Knight's death (Stigler and Becker 1977) and there is no evidence that he was even familiar with the authors' research programs in household production (see the essays collected in Becker 1976 and 1996) and the economics of information (Stigler 1961) upon which the joint article draws. Rather, what follows is my reconstruction of what Knight would say were he to have had an opportunity to reply to Stigler and Becker's article at an earlier point in his career. The reply is written in a style common to Knight's replies and reviews during the 1920s and 1930s – acerbic, deliberately provocative, and engaging the philosophical perspective underlying the authors' article rather than its theoretical conclusions. To heighten the drama of the reply, I have pretended that it was written about the same time as Stigler and Becker's article, thereby allowing Knight to "predict" (and lament in advance) the subsequent rise of economics imperialism within the social sciences – a movement directly attributable to the impact Stigler and Becker's work has had in economics, law, sociology, and political science. Perhaps what is said here is what Knight once said to Stigler and Becker over lunch at the University of Chicago's Quadrangle Club.

Ronnie Davis once remarked that Knight had no need to remember arguments – he would simply rethink an issue and reach the same conclusion as before (Davis 1974: 28). This response is written in the same spirit, and therefore no quotations or citations from Knight's work appear in the main body of the text. Since this is my interpretation of what Knight would have said, however, there is some responsibility to provide a defense. In the places where I have paraphrased Knight's own words, or followed a line of argument found in one or more of his essays, references and some sample quotations are provided in the notes. In the interest of readability, the number of notes has been kept to a minimum; most notes occur where a statement might prompt the reader to wonder where Knight himself made a similar claim.

A speculative piece such as the essay that follows is admittedly an unusual way both to introduce Knight's work and to address the importance of Stigler and

Becker's article for modern economics. Why would one write such an essay? I will address the question with reference to Stigler and Becker's article first, and then turn to Knight.

Economists have been both blessed and cursed by the simplicity of their basic assumption about the nature of human conduct. Individuals, they say, efficiently act to satisfy their preferences with the means available to them, in accordance with the knowledge they possess. A simple statement, perhaps almost intuitively obvious, at least for those of us embedded in the Enlightenment tradition. Yet it is one that provides the foundation for powerful insights into the operation and organization of social interaction, not only in the marketplace but also across numerous other sites of human activity.

But is the economist's basic premise too simple? After all, we know our actions to be tissues of paradox: our rationality abandoned to passion one moment, only to be followed the next by a calculated display of cold-heartedness; our praise for someone's moment of self-sacrifice; our best efforts at goal-setting and strategizing revealed as exercises (yet again!) in tilting at windmills; our willingness to end abruptly a lunchtime conversation with a friend in need in order to catch a sale; our experience of trust betrayed and expectations left unfulfilled. Modern psychology presents numerous theories that provide a more complex self as the starting point for the study of human behavior. Ought we not to at least consider these? And what of social conditioning or genetic programming? Are we really free to act in the rational manner economic theory assumes? Can we determine our own preferences? Do we not follow patterns and rules determined for us by our place in the social framework, which is dependent upon our race, gender, and class? Or perhaps our wants are the result of evolutionary adaptation?

Equally important is the methodologist's concern about claiming scientific status for a theory that depends crucially upon a non-observable phenomenon such as tastes or preferences. How can the empirical claims of the discipline be ascribed scientific validity when the statement "tastes changed" can obviate them?

Economists have struggled with these questions for a long time, of course. Some have pursued alternative frameworks in which to theorize about economic activity: one thinks of American Institutionalism earlier in this century, the economic psychology movement popular in the 1970s, sociobiology's inroads into economics during the1970s, the social economics movement, and the recent post-autistic economics movement. All of these were efforts to construct theories of economic behavior that do not depend on the simple assumption that individuals rationally pursue their preferences within the constraints of the available means and knowledge. Others have resorted to the older argument, usually identified with J.S. Mill (1967), that divides the economic aspect of human behavior from other human tendencies – human action combines many tendencies, one of which is the efficient satisfaction of given preferences. By this account, economics is a partner to the other social sciences in the explanation of human behavior: the explanatory power of economics lies in its relationship to sociology, psychology, history, and other disciplines.

None of these strategies are satisfactory, however, for those who want to construct a science out of economics without fundamentally altering its premises, and who take predictive power as the mark of scientific achievement (Friedman 1953). In order for economics to stand alone as a science, the source of its predictive power must lie entirely within its own domain. How scientific can economics be if its participants must either depend on other disciplines for explanations of preference formation, or shrug their shoulders and say *de gustibus non est disputandum* (there is no accounting for tastes)?

> For economists to rest a large part of their theory of choice on differences in tastes is disturbing since they admittedly have no useful theory of the formation of tastes, nor can they rely on a well-developed theory of tastes from any other social science, since none exists. ... The weakness in the received theory of choice, then, is the extent to which it relies on differences in tastes to "explain" behavior when it can neither explain how tastes are formed nor predict their effects.
>
> (Becker 1976: 133)

Here Stigler and Becker step forward. Their methodological alternative is simultaneously a solution to the scientific economist's problem, and an application of the scientific approach that most economists have adopted (articulated in Friedman 1953). What Stigler and Becker propose is that economists explicitly accept a position they probably implicitly work from already, namely that theories of human behavior which use changes in opportunity cost as the primary explanatory factor provide better explanations than theories that ask us to accept a change in people's tastes, preferences, or values.

To illustrate their argument, assume that a person maximizes a utility function that contains "produced commodities" such as health, social distinction and music appreciation rather than purchased goods and services (see Michael and Becker 1973). Keeping with a simple case, consider a person whose utility function (U) depends on music appreciation (M) and other produced commodities (Z): $U = U (M, Z)$. M is produced by both allocating time to music listening (t_m and accumulating training and techniques that are conducive to appreciating the music that is heard (music capital = S_m); that is, $M = M (t_m, S_m)$. An increase in either t_m or S_m will lower the marginal cost of M. There is no particular reason to expect the marginal cost of producing Z to change while the marginal cost of M is decreasing, so we can predict that the person's production and consumption of M will increase. Most importantly for our purposes, explaining the change in M does not require any reference to (unobservable) changes in the person's musical tastes, depending instead entirely upon (what are in principle observable) changes in the person's conduct or available resources.

The argument that the increase in either t_m or S_m brought about the change in M, however, requires an assumption about the person's tastes: at a minimum, it requires us to assume that the person's preferences among the "produced commodities" remain stable. Stigler and Becker acknowledge this, and argue that economists must accept the assumption that tastes, preferences and values are stable over time and place, and the same for everyone: "Tastes neither change capriciously nor differ importantly between people" (Stigler and Becker 1977: 76). While this is a slight loss of realism in assumptions, it is better than simply assuming that tastes are exogenous, and is a small price to pay for increased predictive power. In this sense, then, Stigler and Becker's proposal is an application of Friedman's methodology: the mark of good science is the empirical adequacy of its predictions, not its assumptions.

> The reason for postulating the assumption of stable and uniform preferences is thus avowedly methodological: it is to produce unambiguously falsifiable predictions about behavior and to avoid, whenever possible, ad hoc explanations on changes in tastes, differences in tastes, ignorance, and impulsive or neurotic behavior.
>
> (Blaug 1980: 242)

The "avowedly methodological" stance provided by Stigler and Becker has not gone without criticism among contemporary economists and philosophers. Although the article receives only passing mention in methodological surveys of twentieth-century economics (apart from Blaug's brief remark quoted above, see Caldwell 1994: 161–2; and Boland 1982: 33–4), two very different lines of criticism have been advanced. On one side, Alexander Rosenberg (1979, 1980) has argued that Stigler and Becker's methodological strategy does not make economics into an empirical science. Urging readers not to be lulled into thinking that Stigler and Becker's strategy removes the economist's reliance upon non-observables such as utility and preferences, Rosenberg points out that their strategy actually adds a new non-observable into the theoretical framework – the "produced commodities" such as "good health" that Becker had introduced first in his theory of consumer choice (Becker 1965; Michael and Becker 1973). While the introduction of good health or other produced commodities may look like a way out of the intractability of traditional utility functions, it fares no better than traditional theory in the test of empirical adequacy:

> The trouble with this supposition is that a given amount of the commodity in question supervenes on many different combinations of market goods. It can be produced by many alternative techniques about which relatively little is known, and each of which is difficult to measure. Therefore, it bears all the problems of incomparability and nonfungibility that utility does. A single, global, directly consumed household good that in effect does nothing but intervene between utility and market goods will be no improvement on the old theory, especially when the "productive techniques" for generating this good from market commodities are so "subjective." To say that smokers and nonsmokers have exactly the same tastes, and maximize utility by maximizing their health, involves either treating health as a mere notational variant on utility, or it raises questions about the efficiency of productive techniques as unanswerable as are questions about the comparisons of utilities.
>
> (Rosenberg 1985: 57–8)

Because we have not found a scientific means by which we can distinguish the effects of a change in price from a change in preferences, Rosenberg's conclusion is that economics needs to strip away its reliance on non-observables in order to become an empirical science.

Rosenberg's more recent treatments of Stigler and Becker's strategy (Rosenberg 1985 and 1992: 112–51) have added two elements to his critique that brings his argument quite close to the one presented here as Knight's. One way to rescue Stigler and Becker's strategy from the trap of depending upon non-observables, Rosenberg argues, is to interpret produced commodities as human needs, and the assumption of stable preferences among those produced commodities as a schedule of needs. Interpreted as a schedule of human needs, the assumption of stable preferences can then be grounded in the knowledge of human needs available through the life sciences: "Needs so understood are as tractable as any variable of natural science, and they really do bid fair to solve the problem of tastes. Or rather to dissolve it" (Rosenberg 1985: 60). Stigler and Becker, then, may have unknowingly provided a means for creating a truly scientific economics. But, as Rosenberg goes on to argue, the switch from "stable preferences" to a "schedule of needs," which is required to render economics scientific, holds moral consequences that Stigler and Becker (and Knight) would find reprehensible. While the traditional formulation of welfare economics could never deal adequately with whether providing a bowl of meal for a starving Rwandan was a better social use of resources than providing a bottle of claret for a banquet in honor of a Nobel laureate (the example is drawn from Knight 1923a: 73 and Stigler 1982: 19), it provided a strong defense against the legislation of morality and censorship of tastes. The virtue of tolerance embodied in *de gustibus non est disputandum* is undermined if human need becomes the tool of imposing moral certainty. Rosenberg closes with a quote from Herbert Marcuse that nicely summarizes one of Knight's problems with Stigler and Becker's strategy: "When tolerance … serves to neutralize opposition and to render men [sic] immune from other *and better* forms of life, then tolerance has been perverted" (quoted in Rosenberg 1985: 65, emphasis added). Stigler and Becker, therefore, appear caught on the horns of the dilemma that Knight will pose for them also: does a scientific explanation of human behavior remove that which we understand to be most human about our behavior – that unsettledness which keeps us questing for a better form of life?

The other line of argument against Stigler and Becker's strategy leads to the same dilemma, but starts from a different place. Unlike Rosenberg (and Stigler and Becker), some theorists have no trouble with intentionality in the social sciences and seek to investigate the consequences of changes in one's choices among tastes and values. For these economists (see Buchanan 1979: 98; Elster 1984; Schelling 1984; Goodin 1990; and Cowen 1989) Stigler and Becker's claim that we can "usefully treat tastes as stable over time and similar among people" (Stigler and Becker 1977: 76) poses a problem because it assumes away the phenomena that they wish to explain. The exploratory nature of human action that fascinates these theorists implies that individuals may be satisfying their current preference ranking efficiently while simultaneously evaluating the quality of that ranking against various conceptions of a "better" preference structure. If we invoke *de gustibus non est disputandum*, either in its traditional form or in its Stigler and Becker alternative, are we not basing our scientific endeavors on a model of "rational fools" (Sen 1977)? Is there any reason to disentangle our explanatory relationship as economists from the other human sciences by an artificial assumption if doing so impoverishes our characterization of human action?

Knight brings with him to the task of writing a criticism of Stigler and Becker's article his own concerns about the scientific status of economics. As we will see in his reply, Knight consciously adopts a wider frame of reference than do most contemporary economists for discussion of methodological issues in scientific economics. More is at stake for him than our methodological starting point. Knight recognized quite early that accepting a methodological assumption like Stigler and Becker's would allow economics to make forays into the explanation of social and political behavior that he believed were not only inappropriate, but in fact dangerous to the future of liberal society. Stigler recognized this difference when he said of Knight in the *New Palgrave*:

> For most present-day economists, the primary purpose of their study is to increase our knowledge of the working of the enterprise and other economic systems. For Knight, the primary role of economic theory is rather different: it is to contribute to the understanding of how by consensus based upon rational discussion we can fashion [a] liberal society in which individual freedom is preserved and a satisfactory economic performance achieved.
>
> (Stigler 1987: 58)

Essential to this task, according to Knight, is keeping open-ended the conversation about the tastes, preferences and values we hold and pursue. Ultimately, liberal society is the field in which we explore, test, criticize, and improve upon our preferences and values. For Knight, *de gustibus est disputandum*.

De gustibus *est* disputandum: A reply to George Stigler and Gary Becker's "De gustibus non est disputandum"

No expression common to economists is as repugnant as the phrase *de gustibus non est disputandum*: if tastes, preferences, and values are not disputable, then what is? Facts? Certainly not, because a dispute over facts is ultimately a question of competing evaluations – which have been ruled non-discussable![1] If we cannot discuss tastes and values, life is one long silence: we might as well write down our wants, employ an army of computers (or, worse yet, economists) to calculate the best means of satisfying those wants under current conditions, and then end it all – leaving the computers to sort out the consequences of any changes in future conditions. That way, society could at least be maximally efficient; which is to say, non-human. In *human* society, economic activity is many things simultaneously: the search for means of satisfying wants, yes; but also a form of creative self-expression; the quest for better tastes, preferences, and values; and it is a game.[2]

Yet here we have two economists arguing that this repugnant expression forms the veritable backbone of a truly scientific economics. The predictive power of economics across a wide range of observable human behavior, Professors Stigler and Becker argue, necessarily rests on the assumption of stable preferences. Rather than throwing up our hands and saying "tastes must have changed" when confronted with alterations in human behavior, Stigler and Becker argue that the assumption of stable preferences allows scientific explanation to continue with the positive analysis of changes in the opportunity costs associated with various alternatives. Equally important to their argument – although less frequently recognized – is their claim that the range of possible preference choices among people is actually quite small – "tastes neither change capriciously nor differ importantly between people," they tell us (Stigler and Becker 1977: 76). If we are to believe our authors, the predictive power of economics rests on the assumption that most people want the same things all the time.

Stigler and Becker's argument is pernicious and dangerous, both for economics and for modern society, because it conveys the mistaken notion that the economic problem – that is, the problem of reconciling the available means to the ends desired in accordance with the knowledge at hand – *is* the problem of life. From a rational or scientific view of life, it must be admitted that this is often the case. But the first question one must ask in regard to scientific economics is exactly to what extent life is rational – to what extent can we reduce the problems of life to the form of using the available means to achieve given ends? I contend that the rational or scientific view of life that Stigler and Becker promote is a partial and limited view. Life is ultimately an exploration in the field of values; an attempt to discover values, rather than an exercise in producing and enjoying them to the greatest possible extent. This fact sets sweeping limitations to any attempt at constructing the kind of predictive economic science that Stigler and Becker desire.[3]

Now I must acknowledge that our authors do have some things right. They recognize, for example, that, as scientists, economists must take the existence of tastes and preferences for granted. Some economists prior to our authors thought that the only way to make economics scientific was to treat tastes and preferences as subject matter requiring explanation. Without providing a litany of failed attempts to provide the science of human conduct with a basis outside of human consciousness, we can applaud our authors' refusal to fall prey to this trap (Stigler and Becker 1977: 76). Economists *qua* scientists can, and must, assume the fact of human consciousness without embarrassment.[4]

Our authors also correctly see that there can be no distinction between "economic" wants and any other wants. All ends are economic, insofar as they all require us to use the resources available to realize them. In this sense, Stigler and Becker point us toward the fundamental scientific question to ask about human conduct – the effectiveness of our adaptation of means to our given ends. And they remind us that in so far as ends can be taken as given, economics is the subject matter of life.[5] It remains for us to ask if ends can be taken as given: *is life economics, or do we need to supplement it with an ethical view of value?*[6]

How far, therefore, can we push this assumption of stable preferences? Because every action involves the use of means – in accordance with our knowledge – to achieve some end, it seems we can take the assumption quite far. Our authors extend their analysis, for example, to choices made in the context of drug addiction, fashion trends, and even music appreciation. One can imagine further extensions to other activities: play (both individual and team sports), art, the academy, religion, family life, gender relations, and even so-called "deviant" behavior. The accommodation of means to any particular end is expensive, in the sense that it requires us to shift means from the pursuit of a different end. And insofar as action is purposeful, it presents us with the problem of economizing – i.e. being efficient in our use of the means at our disposal.[7] It is in this sense, as was suggested above, that we can say that all life is economic.

But life is not all economics. While all three elements of economic behavior – resources, knowledge, and ends – may be taken as "given" at any moment in time, in a larger perspective they are never given, but changing. What is more, producing changes in the elements of economic behavior – but most especially in its ends – is often essential to action itself. Under closer scrutiny, we realize that the ends of activity generally turn out not to be stable at all, but to be themselves the instruments of a search for new ends. Tastes, preferences, and values not only change, they possess an inner intentional dynamism. The thing that people most want, and seek to find in their actions, is not satisfaction for the wants they possess, but more, and *better* wants.[8]

Where does the fact that tastes and preferences have an internal dynamism leave economic science? What is it that economics can explain? Measured by the standards of natural science, where the objects of study can be controlled within definable conditions, and their activity reduced to law, economics cannot go very far. Actual human behavior is provisional, constantly shifting, and individually unique: so much so that generalization regarding the content of human action is practically meaningless. Temporarily, for the time being, people act as if their conduct were directed by the attempt to realize particular ends. But the people are usually aware that their ends are contingent, provisional, and vague: they are not the real ends, only the ends for particular acts at this moment. The person engaged in a game of chess acts as if capturing her opponent's pieces were the supreme value in life; but this is obviously not the true or final end – the conditions under which she accepted it as her "end" are largely accidental and cannot be reduced to law. Most human conduct is analogous to the game in all essential respects.[9]

Economics can be scientific only in so far as it abstracts far enough away from the content of actual human behavior to say something significant about its form. We say that people prefer larger quantities of wealth to smaller because in that statement the term "wealth" has no substantive meaning – it is merely a place holder representing everything that people at this moment provisionally want. As necessary as it is to understand the laws of economics, they have no predictive power in relation to the actual content of human action. Judgments regarding human action are all in the field of art, not science, of interpretation, not objective fact, and as a consequence we do best not to attempt to analyze, measure, and determine the functional relations among activities, but rather to educate ourselves about history and train our intuitive powers.[10] (Need we even speak of the inhumanity of controlling another human being that is implied by the positivists' notion of prediction?[11]) What Stigler and Becker try to do is provide the laws of economics with empirical predictive power by asking us to assume that "one may usefully treat tastes as stable over time and similar among people" (Stigler and Becker 1977: 76); but this we must not do, if we are going to be true to the nature of human action. That way lies perdition.

The fact that human action is simultaneously the attempt to satisfy a want and the search for better wants means that, in our examination of human activity, the science of economics must be supplemented with an ethical theory of value. Solving the economic problem is wrapped up in the larger problem of choosing what preferences to have, what values to hold. What principles will guide us in this realm – what standards assist the restless spirit within us? Are we reduced to the "tolerant" position of saying that one preference is as good as another, or must we avoid the issue altogether by simply asserting that everyone has the same preferences, as Stigler and Becker do? The scientific mind can rest only on one of these two extremes, which turn out to be much the same – *de gustibus non est disputandum*, indeed?[12] Finding science lacking, perhaps we should turn to religion. Here we uncover a common theme: we can achieve harmony between our restless spirit and the world we inhabit by finding the wrong in ourselves and changing our own nature, by suppressing our restless cravings for different wants and accepting the universe as it is given to us. The Christian formulation is the Love command: love God with all your being and your neighbor as yourself. In the Sermon on the Mount, Jesus suggests that, if we embrace righteousness, God will establish the Kingdom on earth and the economic problem (along with any other source of human conflict) will be solved.

And yet can we as modern humans accept the universe as it is given to us? Do we want a life of peace and quiet, of denying ourselves and taking up our cross? Must we give up a life of action, achievement, and even adventure, relinquish our ideals of authenticity and self-development, and refuse to use our energy and intelligence to create better opportunities for both ourselves and future generations? If we must cease to be human in order to solve our problems, then why bother? No, we believe it is better to be humans than to be vegetables, even lilies of the field.[13]

In the end, then, neither science nor religion can provide us with the help we need to create an ethical theory of value. In the scientific realm, intelligence has no meaning other than that provided by instrumental rationality; in the religious realm, it makes no sense to speak of thinking intelligently about our problems and acting to change the world around us. If science and religion cannot help us, where then can we turn? In the short space of time I have left, I cannot develop my response fully, but let me suggest that we begin by turning to our neighbor and talking – finding out what tastes, preferences, and values we share in common and what differences we have, and then discussing the differences to understand what standards we each adopt. In connection with our topic, the fact that we can and do engage in such discussion has decisive implications.[14] The best metaphor for this discussion is neither scientific theorizing (except in the limited sense that scientists discuss competing theories in order to establish the truth – which is itself an interest and must compete alongside other interests for our attention[15]) nor religious moralism, but literary and artistic criticism.[16] We know what forms of art and literature we like, and, if asked, can articulate some of the artistic standards our social and educational backgrounds have given us; others are in a similar position. Through conversation and discussion, we come to appreciate other standards that produce different artistic tastes, and gain new preferences by adapting our own standards in light of the discussion. The art or literature that we buy today expresses the preferences we currently hold, but no one would suggest that they remain constant – the conversation is ongoing and never-ending, and future purchases will express new, and better, artistic tastes. It is futile to try and predict the outcome of the discussion, because there are no permanent rules of judgment available – besides perhaps the rule to use good judgment. But it is equally wrong to assert that any preference is as good as another – to say *de gustibus non est disputandum*; while there are no permanent rules, when we speak of better tastes and higher values, we do make sense.[17]

12 Did the Chicago School reject Frank Knight?

Assessing Frank Knight's place in the Chicago economics tradition

Two stories currently circulate regarding Frank Knight's relationship with the Chicago School of Economics. The first is a story of tradition, emphasizing the continuity of Chicago economics from the time Knight arrived in the late 1920s until at least the early 1980s. The second is a story of new beginnings in the post-war period, suggesting that the rise of the Chicago School had little to do with Knight; indeed, that crucial elements of the Chicago approach involved a modification, if not rejection, of Knight's views. In order to answer the question asked in the title of this paper, we will look at both stories and examine the grounds on which Knight's relationship with the Chicago School can be evaluated. When we're done, we will have a complex interpretation of that relationship that does not yield a yes or no answer to the question asked.

Two stories

To begin, we rehearse the basics of both stories about Knight and the Chicago School. We start with the story of tradition and continuity because it is, well, traditional.

The traditional account[1]

Knight's return to the University of Chicago in 1928, along with several other personnel decisions at about the same time, meant that by the early 1930s the Department of Economics had a critical mass of individuals engaged in what Henry Simons called "a positive program for laissez-faire" (Simons 1934). Despite the programmatic name, however, adherence to the emerging Chicago School involved more of a theoretical commitment than an ideological one. Many commentators on the history of Chicago economics mistake the former for the latter: if one takes price theory seriously, they say, one must be a libertarian – whether a classical liberal or neoliberal is only a quibble at this point. But whether theory and ideology went hand in hand or not (Jacob Viner, for example, could only loosely be described as affiliated with the ideological agenda; the same could be said for T.W. Schultz in the next generation), everyone in the Chicago School seemed to share a commitment to price theory.

In the traditional account, the 1930s was a time of initial consolidation of the Chicago approach. Knight and Jacob Viner were teaching the price theory and history of economic thought courses, and Simons and Lloyd Mints were also active. Although not unified in their understanding of Marshallian theory or its policy implications, the differences among them only heightened the students' awareness of the fact that these Chicago professors provided a perspective on economic organization that differed substantially from what was commonly taught elsewhere. In fact, part of what set Chicago apart was their irreverence for developments elsewhere: Knight's attacks on institutionalism merged into the School's criticisms of the New Deal, Edward Chamberlin's theory of imperfect competition, and, of course, Keynes. Friedman, Stigler, Allen Wallis and Homer Jones – all key members of the postwar Chicago School – were students in the mid-1930s. All of them point back to the unique Chicago perspective at that time as the foundation upon which the School's eventual success was laid. The standard accounts of Chicago economics, therefore, tell a story of continuity from the 1930s to the early 1980s, an unbroken line of apostolic succession, if you will, running from Knight and Simons to Friedman and Stigler to Becker and Lucas, and today to Murphy and Levitt.

Revisionist accounts

Nineteen years ago at a History of Economics Society session at the ASSA meetings in New York, Donald Dewey (1987) asked what place Frank H. Knight had really occupied in the Chicago School of economics. Dewey expressed doubt about the line of apostolic succession; arguing that there were reasons to think Knight's place was uncertain:

> [Knight] purported to believe that ... economic theory is an easy subject and that anything very original ... is probably wrong. He emphasized the differences rather than the similarities between the social and natural sciences. He did no empirical work himself, did not follow it carefully, and sometimes seemed impervious to its results. He doubted that research would have much of a payoff in our power to predict human events. He felt that economists and almost everybody else exaggerated the role of economic motives in human affairs, preferring to stress religion and ideology.
>
> (Dewey 1987: 1)

Dewey did not intend to cut Knight out of the line of succession, however; he merely set out to show that Knight's vision of the role of the economist was different, perhaps smaller, than that of his followers. George Stigler made the same point that same year in his contribution on Knight to the *New Palgrave*:

> For most present-day economists, the primary purpose of their study is to increase our knowledge of the working of the enterprise and other economic systems. For Knight, the primary role of economic theory is rather different: it is to contribute to the understanding of how by consensus based upon rational

discussion we can fashion [a] liberal society in which individual freedom is preserved and a satisfactory economic performance achieved.

(Stigler 1987: 58)

More recently, Rob van Horn and Phil Mirowski (2008) have argued that Knight had very little to do with the founding of the Chicago School. They give credit for the formation of the School to the generation of economists that followed Knight at the University of Chicago. While they include Friedman and Stigler in that group, they point in particular to Aaron Director. The Chicago School, they argue, had its roots in the Free Market Study, which the Volker Fund initiated, and which Director returned to Chicago following Simons' death to direct. That Study provided the research infrastructure that spawned both Chicago's new theory of industrial organization and the law and economics movement.

Dewey and Mirowski/van Horn argue that Knight's place in the history of the Chicago School is uncertain at best, and perhaps even non-existent. But they provide different reasons for the tenuous relationship. Dewey argued that Knight's place in the Chicago tradition was uncertain because of his methodological and theoretical differences with the Chicago approach developed by Friedman, Stigler, and Becker. In Mirowski and van Horn's account, discontinuities in theory and methodology are seen more as the product than the cause of the reasons why Knight is not really part of the School. New developments in theory and methodology emerged from an agenda set by a privately funded research study that had the explicit purpose of defending corporate capitalism, or what they call neoliberalism.

Conflicting foundations

Looking back at these competing stories, we see that the argument for continuity in the traditional story is based on theory (Knight the price theorist), ideology (Knight the defender of liberalism), and teaching (Knight's role in teaching price theory and the history of economic thought, and his irreverent pedagogical style). The revisionist accounts, on the other hand, focus on methodology (Knight the pluralist), ethics (Knight the philosopher), and changes in the research infrastructure of economic research at the University of Chicago. These six issues, then, divide the stories: Chicago's price theory tradition, its methodological approach, and its research infrastructure; as well as Knight's role as a teacher at Chicago, his understanding of ethics and economics, and his defense of liberalism. In order to adjudicate between the conflicting founda-tions of the traditional and revisionist stories, we need to explore these issues in greater detail. The next two sections combine consideration of these issues into two groups: price theory, teaching and ideology; and methodology, pluralism and ethics.

Price theory, Knight's role as a teacher, and the defense of liberal society

If there is anything that distinguishes Chicago economics from other schools of economic thought, it is the Chicago tradition's assumption that all you need is price theory. Chicago's methodological approach depends upon, and reinforces, this assumption. Chicago's training of students is designed to inculcate a price theoretic way of seeing the world. Chicago researchers use basic price theory to explain an expanding range of human behavior and social outcomes. Policy proposals put forward by Chicago economists invariably involve the application of price theory. In short, taking price theory seriously is at the core of Chicago economics.

I once asked Al Harberger what he thought accounted for Chicago's success. He first gave a typical department chairman's answer: the continuity in the chair from the mid-1940s to the mid-1980s (T.W. Schultz to Harberger to D. Gale Johnson). But then he said that the continuity in the teaching of Price Theory – Econ 301 – over the same period was equally important. From the late 1940s to the mid-1980s, he pointed out, Econ 301 was primarily taught by three individuals: Milton Friedman, Gary Becker, and Al Harberger (Harberger 2002).[2] When you combine that with the fact that the same course was primarily taught from the late 1920s to the mid-1940s by Frank Knight and Jacob Viner, you have a 50-year or more time-span during which generations of Chicago students received Marshallian price theory from five individuals. The legacy of continuity in teaching price theory in Econ 301 is the cornerstone of the Chicago School.

No one will disagree with the statement that Frank Knight took price theory seriously. *RUP* showed that Marshallian price theory could still reveal essential insights about market economies at a time when many economists were ready to cast it aside. In the 1920s, he defended the autonomy and legitimacy of price theory against the Institutionalists and other social scientists (Knight 1924a). In the 1930s, he returned to Marshall's *Principles* as a text after realizing that no more recent textbook provided an adequate alternative. His own exposition of the basics of price theory that was used in the College as well as in undergraduate courses in the department – *The Economic Organization* (Knight 1933c) – helped put price theory at the center of economics education at Chicago. His debates during the late 1930s and early 1940s with Viner over the neoclassical theory of cost – carried out not in person but in their respective classes, with students shuttling back and forth to see what it was all about – as well as Henry Simons' famous "syllabus," which created a set of problems to go along with the students' reading of *The Economic Organization*, made price theory a vibrant intellectual exercise for Chicago students. Knight's role as creator of the Chicago price theory tradition is symbolized today by the fact that the first chapter of *The Economic Organization* ("Social Economic Organization") remains on the reading list for Gary Becker's and Kevin Murphy's Econ 301 class at Chicago today. If the legacy of Econ 301 is the cornerstone of the Chicago School, then Knight is largely responsible for laying it!

Oh, but there's more. As co-editor with Viner of *The Journal of Political Economy* (*JPE*) for almost 20 years, Knight also played a role in the development of that journal as the foremost organ for the advancement and application of a price theoretic perspective on economics. Price theory occupied little space in most economics journals during the 1930s and 1940s, *The Quarterly Journal of*

Economics and the *American Economic Review* included, but that was not the case at the *JPE*. Also, Knight's published attacks on almost every significant opponent of neoclassical price theory cleared the deck for his students to apply price theory to a variety of issues that previous economists would not have dreamed possible.[3]

Notwithstanding Knight's rich pedigree as a Chicago price theorist, however, there is a significant difference between his understanding of what it meant to take price theory seriously, and the understanding that has operated within Chicago economics since his time. For most Chicago economists, taking price theory seriously means: (1) that economics is an applied policy science; and (2) that price theory was applicable to the regulation of economic activity; and (3) its application to the regulation of other aspects of human conduct was a legitimate social scientific activity. For Knight, taking price theory seriously meant: (i) that economic policy discussions must be informed by a deep understanding of price theory; (ii) that price theory was necessary but not sufficient for our understanding of the regulation of economic activity; and (iii) price theory could be useful in understanding many other aspects of human conduct, but only as one factor among many. We'll explore the first of these now, and then examine the second and third issue in the next section, on methodology.

Economics and policy

Another way to express the difference between Chicago economics and neoclassical economics more generally is that the Chicago tradition was less concerned with economics as a pure science, and more concerned about economics as an applied science. This is not to say that Chicago is unconcerned about being scientific; as we will see later, Chicago takes great pains to insist that its approach is scientific. But Chicago takes for granted that the purpose for being scientific is to improve the policy analysis of human societies. Knight actually sets the tone for this approach to economics as a policy science. Intelligent action in society, he argued, requires both the education of the citizenry regarding the fundamentals of price theory (which he thought of as basic common sense) and the commitment of the economics profession to work toward common agreement on what those fundamentals meant with regard to particular policy areas. In this context, nothing should be viewed as outside the bounds of economic thinking (Knight 1924a, 1960a).

Knight also thought that intelligent action in society required an appreciation for the limited relevance of economics to policy, however. As he said in *Intelligence and Social Action*: "there are two sets of problems for policy or action: problems arising because the system does not work in accordance with the theoretical description, and problems arising because it does" (Knight 1960a: 96). For most economists of the twentieth century, the former set of problems (externalities and public goods, for example) occupied the entirety of their attention. Knight called these problems the "mechanical" limitations of market organization (Knight 1923a), and argued that, as difficult as they were to resolve, the price system's mechanisms could internalize these limitations in ways that regulated their effects as well (if not better) than any other mechanism could (Knight 1924a).

The second set of problems – arising from the fact that the economy does not conform to its description in competitive theory – were Knight's special concern. Even when the economic system works according to theory, it raises political and ethical concerns – increased inequality, for example, or the reduction of democratic discussion to the mere adjudication of conflicting interests. Public policy in a democratic society, Knight argued, also required a political appreciation of democratic processes and ethical judgment regarding the relevance of conflicting values like freedom, justice, and equality (Knight 1951b, 1967).

Knight's early writings focused primarily on the ethical side of the argument. His famous two-part lecture at Harvard University in 1922 set out the basic argument: economic theory reduced the human person to a want-satisfying machine. Insofar as we seek to satisfy our existing wants, economics is a necessary part of the explanation of the social outcomes of human action. But, while all of life may be economic, economics is not all of life. Life is more than the satisfaction of existing wants and desires; what we want is not just to satisfy our wants, but to find better wants (Knight 1922). Furthermore, because market exchange reduces human interaction to want satisfaction, it may deteriorate the character of its participants: playing a game, even in a sporting fashion, is not the same as seeking the Good. Thus, in market society we become something less than the people that our ethical systems call us to be (Knight 1923a).

If we dwell – as we are prone to – on the skepticism of Knight's assessment of economics and the market system in "Ethics and the Economic Interpretation" and "The Ethics of Competition," however, then we miss the point, which Knight makes clear later in his life when he incorporates a theory of politics into his analysis. Life is more than just economics, fortunately, and what little hope there is lies in the "more." The political problem is to construct a society that allows individuals the freedom to pursue their desires, including the desire to have better wants, while also ensuring that that policy-making does not become merely the adjudication of competing interests. Knight frequently quoted Viscount Bryce's remark that "democracy is government by discussion." Liberalism's goal, for Knight, is to ensure that the discussion is about what our wants and values could be, not just backroom deals in regards to what they are (Knight 1944c, 1946, 1956b).

For the last 25 years of his life, Knight worked on a book manuscript built around three chapters: the first on the economics of policy in a liberal society, the second on its ethics, and third on its politics. These three chapters provide a convenient way to summarize our comparison of Knight and the Chicago School on what it means to "take price theory seriously" in regard to public policy. Both would agree on the contents of the first chapter; and the portion of the third chapter that came close to a public choice theory could also be shared. But the remainder of that third chapter – on discussion, and almost all of Knight's second chapter – on ethics as an "exploration in the field of values" (Knight 1924a) – would separate him from the Chicago School. For Knight, price theory was necessary, but not sufficient, for public policy formation. The Chicago tradition since Knight, on the other hand, has often acted as if price theory were both necessary and sufficient for public policy formation.

Chicago's methodological approach, Knight's pluralism, and ethics

Since Knight, Chicago economics has developed a methodological approach that supports its task of making price theory an "empirical" applied policy science. The empirical element of Chicago economics emerges from two post-Knight methodological assumptions that Chicago economists introduced. Both are familiar to every economist today, and are frequent topics of methodological discussion. They are, of course, Friedman's methodological principle and the Stigler/Becker principle of *de gustibus non est disputandum*. More relevant to our consideration is the fact that Knight would reject both assumptions.

Friedman first (his essay was, after all, written 20 years before the other). A "positive economics" – i.e. one that could be free from prior value judgments – requires that theory is "judged by its predictive power for the class of phenomena which it is intended to 'explain'" (Friedman 1953: 8), rather than its aesthetic appeal to the mathematician or even the realism of its assumptions. Marshallian theory should be kept in the economist's toolkit, whether its assumptions are realistic or not, because more often than not it works; tools that have repeatedly not worked should be discarded, despite their greater realism.

So much discussion of Friedman's principle has focused on its philosophical and methodological dimensions that we often overlook its *pedagogical* orientation. Friedman is instructing us – his students – to confront theory with the evidence. Unlike Knight, who thought economic theory was fairly easy, its insights basically an extension of human common sense, and its predictive capacity practically empty, Friedman responds to each student's claim: "Prove it."[4] Thus, just as Knight and Viner brought analytical excitement to the study of price theory, Friedman (and Harberger and the agricultural/development economists like Schultz and Johnson) brought an empirical and policy-focused excitement to its study. Beyond the prelims, a student at Chicago engaged in the exact same discipline that a faculty member at Chicago engaged in: confronting hypotheses about market outcomes with the evidence (see the discussion of workshops below). By the late 1940s, if you were doing something else – say, Walrasian general equilibrium theory – you belonged in the Cowles Commission or at Harvard/MIT.

But could one really be "empirical" in the Chicago sense if a rejected hypothesis could always be rescued by the claim that tastes had changed? If opportunity cost is the essence of price theory, and cost structures matter, then Chicago needed a methodological principle that instructed the theorist to focus her attention solely on changes in cost structures. In 1977, Stigler and Becker gave articulation to a second methodological principle, which Chicago had operated on since the late 1940s: *de gustibus non est disputandum*. According to the *de gustibus* principle, better predictions result from assigning explanatory power to the cost structure that constrains people's choices than to changes in preferences or tastes. Put the other way around, better predictions result from assuming that people across time and place have essentially the same set of preferences (Stigler and Becker 1977).

Once stated, Stigler and Becker's *de gustibus* principle seemed an obvious complement to Friedman's principle. Start with models that focus on changing costs, and resort to explanations that depend upon changes or differences in taste only as a last resort. Few Chicago economists have seen the need to use the fall-back position since. In fact, the Stigler–Becker principle has allowed Chicago economists to expand the realm of human conduct explained in price theoretic terms – what some call "economics imperialism" (Becker 1976, 1996; Becker and Murphy 2000; Lazear 2000).

We have no evidence that Knight ever read Friedman's essay, and he never had the opportunity to respond directly to Stigler and Becker. I have summarized his argument against the *de gustibus* principle, which runs throughout his work, in Emmett (2006a). The *de gustibus* principle was a rejection of Knight's most basic assumption about value theory: that human values are dynamic and explorative. While economic theory had to assume that preferences were given in order to reveal the underlying order that the price system generated, economic policy could not function with such an assumption. The assumption rendered the notion of "government by discussion" meaningless, because it implicitly assumed that the end that a policy promoted was already known. In *The Economic Organization* (Knight 1933c), the first function of economic organization is the establishment of a "value scale" – a means by which society could adjudicate among values. A liberal society, Knight argued in *The Economic Organization* and elsewhere, was one which sought to keep the value scale open as long as possible, allowing as diverse a set of values as possible, and ensuring that participants could change values as they learned what was best for them. Policy-making, therefore, was a discovery process, in which we found, by discussion, not only the best means for satisfying our goals, but also what our goals ought to be. Of course, as Friedman makes clear at the beginning of his essay, the "ought to be" is exactly what his methodological principle was designed to avoid. Our ends are known and given, Friedman suggested; the real issue is our disagreement over the policy means by which to accomplish them. That disagreement, he argued, can be settled only by an increase in the positive knowledge of economics.

Thus the two assumptions which form the methodological core of postwar Chicago economics are both an implicit rejection of Knight's understanding of the relation of economics to liberal economic policy.

Research infrastructure

In the 1940s, economists at the University of Chicago began to build a framework for postwar economic research that was largely unparalleled in the social sciences. For the most part, the infrastructure they built went unnoticed by theorists and historians of economics during the postwar period. Perhaps this should not surprise us. Chicago economists knew that what they did was unique, but were often more focused on what the results of "taking price theory seriously" could mean for theory and policy than they were on the institutional processes that generated those results. Many historians of economic thought were also focused on those results in order to differentiate Chicago from other "schools" of thought. While we sometimes heard about Chicago's unusual practices, we seldom identified them as central to what made "Chicago School" a school.

I think it fair to say that we now know that to be a mistake. Where it was common to think of a "school" of thought as a group who thought alike, we now often identify a "school" by the institutions and rules by which it "disciplined" its members. We have already seen that Chicago economics is more identified with a methodological approach than it is with ideological conformity. We can now carry that further. Chicago's methodological approach was established early in the educational process, and reinforced by the structure provided for faculty and student research. In fact, Chicago economics melded the education of graduate students with the research process of faculty in such a way that one not only led to the other, but in many cases *was* the other. We often say that the social sciences lack laboratories, but at Chicago, the workshop model accomplished the same result: graduate students learned the basics in their first year; apprenticed in the workshops for the next couple of years while finishing their coursework; and joined the central core of the research team by the completion of their dissertation. Today, many economics departments incorporate elements of the Chicago workshop model. Between the 1950s and 1970s, only Columbia came close to Chicago.

The development of the Chicago workshop model in the 1950s was primarily inspired by the department's applied policy specialists – the agricultural economists and their labor economics allies. T.W. Schultz brought an externally funded research program in agricultural economics and development with him from Iowa State University in the 1940s, and H. Gregg Lewis proposed the adaptation of Columbia's fledgling workshops in the late 1940s. The first two non-agricultural economics workshops were the "Money" workshop that Friedman ran, and the "Public Finance" workshop run by Harberger. Many more followed: Deirdre McCloskey counted almost 20 workshops in the late 1970s (McCloskey 2001), which is about where the number of workshops remains today. Most of the workshops followed a common pattern: weekly meetings, paper distribution prior to the meeting, and presentations by the professors who led the workshop, seasoned graduate students, and invited guests. Workshop meetings ran on some version of "Chicago rules": an opening statement by the presenter, followed by open discussion often dominated by the workshop's professors. Tales of merciless dissection of presenters are somewhat exaggerated,[5] but invited guests were certainly at a disadvantage because they were not used to the effort to "uncover where the bodies were buried" in their papers (McCloskey 2001). Graduate students and faculty frequently attended several workshops each week, fueling an intensity of debate which refined the ideas and methods of all its participants.

While it is possible to argue that ideas alone drive great advances in science and policy, it is far more likely the case that the ideas thrived because they were refined by the fire of intense disciplinary debate. Chicago economists had their ideas refined by such a fire every week. No one can doubt that postwar Chicago economics owes much to the workshop model.

But the workshops cost money, and require an administration willing to support such a structure financially. Remember that there were a couple hundred graduate students every year working their way through the program in the department and in associated workshops in the Graduate School of Business and the Law

School. Foundation support for the workshops, for individual students, and particular faculty research programs was sought early on, and the Ford, Rockefeller, Sears Roebuck, Volker, and Earhart foundations were regular contributors. Several endowments were also set up at the University of Chicago for support of institutes, such as the Norman Wait Harris Memorial Foundation, established in 1923, and the Charles R. Walgreen Foundation for the Study of American Institutions, established in 1937.

Knight played almost no role in the creation and maintenance of the infrastructure which supported the postwar Chicago research program. By the time the workshop infrastructure was constructed in the 1950s, he had retired and had little to do with departmental affairs. In the late 1940s, his influence in libertarian circles was useful in obtaining funds from Volker and other funds, but as Mirowski and van Horne have shown, he had little to do with the uses to which those funds were put. It is possible that Knight's opposition to Hayek's view of liberal society, which came to be closely associated with the Chicago program, had something to do with this (Emmett 2007), but it is more likely that Knight was simply not involved in the postwar Chicago economics program. His energies went into his own writing, almost all of which was related in some fashion to the argument of his book on the economics, ethics and politics of policy formation in a liberal democracy.

Conclusion

Our re-assessment of Knight's relationship with the Chicago School of Economics has examined six issues that emerged from the traditional and revisionist stories of that relationship. We found the following:

(1) Taking price theory seriously is the core of the Chicago approach, and the legacy of continuity in the teaching of price theory in Econ 301 is the cornerstone of the Chicago School. Knight's role in initiating the teaching of that course, and encouraging the development of a strong price theoretic tradition at Chicago generally, cannot be exaggerated.
(2) But Knight took price theory seriously in a different sense than did significant strands within the Chicago tradition after him. Where those who followed Stigler and Becker assumed its sufficiency for the explanation of human conduct, Knight assumed only its necessity, and argued that economics alone was insufficient for the explanation of human behavior and the conducting of economic policy in a liberal democracy. Methodologically, this meant that much of the Chicago tradition rejected Knight's understanding of the role of ethics and politics in human conduct and the formation of public policy.
(3) Although Knight was central to the establishment of a price theory tradition at Chicago, he was not instrumental to the creation of the research infrastructure that supported the postwar Chicago School.
(4) Chicago economics built a research program that responded well to criticisms of price theory that focused on how poorly it explained the real world's

departure from the ideal of perfect competition. But that program was not a response to Knight's concern that the perfect competition itself fell short as an ethical ideal. In addition, he argued that a liberal democracy could not yield its freedom to the authority of any standard outside the "discussion" that defined democracy itself, even if that authority wore the mantle of a science. Thus his ethics and his ideology came together in agreement on the need for a pluralistic approach to social problems that was the opposite of what Chicago economics sought in its straightforward application of theory to policy.

Ironically, then, the Chicago School can be said to owe everything, and nothing, to Knight. Without his initiation of teaching price theory and persistence in defending it against its numerous opponents in the interwar years, there would be no Chicago tradition. Yet the methodological approach and research infrastructure which propelled the Chicago School to its central position in the economics profession and among policy-makers across the globe by the 1980s owe little or nothing to him. In fact, the two central methodological principles of Chicago economics – Friedman's principle of positive economics, and the Stigler/Becker *de gustibus* principle – combine to deny the pluralism Knight advocated for social science in a liberal democracy.

Section IV

Economics, religion, and politics

13 Frank Knight

Economics versus religion

In their recent history of American sociology, Arthur Vidich and Stanford Lyman argue that the central problems and concerns of American social science "emanate from the dilemmas and contradictions in the relationship between God, the state, and civil society." (Vidich and Lyman 1985: 281) Called upon to explain, and justify, the ways of American society to those within it, *without reference to God's divine providence,* social scientists have been led to examine "the kind of folks people are" and "the kind of world it is" (Knight, quoted in Dewey 1987: 9), to judge what it means to live intelligently in a world of illness, inequality, death, and scarcity, and to recognize that intelligent social reform will never be wholly realized in this world. Although social scientists seldom understand themselves to be preaching, and would eschew the title of "theologian," their work encompasses the roles of both minister and theologian in a secular society.

Of course, few modern economists understand their work as social scientists in these terms. Most economists work from an understanding of economics that emphasizes the independence of the economics profession as a scientific community and the contribution that the technical expertise of the profession makes to public policy formation. Furthermore, in the contemporary economist's understanding, social choice is ultimately synonymous with public policy-making; that is, in the final analysis social choices are decisions made by public officials regarding the coordination of conflicting ideas about the best means to select for the accomplishment of some given objective. In the context of this understanding of economics and society, it is primarily the individual economist's participation in a scientific community, rather than the person's status as a citizen, that forms the basis of his or her participation in society's discussion about its problems. Hence the economist's primary responsibility is to contribute to the growth of the scientific knowledge of the community. The individual economist's own social values may have some effect upon the choice of research topic, of course, but the nature of the inquiry conducted is disciplined by the rules and conventions of the scientific community.

This is not the place for an extended examination of the relation between the modern economist's understanding of the work of an economist as a social scientist and the claim of Vidich and Lyman regarding the fundamentally theological nature of American social inquiry (see Nelson 1991). Instead, the purpose of this chapter is to show how the work of one economist who is central to the development of American economic thought in the twentieth century – Frank H. Knight – illustrates that claim. How might "the dilemmas and contradictions in the relationship between God, the state, and civil society" have shaped the understanding of the nature and significance of economics that Knight articulated?

Knight on economics and religion

We can begin by recognizing that Knight is a prime candidate for examination in a case study such as this. Not only did he write more on religion that most other modern economists – some mention of religion appears in many of his articles, but it is the focus of his attention in Knight (1923b, 1923c, 1924c, 1939a, 1941b, 1963, n.d.); and Knight and Merriam (1945) – but his lifelong preoccupation with, and frequent antagonism toward, religion in general and Christianity in particular has become one of the central elements in the "image" that his students at the University of Chicago and his interpreters have constructed for us. We have been told, for example, that Knight's unflagging scepticism can be attributed to "overexposure in early life to the hell-fire and brimstone of prairie evangelism" (Buchanan 1968: 427), and that his decision to seek a career as a social scientist emerged, at least in part, from his rejection of conservative Protestantism (Emmett 1991: 114–53; Dewey 1990). Don Patinkin (1973) has told us that the unique contribution that Knight made as a teacher lay in his digressions on the problems of the human condition, which were often laced with stories about the follies of religion. And some of the anecdotes about Knight's opposition to religion which circulated at the University of Chicago during his lifetime have been passed on to us (e.g., Patinkin 1981; Stigler 1987: 55). When we put these indications of Knight's interest in religion together with the frequent discussions of religion we find in his writings, we can appreciate Donald Dewey's remark that "One cannot discuss … Frank Knight without attention to his views on this cosmic subject" (Dewey 1990: 2). There are not many other twentieth-century economists of whom the same could be said.

But there is another, and perhaps more important, reason why Knight should be considered in a study such as this one. As Dorothy Ross recently said in her history of the origins of American social science, Knight stood "at a fundamental turning point" in the history of American economic thought (Ross 1991: 427). Behind him lay the history of a community of economists who understood their discipline to be a part of a larger social, historical, and even moral undertaking, and whose world was shaped by the reality of God's providential presence; before him lay the modern development of a community of economists who understood the discipline to be a positive science, independent of history and of social or moral concerns, and whose world was shaped by the reality of God's absence. Often individuals who write at fundamental turning points in intellectual history, and who are able to capture something of both the old and the new in their writing, continue to speak to the new tradition long after their theoretical insights have been assimilated, because they raise anomalous or problematic issues for the normal discourse of the new tradition. Knight is no exception: his importance to us lies in the way he held the concerns of the passing tradition of economics in tension with the insights promised by the new tradition. To put it in theological terms: Knight's work expresses the tension between the need to get on with the work of making sense of a world in which God is absent, while remaining acutely aware of what we have lost because God is no longer present. Despite his frequent inability to sustain the tension between the old way of seeing the world and the new, Knight's attempt to do so created an ambiguity in his work that increases his importance for us. As James Buchanan pointed out in a recent article on Knight's critique of competitive society, it is the ambiguity that results from Knight's attempt to hold these two different ways of understanding economics in tension that makes his work so fascinating to us (Buchanan 1987: 74).

The question which needs to be addressed here, therefore, is whether Knight's lifelong preoccupation with the role of religion in the modern world is in any-way connected with the methods or results of his economic analysis. Are Knight's perpetual musings on religion simply the product of his childhood experience of "prairie evangelism," his general philosophical bent, and his personal preferences, or are they essential in some fashion to his work as an economist?

In order to answer that question, we need to examine Knight's understanding of the nature and significance of both religion and economics in modern society. Religion, we see, has little place in the public realm of a modern society because it is perceived to be inimical to that free discussion of values that Knight believed is the essence of democracy. Economics, on the other hand, is inextricably bound up with the valuation process in a liberal society; in fact, Knight believes it has little relevance outside the context of a modern liberal democracy. Common to Knight's understanding of both religion and economics, therefore, is his belief that their functions in a modern liberal society are defined and circumscribed by their respective relations to the social discussion of values which lies at the heart of the liberal society. The identification of this common theme in Knight's treatment of religion and economics will enable a direct connection to be made between Knight's opposition to religion and his understanding of economics. The conclusion that will be reached can be stated clearly at the outset: Knight's opposition to any form of Christian social thought is directly related to his economics because his opposition is grounded in the belief that modern society, of which economics is an integral part, cannot be analyzed from a religious perspective. Ultimately, economics is not susceptible to theological reflection because modern social relations are not open to theological speculation.

At the same time, however, an analysis of Knight's understanding of the nature of economics will uncover a theme which must be held in tension with the conclusion just stated. That contrary theme, namely the limited relevance of economics to the fundamental problems of social choice in a liberal democracy counterbalances Knight's opposition to Christian social thought with his belief that the problems of a liberal society are ultimately ethical in nature, and, as such, require a sense of critical judgment that lies beyond the purview of economics. In fact, addressing these problems at their root may require us to return to spirituality, for "religion *is* life, at its highest and best" (Knight 1923b: 9, italics in original).

Knight's opposition to Christian social thought

The basic structure of Knight's argument against Christian social thought is well known and has been described in several recent articles (Kern 1988; Raines 1989; and Raines and Jung 1986). In Knight's estimation, the Christian gospel of love is directed *at personal relations,* where good intentions matter, whereas the central problems of a liberal society revolve around issues of *social relations,* where it is the consequences of an action rather than the intentions behind it that matter. Claiming that the core of the gospel message was originally an "interim ethic" – which is to say that we should live now in the expectation of God's imminent reversal of scarcity, by which all the ordinary earthly problems of life will be transcended (Knight and Merriam 1945: 29) – Knight argued that the gospel was never intended to provide guidance for the collective actions of a large, pluralistic society. "Indeed," he claimed, "the standards set [are] impossible to maintain without destroying the material and social basis of life" (Knight and Merriam 1945: 29).

The only way the original gospel message could possibly be translated into a modern pluralistic society, Knight believed, is through reference to the two-fold command to love God and neighbor: "If Christianity does not mean this, there is nothing that it can be said to mean" (Knight 1939a: 48). But however fine "personal affection and abstract mercy" are as motives, "they are notoriously unreliable as guides to action" (Knight and Merriam 1945: 35). Of course, in a society that believes that the hand of God is at work in ways that are often invisible to human perception, good intentions may be enough; although the problem of explaining why the wicked prosper at the expense of the righteous cannot easily be dismissed. But in the modern social world, which does not have recourse to the providential nature of a divine Being, the moralistic call for good intentions is definitely not enough. What such a society requires, Knight argues, is attention to the consequences of any action. In the case of social action, paying attention to consequences means that right action requires knowledge of the relations among people created by the institutional arrangements of society. Because action always involves the use of power, which can cause irreparable harm if it is not used intelligently or remains unchecked, the ethical person in modern society:

> … must seek and intelligently use power, in business and politics and other social relations … Neither love nor the Golden Rule shed any significant light upon the problem of organized social relations. Differences usually involve a conflict of rights as well as desires. … Love cannot replace justice, in practice or as an ideal.
>
> (Knight and Merriam 1945: 49–50)

Knight's earliest reflections on Christianity and modern society focus primarily on the relation between the love ethic and the use of power, and suggest that the central problem with the love ethic emerges from its failure to recognize the inevitable need to use power. Because Christianity refuses to recognize the presence of power in all human relations, and therefore provides no guidance for using power rightly, the existing power relations in society are absolutized, and the gospel of love converted into a form of coercion. Thus, "love is equivalent to force in human relations, is in fact but a variety of force" (Knight 1924c: 1; see also Knight 1923c; and Knight and Merriam 1945: 42–7). As his thinking on the nature of a liberal society developed, however, Knight realized that social action requires more than the knowledge of the effects of action on others in a particular institutional framework. It also requires *discussion*. The new element in his thinking about the nature of a liberal society adds an extra dimension to his critique of Christian social thought.

The term discussion is an important one for Knight, and mention of it can be found throughout his writing on both economics and social philosophy. He is fond, in particular, of quoting Lord Bryce's definition of democracy: "government by discussion." No matter where he employs the term, however, he always uses it to imply reference to a two-tiered process. At one level, discussion for Knight means dialogue about the appropriate institutional mechanisms that society should use in order to coordinate individual action. For the purpose of social action, society is "a thing of institutions" far more than it is of humans (Knight 1939a: 60), and the choice of social institutions is essential to ensuring that individual actions contribute to the general good. "The broad crucial task of free society," Knight tells us, "is to reach agreement by discussion on the kind of civilization it is to create for the future" (Knight 1956b: 407).

But the discussion of what coordinating mechanisms to choose must be undergirded by a deeper level of discussion, Knight reminds us, if it is to avoid becoming merely "a contest between individuals or interest groups in getting what they want at the cost of others" (Knight 1956b: 407). The deeper level of social discussion required is an ongoing dialogue about the values and ideals which inform our choice of institutional arrangements:

> The chief thing which the common-sense individual actually wants is not satisfaction for the wants which he has, but more, and *better* wants. … [For this reason, i]t is the higher goal of conduct to test and try these values, to define and improve them, rather than to accept and "satisfy" them.
>
> (Knight 1922: 42, 55)

Because our values are fluid and dynamic, rather than static, we can never presume that we have fully captured the ideals that our values express in our choice of institutions. Hence the ongoing discussion and reformulation of values "is the social problem in the strict sense" (Knight 1939a: 51). Viewed from the perspective of the long run, the social problem for Knight is not so much the creation of greater freedom through the evolution of social institutions as it is "the creation of individuals fit for membership in a free society" (Knight 1943: 181). Freedom requires responsibility, and only constant discussion about our values and ideals (for example, what kind of people we want to become) will insure that changes to society's institutions will be improvements in the sense that they contribute to the production of more responsible citizens. Neglect of the deeper level of discussion, Knight believed, would inevitably lead to the downfall of liberal society. His perception of this neglect, in fact, was the basis of his pessimistic attitude toward liberalism in the mid-1930s (Knight 1922, 1934b, and especially 1991).

The importance of an evolving social discussion of values and their institutional expressions suggests another way in which the Christian gospel of love is at odds with the ideals of a liberal society. Christianity cannot contribute to the discussion that lies at the heart of a liberal society, Knight tells us, because it takes the existing social structure as given. The maxim, "Render unto Caesar the things that belong to Caesar, and unto God the things that belong to God" provides no help, for example, in showing us which things are best coordinated by government, and which are best left to a market (Knight 1922; and Knight and Merriam 1945: 26–50). Because Christianity fails to address the inequities and inefficiencies of the prevailing social structure, it can easily be used as a defense of the existing social order. And whenever a change in the structure of society is accomplished, the new order will soon be proclaimed to be "gospel" truth. Speaking of the way Christianity has been used historically to sanction both the existing order and the establishment of any new order, Knight remarked that:

> [a]s soon as any issue in politics or economics became openly controversial, Christianity was used as an argument on both sides with equal assurance. And as soon as any change was definitely accomplished, the result became the state of affairs called for by the original Gospel, and a product of its teaching.
>
> (Knight and Merriam 1945: 24)

For Knight, an ethic that can be used to sanction any social order is no ethic at all; and liberalism, which must constantly evaluate the existing order, will do well to avoid appeal to religious beliefs. Christianity, therefore, has no place in the social discussion of values in a liberal society.

What a liberal society needs, Knight argued, is a free and open-ended discussion of the values to be pursued by individual and collective action, the evaluation and improvement of our institutions in light of the discussion of our values, and measures by which we could weigh the consequences of actions within any particular institutional arrangement. Christianity's failure to provide an ethic relevant to any aspect of the overall problem of organized social relations means, for Knight, that it has nothing to contribute to a liberal society. Indeed, any attempt to apply the Christian love ethic in a liberal society would produce less-than-satisfactory, perhaps positively evil, results:

> ... the teachings of Christianity give little or no direct guidance for the change and improvement of social organization. ... Indeed, evil rather than good seems likely to result from any appeal to Christian religious or moral teachings in connection with the problems of social action.
>
> (Knight 1939a: 46–7)

As Anthony Waterman (1987: 59) has pointed out, Knight's argument is one of the most radical attacks on Christian social thought yet produced by a modern economist, because he goes beyond the usual criticism of specific policy proposals presented by church bodies or individual Christians to undermine the very foundations of religiously based social reform. For Knight, the use of the term *Christian* in conjunction with *social thought* is, in the context of modern liberal societies, a logical impossibility.

Knight on the nature and significance of economics

In the previous section, we saw that Knight's attack on Christian social thought emerged from his understanding of the antithetical character of the relation between religion and liberalism. In a world where the assurance of divine providential care cannot be assumed, the consequences of human choice matter much more than the intentions behind them, and the choice of institutional mechanisms for facilitating discussion and coordinating choices becomes a matter of great significance. Religion has no place in such a world, because it cannot provide the necessary social standards to assist in the discussion of values or in the evaluation of institutional coordination mechanisms. In the context of a liberal society, Christianity (which Knight usually equates with religion) has nothing to say to the central social problems because it has no truly *social* thought.

The purpose of my investigation, however, is not primarily to examine Knight's treatment of religion and liberalism. I have pursued that examination in order to draw the connection between Knight's understanding of the antithetical nature of the relation between religion and liberalism and his understanding of the relation between religion and economics. The next step we need to take is to examine Knight's discussion of the nature and significance of economics, in order to see the connection he made between liberalism and economics. Only then will we be able to see why he rejected any connection between religion and economics, and why, at the same time, he believed that economics has only a small role to play in the most important aspect of a liberal society – its ongoing discussion of the values and ideals that will guide its social action.

When addressing Knight's approach to economics, most commentators begin with his writings on methodology: in particular, his review of Terence Hutchison's *The Significance and Basic Postulates of Economic Theory* (Knight 1940a; for commentary on Knight's methodology, see Gonce 1972; and Hirsch 1976). The central questions posed from this perspective are ones such as these: Did Knight believe that the fundamental postulates of economics were a priori truths? Did Knight view the laws of economics as tendencies? How did Knight employ Weber's concept of *Verstehen*? And what were Knight's views on the empirical testing of economic models? Though these questions are interesting, and though their pursuit of them might bring us close to the questions at the heart of our investigation (see Hammond 1991), I propose to begin at a different point.

In order to come at his approach to economics from an angle that will enable us to appreciate the way in which he practiced and taught economics, as well as what he said in his methodological writings, let us consider the understanding of economics expressed in *The Economic Organization* (Knight 1933c). This famous little textbook, which circulated throughout Knight's classes as an unpublished set of readings for most of his career (see Emmett 1991: 280), encapsulated Knight's understanding of economics in four short chapters. For our purposes here, we can focus on the first chapter, "Social Economic Organization," in which Knight identified economics as a subject which "deals with the *social organization* of economic activity" (Knight 1933c: 6; italics in original).

After opening the chapter with "a warning against attaching too much importance" to economics (Knight 1933c: 3), Knight sets about distinguishing economics, which is necessarily linked with the economizing activity of humans, from the study of rational human activity. For Knight, economics is not equivalent to the science of rational action, for two reasons. The first reason Knight gives is that economics deals with the social organization of human economizing activity – "the concrete means or mechanism for dividing the general function of making a living for the people into parts and bringing about the performance of these parts in due proportion and harmony" (Knight 1933c: 7) – rather than with the process of making a living itself. The care Knight takes to distinguish economics as a *social* science from the study of individual economizing behavior suggests that he places far less emphasis on the attributes economists ascribe to individual behavior than he does on the attributes ascribed to the price system which coordinates that behavior. In other words, for Knight, economics is less the study of maximizing behavior than it is the study of the exchange process (on Knight's ambiguous relations with the maximizing tradition, see Buchanan 1987, and Emmett 1991: 197–245). It is no mistake that the second chapter of the textbook is entitled "The Price System and the Economic Process," and that there is no intensive examination of demand theory in the book.

Furthermore, as he makes clear in the first chapter, economics deals primarily with only *one* specific form of social organization – the free market. Despite the fact that economic activity has been organized according to tradition, command, and voluntary association in many societies, modern societies that take personal freedom seriously generally adopt the free enterprise system as their central form of economic organization. "Consequently it is the structure and working of the system of free enterprise which constitutes the principal topic of discussion in a treatise on economics" (Knight 1933c: 6).

Knight's definition of economics as a social science that studies free enterprise means that economics makes little sense apart from in the context of a liberal society. In a lecture published near the end of his career, he said, "Economics as a discipline is a quite recent arrival on the scene, because it assumes individual freedom and hence there was no place for it in earlier forms of society" (Knight 1961: 185). Despite the existence of exchange relations in other and earlier forms of society, economics as a scientific discipline could not emerge until the free enterprise system that it studies developed as a significant form of social organization. The strong connection Knight draws between economics and free enterprise economies allows him to claim (later in his life) that:

> The purpose of teaching and writing on economics I take to be to give the public a general understanding of the "economic order" or organization

that prevails in a modem "free" nation, for their guidance in social action affecting it.

(Knight 1961: 185)

The second reason that Knight gave for his argument that economics is not the science of rational action emerges from his claim, made in the first chapter of *The Economic Organization,* that rationality is something more than efficient "economizing," understood as the accommodating of available means to achieve a goal. Human rationality, Knight suggested, also includes discussion about what goals to pursue. Contrary to the assumption that economists often make – *de gustibus non est disputandum* – Knight believed that it is precisely tastes, preferences, values, and beliefs that are, and should be, subject to intense rational discussion.

> Living intelligently includes more than the intelligent use of means in realizing ends; it is fully as important to select the ends intelligently, for intelligent action directed toward wrong ends only makes evil greater and more certain. … Not only are the objectives of action in fact a practical problem, as well as the means of achievement, but intelligent discussion of the means cannot be separated from the discussion of the ends.
>
> (Knight 1933c: 4)

As we saw in the previous section, the notion that rationality consists of more than economizing behavior is a theme that runs throughout Knight's work (for its relevance to economics, see Knight 1922 and 1923a). This theme sets up an interesting tension in his understanding of the relation between economics and liberalism, however. On the one hand, because any choice that an individual makes is simultaneously a decision about means *and* ends, the price system, which coordinate individuals' economizing choices, is itself a part of the process of social valuation. Economic exchange is inextricably a part of the broader social discussion of values in a liberal society:

> The system of social organization does more than reduce individual values to a common denominator or scale of equivalence. In large part the individual wants themselves are *created* by social intercourse, and their character is also largely dependent upon the form of organization of the economic system upon which they are dependent for their gratification.
>
> (Knight 1933c: 9, italics in original)

On the other hand, Knight's assumption that rationality is more than economizing behavior also imposes a severe limitation on the relevance of economics to the social discussion of values. For although the price system can be described *as if* the decisions being made were simply choices over means and not ends, and even though such an analysis is probably a necessary "first stage in the discussion of economic problems" (Knight 1921d: 146; see also Knight 1923a), it is still necessary to remember that price theory can never wholly subsume value theory. Thus

Knight wanted economists to keep the intimate connection between price theory and the social valuation process in the foreground of their analysis in order that they should recognize the significant limitation placed on their contribution to the social valuation process. "But should it not be kept in mind," he asked in a book review written at about the same time as the earliest versions of the material in *The Economic Organization*, "that the ultimate object of economic theorizing is a criticism in ethical and human terms of the workings of the economic machine, and that a theory of value as well as price is indispensable?" (Knight 1921d: 146). The fact that economics must take human values as given in order to generate a theory of exchange relations meant, for Knight, that its contribution to the social discussion of values was extremely limited.

The tension between these two sides of Knight's understanding of economics has been described quite well by George Stigler, who said that:

> For most present-day economists, the primary purpose of their study is to increase our knowledge of the workings of the enterprise and other economic systems. For Knight, the primary role of economic theory is rather different: it is to contribute to the understanding of how by consensus based upon rational discussion we can fashion [a] liberal society in which individual freedom is preserved and a satisfactory performance achieved. This vast social undertaking allows only a small role for the economist, and that role requires only a correct understanding of the central core of value theory.
>
> (Stigler 1987: 58)

From religion to economics (and back again?)

In the previous section, we saw that Knight viewed economic exchange as a part of the larger social valuation process, and hence understood economic theory to emerge from, and exist within, the social discussion of value. Because economics is an integral part of the intellectual culture of a liberal society, and because religion is not, we can conclude that for Knight, religion and economics have no relation. In fact, we can say that because of the particular way in which Knight understood religion to be antithetical to liberalism that he believed religion can *never* be related to economics. Economics, which is the study of social organization in a liberal society and its consequences for human action, cannot be connected to an ethical framework that refuses to consider the consequences of actions and simply accepts (if not sanctions) an existing social order. Ultimately, the reason why economics and religion are unrelated is because religion contains no resource for the evaluation of social change, which is the one thing most needed in a modern society.

At the same time, however, our examination of Knight's understanding of the nature of economics has uncovered another theme that must be held in tension with the fundamental antithesis between religion and economics that characterizes so much of his writing on the relation between the two realms of thought. The notion that economics might be an integral part of the social discussion, but that it has no claim to dominate that discussion because of its assumption about the givenness of human preferences, implies that there is some room in a liberal society for an independent field of ethics. By its very nature, an ethic suited to the needs of a liberal society would reject the absolutized standards of Christianity and most other religions. But would it be anti-religious in every sense?

In most of his writing on ethics, economics, and liberalism, the answer Knight gave to that question, as we have seen, was "Yes": religion and liberal ethics are antithetical. But early in his career, while he was still sorting out his relations with the religious environment of his youth, he offered a tantalizing suggestion of a different answer. After considering many of the themes touched on here in a paper that appears to be a public address, Knight added:

> My concluding thought would be that in spite of all that I have said about the difficulties of these [religious] ideas for the modem man and the inhospitability of his mind toward them, his penchant for tough-mindedness and fear of being fooled ... the world is ripe for the fearless preaching of a spiritual gospel. At heart it is hungry, and is looking for the man with the courage to "break the bread of life" and "pour out the living water." It is dimly aware of the existence of a realm of values where to seek reverently is to find, and wants nothing so much as confident guidance on the path toward that country, which has no immigration restrictions or naturalization laws, no boundaries even, for it is co-extensive with time and space, the City not made with hands but whose builder and maker is God.
>
> (Knight 1923b: 9–10)

Despite the fact that he never again felt comfortable putting his ideas in quite the same form – because he came to reject the presence of God – we would not stretch the truth too far to suggest that Knight spent the rest of his life seeking ways to preach that "spiritual gospel" to modern society.

Conclusion

At the beginning of this chapter, I suggested that Frank Knight's work could be used to illustrate Vidich's and Lyman's claim regarding the fundamentally theological nature of social inquiry. After our examination of the relation between Knight's opposition to Christian social thought and his understanding of the nature and significance of economics, we are ready to return to that claim and to summarize what we have found.

One of the central elements of Vidich and Lyman's thesis is that even in a society that has no recourse to the providential nature of a God who is present in human history, the provision of a justification for the way society works is a "theological" undertaking. Despite the fact that modern economists often forget it, their investigation of the universal problem of scarcity and its consequences for human behavior and social organization is a form of theological inquiry: in a world where there is no God, scarcity replaces moral evil as the central problem of theodicy, and the process of assigning value becomes the central problem of morality. Knight's (implicit) recognition of the theological nature of economic inquiry in this regard is one of the reasons for his rejection of positivism in economics and his insistence on the fundamentally normative and apologetic character of economics. In some sense, therefore, it is appropriate to say that Knight understood that his role in a society that did not or could not recognize the presence of God was similar to the role of a theologian in a society that explicitly acknowledged God's presence. As a student of society, he was obliged to contribute to society's discussion of the appropriate mechanisms for the coordination of individuals' actions, and to remind the members of society that their discussion could never be divorced from consideration of the type of society they wanted to create and the kind of people they wanted to become.

Vidich and Lyman's belief in the theological nature of modern social inquiry has another element which is also relevant to our examination of Frank Knight's work. In a world where God is absent, some individuals will continue to be troubled by that characteristic of reality, and will need to explain its significance. Frank Knight was such a person. Whether because of his own experience or because the intellectual world in which he lived was still coming to terms with it, God's absence was a theme that ran throughout all of his work. The most visible form that the theme took was his opposition to Christian social thought, but it also permeated his social philosophy and complicated his ethics. Perhaps paradoxically, the economist whose attack on religious approaches to economics poses some of the most difficult questions for those who continue to argue that religion has any contemporary relevance, is also one of those who most acutely recognize the significance of what has been lost by religion's irrelevance. The tension that this paradox produced in Knight's work is one of the reasons his work continues to engage us today.

Students at the University of Chicago used to say, "There is no God, but Frank Knight is his prophet" (Buchanan 1982: xi). I have already suggested that Knight's recognition of the theological nature of economic reflection could allow us to call him a "theologian" of liberalism. If there is also a prophetic quality to Knight's work, it lies in his questions regarding our ability and willingness to live in a world where there is no God. In typical Knightian fashion, he rather doubted that we were either able or willing, but insisted that we owed it to ourselves (and perhaps to God?) to make the effort.

14 Is economics a religion?[1]

In their history of sociology in the United States, Arthur Vidich and Stanford Lyman (1985: 281) argue that the central concerns of American social science "emanate from the dilemmas and contradictions in the relationship between God, the state, and civil society." Social scientists in America are asked to explain the "ways of society" to those within it, although in a modern secular society they are asked to do so without reference to God or divine providence. Social scientists may not be theologians, but in modern society their work plays the same role religion played in prior societies.

In *Economics as Religion,* Robert Nelson (2001) extends Vidich and Lyman's argument to economics in the twentieth century. While most economists avoid reference to God or divine providence, throughout the twentieth century they have devoted themselves to explaining the "ways of the market" – for example, how the market mechanism works, and the relationship between the market and the state – to members of contemporary society. Because the market has become the central coordinating mechanism in modern society, economists have become the theologians of modernity. Nelson's book, therefore, "offers a theological exegesis of the contents of modern economic thought, regarding the economic way of thinking as not only a source of technical understanding of economic events, but also for many … a source of ultimate understanding of the world" (Nelson 2001: xxv).

Does Nelson's "theological exegesis" succeed? If the purpose were to remind economists that their science was first and foremost a human activity and that the line between science and other human activities may be smaller recognize than they realize, the answer might be "Yes". But Nelson sets out to do much more, and it is the "much more" that causes some trouble. The purpose of this review, then, will be to assess Nelson's use of the religion as an organizing metaphor for twentieth-century economics and evaluate his claim that economics is the religion of modernity. Regarding his account of the discipline of economics as a religion, we will ask what the benefits and limitations of the metaphor are. Is it more appropriate to think of economics as a religion than as a science? Regarding Nelson's story of the history of twentieth-century economics, we have to ask if the metaphor of Northern Ireland's cultural divide, based on the religious differences between Protestant and Catholic, is appropriate for telling the story of economics in the melting pot of the USA? And why does he exclude the new institutional economics from a theological exegesis?

The organization of *Economics as Religion* is straightforward. After considering what it means to say that economics is a religion (part one), Nelson turns to a theological exegesis of the two main strands of the economics religion in twentieth-century America: the Progressive Catholicism of Paul Samuelson and MIT economics (part two) and the Calvinist Protestantism of Frank Knight and the Chicago School (part three). The identification of Samuelson with both Catholicism and the American Progressive movement, and of Knight with Calvinism, provides a link between the argument of this book with that of Nelson's first book on this theme, *Reaching Heaven on Earth* (Nelson 1991), which traced similar concerns through pre-twentieth-century economic thought. While there are differences in the way Nelson characterizes economics as a religion in the two books, the overall message is the same: economics is theological (absent God), both because it addresses questions similar to those faced in theology (explaining the mysteries of the "ways of society"), and because it plays a social role of validating the existing (or an alternative) social order. The fourth part of *Economics as Religion* examines the changes in American economics during the past 30 years stemming from the emergence of New Institutional Economics. While suggesting that the new economics re-writes economics in ways that avoid the Cambridge–Chicago split of the previous 50 years, Nelson also examines what the new economics has to say about the role of religion in fostering a culture conducive to economic development. The book concludes with another look at economics as religion at the beginning of the twenty-first century. Is the market "God"? Is the notion of "progress" under enough attack to call into question economics' role as the religious validation of modernity? Where should we then turn?

Nelson's characterization of economics as religion is built upon the observation that economics provides for a modern secular society the types of answers and validation that various religions provided for prior societies. As Nelson says, "To the extent that any system of economic ideas offers an alternative vision of the 'ultimate values,' or 'ultimate reality,' that actually shapes the workings of history, economics is offering yet another grand prophesy in the biblical tradition" (Nelson 2001: 23). And again, later in the book, he argues that with the loss of confidence in traditional Christianity in the wake of scientific discovery:

> Social science ... became the religion of the modern age in regard to the conduct of affairs in this world ... , and in this capacity social science became responsible for resolving the collective action problems of the economic system that only a common religious bond ... can resolve.
>
> (Nelson 2001: 266)

The example of Marxism, which Nelson uses (Nelson 2001: 24–7), is instructive. Marxism provides a framework in which one can understand not only how society works, but why it works the way it does, and what future one might expect. Underlying the story that Marx tells, of course, are the omnipotent economic laws of history. Although most twentieth-century economists are quick to point out that Marxism's inability to provide testable hypotheses render it more of a religion than a science, they must also face the uncomfortable fact that some of their implicit assumptions are similar to those of Marx. Nelson mentions the similarity of Marx's and Keynes' visions of the future (ibid. 2001: 30–4), but a similar observation was made about Chicago economics and Marxism by Robert Fogel, the formerly-Marxist Chicago economic historian. Fogel apparently once remarked to George Stigler, "George, did you know you are a Marxist?" The question brought a sharp retort from Stigler, but Fogel then explained: "George, your economics may be different, but you both believe that all human activity is ultimately determined by economics."

It is on this uncomfortable fact – that the implicit assumptions of an economic approach may be held as commitments akin to religious beliefs – that Nelson builds his exegesis of the two main currents of American economics in the twentieth century. While the schools have different emphases, Nelson's treatment of them follows a similar pattern. He focuses first on the religious commitments implicit in the work of one of the school's masters – Paul Samuelson in the case of Cambridge; Frank Knight for Chicago (in Chicago's case, he also includes a chapter on Friedman, Stigler, and Becker). Then he picks up a particular theme in the school's work and organizes his consideration of the school's policy orientation around that theme. The Cambridge School is interpreted as a continuation of American Progressivism, seeking to use the tools of scientific management to realize a better world here on earth. Nelson's interpretation of the Chicago School is organized around the School's commitment to the rationality inherent in economic self-interest, an emphasis compared by Nelson to Calvinism. We will consider each of these in turn.

Using Samuelson's famous textbook as his primary source, Nelson suggests that Samuelson's economic arguments fit together only when one uncovers the implicit assumptions he holds about the market, inequality, and the role of the state. The key assumptions are: (1) Samuelson's belief that the market provides a natural order for society; (2) that economics understands how the market mechanism works (and does not work, in the cases of externalities and public goods); and (3) that the natural order of society can be scientifically managed to create the best social order possible given the available resources. How do these assumptions function as religious beliefs? One example of Nelson's exegesis will suffice. In a number of places in *Economics,* Samuelson deals with the benefits and costs of economic progress, whether it be the adoption of free trade or alterations to land use. Nelson argues that, in these cases, Samuelson always weighs the benefits of progress as greater than the costs of remaining in the present economic state. But there are costs Samuelson does not consider – including the stress and psychic pain caused by economic transition. For Nelson, Samuelson's willingness to discount the costs of economic progress reveals his fundamental commitment to progress through scientific management. The closing paragraph of *Economics* reaffirms the hope that economic progress will lead to a day "when everyone has the opportunity for a good job, an adequate income, and a safe environment" (Samuelson, quoted in Nelson 2001: 112). Nelson suggests Samuelson is best understood as a latter day prophet of this secularized version of the Judeo-Christian vision of heaven on earth.

More attention is devoted in *Economics as Religion* to the Chicago economists than to Samuelson's extension of the Progressive movement's vision of the perfectibility of the social order. Perhaps this is because the Progressive themes are ones he has developed elsewhere (Nelson 1991), or perhaps it is because Frank Knight fascinates him. In any case, in part three Nelson examines Knight's focus on uncertainty and human depravity, and the extension of his ideas in the work of Friedman, Stigler, Becker, and others in the Chicago School.

While the temptation to discuss Nelson's view of Knight at length will be avoided, a few comments should be made. First, Nelson's interpretation of Knight's understanding of the relation between religion and economics is largely compatible with my own (Emmett 1994a), which is not surprising given our shared appreciation for Vidich and Lyman's (1985) framework. Second, the contrast between Samuelson's desire to create heaven on earth and Knight's appreciation for uncertainty and the tension between self-interest and social progress provides a contrast that runs throughout the history of American (and perhaps all) economics. Is economics the science which will steer us to prosperity, or does it remind us that even the best-laid human plans go awry? Third, Nelson's identification of Knight with the American tradition of Puritanism provides an intellectual history that is frequently missed when commentators try to understand his skepticism. His skepticism is often attributed to his rejection of religion, when in fact it may emerge from the religious perspective he gave up.

Yet it is surprising that Nelson himself misses the importance for Knight's thought of his upbringing and education in the Disciples of Christ. The Disciples were an indigenous American religious movement to restore New Testament Christianity, which rejected key aspects of Calvinist theology (election and predestination) and sought a non-creedal basis for unity among Christians. Knight's background in the Disciplines helps us understand at least a couple of aspects of his social philosophy: his virulent attacks on Catholic social thought (anti-Catholicism was a common feature of restoration movement tracts), and the passionate call for the economics profession to speak publicly only when it could do so with a unified voice (Knight 1935b). The dictum "we speak where the Bible speaks, and are silent where the Bible is silent" is rivaled in restoration circles only by the Augustinian motto, "in essentials, unity; in non-essentials, liberty; in all things, charity" (although it must be admitted that Knight was not known for charity towards fellow academics).

It is clear from the chapter on Knight, and comments elsewhere in the book, that Nelson is fascinated with Knight's complex understanding of human conduct and social organization. That fascination does not, however, carry over into his interpretation of the rest of the Chicago School. Chicago, Nelson argues, has a narrow and simplistic understanding of human conduct and social organization. If Samuelson is chastised by Nelson for an idealistic belief in progress, Nelson thinks that he at least had a vision which led him to think beyond the confines of narrow self-interest. The Chicago School preached self-interest as the gospel; the rich young man of Matthew 19 would have been happy to join their company. Friedman (the social responsibility of a business is to increase its profits), Stigler (whose orientation we have already seen), and Becker (theft may be rational if the constraint set is appropriate) seemed to enjoy rankling those who subscribe to moral codes like the Ten Commandments (chapter 7 is entitled "Chicago and the Ten Commandments"). Yet Nelson seems even more concerned about the methodology of Chicago: the willingness to build an entire social science on the basis of a narrow conception of human nature. We will return to both his moral and methodological concerns shortly.

So where might the problems with Nelson's view of economics as religion be? The parallels Nelson draws between medieval Catholic natural law theology and the Cambridge School, or Chicago economics and Calvinism, are not the problem. Nor is his use of religious imagery to explain the rhetorical power of Samuelson's and Knight's visions of the world. Nelson's interpretative framework also provides several ways of seeing the continuity between modern social science and the Western intellectual tradition, and his approach fits well with the current interest among historians of science and economics in breaking down the barrier between science and other human activities (see Golinski 1998). The problem appears when he claims that economics is a religion.

To argue that x (economics) is analogous to y (religion) because x plays the same role in society w that y plays in society z is different than arguing that x and y are the same thing. Vidich and Lyman (1985; and myself in Emmett 1994) make the former argument regarding the social sciences and theology. Nelson's book is frustrating because he often slips into the argument that economics, at least in some of its forms, *is* a religion. Dangers of which Nelson does not seem aware lurk close when he moves from the analogy of economics *as* religion to the metaphor that economics *is* religion. The clearest instance where Nelson's slip across this line brings him close to danger is in his exegesis of the Chicago School.

At the heart of Nelson's problems with the Chicago School is the Chicago propensity to extend self-interested rationality as far as possible, and to discount the possibility of irrationality, altruism or other such non-rational behavior as separate aspects of human conduct (see Lazear 2000 for a recent Chicago statement of this view). Sarcastically, Nelson remarks:

> If something cannot be explained today in a narrowly individualistic framework of economic analysis, it is the belief of the "Chicago project" that in the future there will be a smarter graduate student, a more insightful theory, a better statistical method that will permit us to show the full workings of the forces of self-interest in more and more areas of life.
>
> (Nelson 2001: 168)

For Nelson, this approach is the Great Idolatry, leaving no room for God:

> From the Chicago perspective, ... any claim that, say, 40% of human behavior in some realm is irreduceably noneconomic, would be virtually to say that science is in principle restricted in its scope – that in some domains of life perhaps God has simply reserved them for his understanding alone. ... Clearly,

there can be no such "stopping points" within the value system – the moral philosophy – of the Chicago project today.

(Nelson 2001:170)

But let us ask the question, is the Chicago understanding of economic science any different than, say, that embedded in evolutionary theory? Religion has always faced the challenge of science seeking to explain every aspect of natural and human activity. The worst response to science by religious thinkers was the attempt to "rope off" some aspects of human life – the human psyche or the personal – from scientific inquiry. Either God is in all or not at all. Either science explains all or it is not science. Herein lies the fundamental paradox of faith in the modern world.

Nelson cannot understand how someone might affirm both sides of this paradox. His response to the Chicago School is reminiscent of the debate in the early 1800s over the relation between classical political economy and the Philosophical Radicals (Utilitarians). Because the Philosophical Radicals combined classical political economy with atheism and a social policy agenda which the Church opposed, many argued that Christians must reject the emerging science as well. Richard Whately's *Introductory Lectures on Political Economy* (Whately 1832) responded by distinguishing between scientific and religious knowledge on epistemological grounds, arguing that they represented two different *types* of knowledge. Whately's characterization of the difference between religious and scientific knowledge constituted the first formation of what economists today know as the positive–normative distinction (Waterman 1994). While there are problems with later formulations of that distinction, Whately's basic intuition that religion and science are different language games has saved many Christian social scientists from making the mistake of doing what Nelson seems to want them to do: form a "Christian economics" to compete with Chicago (and other) economics.

Of course, Nelson might want to claim that this is not exactly what he meant, and that, even if he was overzealous in identifying economics with religion, it is still the case that the economics of Chicago supports the basest human values rather than our highest values. Religions call us to rise above self-interest for the sake of others, and advance better human values. Economics destroys such values. Surely the realm within which economics and the market are allowed to operate must be restricted?

Why should we assume that the market will only benefit people's baser values, however? The ideal in a liberal society is neutrality toward values – live and let live. The market enhances that neutrality by regulating the allocation of resources across preferences in such a way as to broaden the range of values that can be satisfied. This broadening of values allows individuals to pursue both "better" and "worse" values. Won't some people pursue better values? Even Frank Knight, who was known to criticize the market on this score (Knight 1923a), once said that "the chief thing which the common-sense individual actually wants is not satisfaction for the wants which he has, but more, and better wants" (Knight 1922: p. 42). Those who want to restrict the range of values available to people in a market society may be surprised at the unintended outcomes of their restriction. Or, to flip the argument around, those who wish to enforce the "best values" on society often find it hard to accept people's willingness to exit a restricted-choice society for the wider range of values available in a liberal society.

Nelson has another argument that is closely connected with his claim, contra Chicago, that the market is destructive to human values. His second argument is similar to the one made in Francis Fukuyama's *Trust* (1995): the market itself depends upon the trust built among individuals in non-market settings, such as religion (Nelson 2001: 245–60). This argument has received a lot of attention recently, especially in the context of the debate over whether culture matters in economic development (Harrison and Huntington 2000). Rejecting Adam Smith's argument in the *Wealth of Nations* that the market creates interdependencies among the members of a market society, which bind people with disparate values, beliefs and commitments to each other, these scholars argue that prosperity requires a "deeper" commonality. Smith argued that trust emerges from the interdependency built upon the division of labor, and that no underlying commonality is required to produce social order because a self-regulating order will spring – as if by an "invisible hand" – from the market process itself. Nelson and company imply that the market only provides order when an ordered set of values are already present.

Most economists would side with Smith: people will trade where they judge there to be an advantage to do so, and such trades will contribute to all participants' prosperity. Society is bound together by the mutually beneficial advantages that individuals find from exchange with one another. This argument has only gained strength from its appearance in game theoretic form: if we limit our trade to a group with whom we share common bonds, we may increase the prosperity of that group relative to other groups, but we will also curtail the total prosperity of all groups. Group-based differences may alter one's estimation of the benefits or costs of trade, but where a net benefit is seen, trade will occur, as Smith said it would.

The majority of *Economics as Religion* is devoted to exploring the religious aspects of Cambridge and Chicago economics. The fourth part of the book, however, examines the ideas of New Institutional Economics. Nelson's purpose in bringing this emerging school of economic thought into his discussion is unclear, and in some cases seems to undermine the argument made throughout the remainder of the book. Three elements of his examination of the New Institutionalism warrant our attention.

First, Nelson suggests that New Institutionalism should be considered a viable option for economists today, despite its return to historical and institutional analyses that economics abandoned in the postwar period. Nelson argues that many economists view these methods of analysis with suspicion because they have been taught that the older institutionalists were non-scientific both in their methodology and in the fervor of their search for mechanisms of social control. But, as Nelson's exegesis of Samuelson and Chicago suggests, neoclassical economics has its non-scientific aspects. Hence the economist should not fear that they are leaving the realm of science if they pursue New Institutionalist approaches: "They may think they would be losing their scientific virtue, but it would be more correct to say that they would be abandoning their scientific hypocrisy" (Nelson 2001: 229).

The mention of hypocrisy should set off warning bells. Is Nelson once again treading close to the danger of mistaking the similarities between theology and economics as human activities for the religiosity of economics? The problem that this question raises is reinforced by the second thing that warrants our attention, namely Nelson's unwillingness to undertake the same kind of theological exegesis of the New Institutional Economics that he does for Chicago and Cambridge economics. There is no suggestion that the New Institutional Economics might play the same type of religious or theological function in modern society as earlier forms of economics. Nelson must recognize that the New Institutionalism addresses the same kind of "ultimate" questions that he thinks Cambridge and Chicago did. If he accepts his initial idea that any economics plays a theological function in a modern society by providing an explanation of the "ways of society" for those in it, then he should have at least attempted a tentative theological exegesis of New Institutionalism. Of course, if Nelson really thinks that only Cambridge and Chicago were religious, because of their religious commitment to the underlying assumptions of their system of thought, then he needs to be reminded that the New Institutionalism is not without its committed. An example of the kind of "religious" commitment that may exist in the New Institutionalism was recently relayed to me by Patrick O'Brien, the British economic historian. At a meeting several years ago to consider the impact of institutions in economic history, Doug North impatiently remarked at some point that, "surely there was an institutional framework that could have been set in place to avoid the French Revolution."

Despite Nelson's lack of a theological exegesis of the New Institutionalism, he compliments the School for providing economists with a means to appreciate the positive role that religion might play in economic development. This third element of his investigation of New Institutionalism is, however, a two-edged sword. On the positive side, the focus on institutions, and in particular on the role of institutions other than markets and the state, allows New Institutionalism to ask questions that economists have largely avoided since the time of Max Weber. What is the relationship between the institutions of religion and economic systems? What relationship does religion have to law and constitutional questions? And are certain religions more conducive to the establishment of markets and of liberal democratic institutions than others?

Unfortunately, there is a lot of sloppiness in Nelson's treatment of this last topic. There is a tendency to look for an "efficient religion" – the title of the chapter – rather than simply point out that these questions take us beyond neoclassicism into economic sociology and history. Also, Nelson does not recognize that the New Institutionalism may be more threatening to religion than neoclassicism. Neoclassicism, like liberalism, is neutral toward religion, allowing one to find one's values wherever they might be found. The New Institutionalism, on the other hand, seeks to provide an explanation for religion, and, if one is committed to economic progress, may provide an independent means of adjudicating among religions (Protestantism is good for economic progress, Hinduism may not be).

Can someone who has made a faith commitment to a religion accept an argument which provides a non-faith-based explanation for that faith commitment? These questions return us once again to the fundamental paradox of faith in the midst of modernity, and remind us that solutions that try to divide the world between religion and science are fundamentally problematic.

On balance, then, what assessment can we provide of Nelson's book? One way of expressing the positive and negative aspects of the book is to say that Nelson succeeds where he makes the weakest claims, and fails where he most wants to succeed. The rhetorical device of comparing economics with religion effectively reminds economists that they also have commitments, and that their science is simply another human activity. Yet the argument that these commitments have led economists astray by making their economics a religion makes a fundamental category mistake. Economics is not a religion, although it may be like religion in the context of modernity. And religion is not a social science, even when its practitioners wish it were.

15 The idea of a secular society revisited

Christian economists should [...] read Munby [...] for guidance and inspiration in the difficult intellectual and spiritual enterprise of relating economics to the faith.

(Waterman 1988)

In March 1962, Denys L. Munby gave the Riddell Memorial Lectures at King's College, University of Durham. The lectures were published a year later, under the title *The Idea of a Secular Society: And its Significance for Christians.* Munby was an applied economist, a fellow of Nuffield College at Oxford, and a Christian (Waterman 1988). The latter was of particular importance for Munby's lectures because they were designed as a response to T.S. Eliot's famous lectures entitled *The Idea of a Christian Society* (1939). Schooled in the Christendom movement, which claimed Eliot as its own, Munby's eventual training in economics brought him to a different understanding of the relation between social science, religion, and social policy. Where Eliot argued for a state that functioned according to Christian principles, Munby said that the church, had little to say about the functioning of the state, and made the case for specialized roles for religion and economics. Where Eliot believed that the church should comprehend the entire nation and that religious symbols and images were necessary for social unity, Munby argued that a secular society must accept religious diversity and reject unifying symbols that bore the stamp of particular religions. Where Eliot affirmed the permanence of traditional Christian values, and worried that the secular trend of social change would lead to a society that worshiped "gods that are not gods," Munby believed that economic progress would lead to the enhanced satisfaction of many social values and could be pursued without necessarily threatening traditions and religious practices. In short, the differences between these two Christians' understandings of society could not be more stark.

While the language of both Munby and Eliot sounds naïve and optimistic to us today and was clearly shaped by the contingencies of their historical settings – Britain in the 1930s and the early 1960s – their discussion of the relationship between religion and economics remains relevant to us today. We have seen in recent years that religion has not diminished in the face of secularization and that, far from losing its public authority, it once again shapes global politics. We are now told that the modern political world is a "clash of civilizations" (Huntington 1996), shaped by the religious divide between the Judeo-Christian civilizations of the West and the Islamic and Sinec civilizations of the East. Rather than ending history (Fukuyama 1991), the conclusion of the battle between the *ideological* West and East – capitalism versus socialism – has transformed global conflict into a clash between the *religious* West and East. In this post-September eleventh world, is there any place for a secular society? Can a society that is neutral to religious beliefs survive in a world shaped by religious difference?

At the same time, we are also told that Munby's chosen profession – economics – is itself a religion, or at least the theology that undergirds the religion of economic progress and the market. In his book, *Economics as Religion: From Samuelson to Chicago and Beyond,* economist Robert Nelson argues that "the most vital religion of the modern age has been economic progress. If economists have had a modest impact in actually generating this progress, or even understanding the actual mechanisms by which it has occurred, they have had a large role in giving it social legitimacy. They have been the modern priesthood of the religion of progress" (Nelson 2001: 329).

Can Munby's argument for the specialized roles of religion and the social sciences be upheld in light of the critique offered by Nelson? Does a secular society simply substitute material progress for religious tradition, the market or money for God? Does Munby's vision mean that Eliot's greatest fear – that society will serve Mammon, not God – will be realized?

What is a secular society?

An appropriate starting point for our consideration of Munby's view of the secular society is to contrast his understanding of such a society with that of his contemporaries, whose views are more familiar and have shaped our common understanding of secularization. It was Dietrich Bonhoeffer who spoke of "man's coming of age" – of the human race's maturation to the point where we no longer needed God as a comfort in pain or sorrow, a source of inspiration to act for good, or as someone to blame for the world's misfortunes. We could turn our attention from another world and focus it on the joys and trials of this world, from emancipation *from* this world to emancipation *in* this world (Cox 1965). From the perspective of a secular society, religion "gives not help but hindrance as it keeps man in a state of puerile dependence and holds him back from his maturity" (Ramsey 1969: 17). These observations led to the secularization thesis: belief in traditional religion would decline as modern society developed a variety of means to enable its members to live without it. Social scientists and liberal theologians alike adopted the secularization thesis: the former assumed it meant that they could ignore religion as a factor in social and economic development; the latter began to construct theologies more relevant to a secular world than the orthodox formulations.

It was the increasing loss of common beliefs and rationalization of life that Eliot protested in *The Idea of a Christian Society.* Munby puts Eliot's case well when he says that, according to Eliot, a secular society:

Undermines the cultural values without which men cannot remain permanently satisfied. It uproots men from their traditional stabilities, demands of them a rationality they cannot bear, and continuously disassociates them from their fellow men, as the changing social and economic forces break up any grouping, whether regional or professional, at work, or in the places where people live, almost as soon as they are able to form them. [...] Far from being enriched by the new powers, men become the slaves of new and more compelling social and economic processes.

(Munby 1963: 46–7)

The notion of a secular society that Munby defended is somewhat different from the one that Eliot attacked, however. Munby's notion differs from the common understanding of secularization in three ways. The first difference emerges from his use of the term "neutral" as a synonym for secular. A neutral society is one in which the state does not privilege one religion over another (Munby 1963: 11–12). Munby extended neutrality to imply that a secular society's decisions about the production and distribution of resources and the administration of human, natural, and financial capital were made via mechanisms that do not depend upon the organization or beliefs of any particular religion. The analogy of the American notion of the separation of church and state comes to mind, but, for Munby, the separation is between church and any form of social macro-organization. At the micro level, individuals retain the right of free association. One of the implications of Munby's identification of secularization with religious neutrality at the macro level is that his notion of the secular society does not necessitate the same decline of traditional religious belief that the secularization theorists posited. In fact, he suggests that secularization brings the enlargement of human choices over their beliefs and values rather than the loss of traditional beliefs (Munby 1963: 77). The difference between a focus on the decline of belief and the enlargement of choice plays a central role in Munby's argument for the secular society.

If we combine Munby's focus on religious neutrality at the macro level with his assumption that totalitarian states privilege "Communist dogma," then we can identify a second difference between Munby's understanding of a secular society and the secularization thesis: the close relationship between liberalism and secularism. While it is never explicitly stated, this close relationship is another underlying theme in Munby's argument. When secularization was seen simply as the decline of religious belief, it could be interpreted to include the totalitarian societies of the post-World War II era. Munby's focus on neutrality provides a different perspective on the communist régimes. These régimes were not neutral, choosing to restrict religious choice and privilege their own dogma. According to Munby, the secular society will not flourish in collectivist environments but only in the liberal societies of the West. Munby suggests that communist societies could become secularized if "Communist dogma becomes as irrelevant to the concerns of the common man as have the theological pretensions of the Christian Church in the West" (Munby 1963: 12). In hindsight, one wonders if the secularization of communism, in Munby's sense, helped to bring about its downfall.

Finally, Munby sees secularization as offering new opportunities for orthodox faith. Eliot saw secular society as aiding the onslaught of Paganism against the stronghold of orthodoxy (perhaps an appropriate metaphor during the dark days of 1939). Despite the spread of communism, Munby thought:

> It is less easy to be pessimistic about the inherent possibilities of our society, however much we may detest the complacency and vulgarity of the Macmillan era in decline. In spite of the theological prophecies that a people without God will perish, in spite of the condemnations of moralists who point to the allegedly growing laxity of sexual mores and the supposed increase in neuroses, our society has shown signs of vigour that would hardly have been believed in the thirties. The Neutral Society has become more neutral, without as yet showing signs of becoming more aggressively "pagan," at least in the Communist or Fascist/Nazi sense, in which Mr. Eliot may be supposed to have intended his phrase to be interpreted.
>
> (Munby 1963: 10–11)

Like Bonhoeffer, Munby perceived that true Christianity could flourish in a world that had come of age. God's presence in the world meant that the secular society was not to be feared and resisted, but welcomed.

It may be worth noting that Munby's positive view of the prospects for religion in the secular society has been reinforced by recent studies in the sociology and economics of religion that challenge the secularization thesis. These studies have shown that religious activity has increased over the past several decades, although lower growth occurred in countries or regions with an established or dominant church (see Iannacone for a summary). Where the scholars who undertook these studies usually interpret their results as an attack on the notion of the secular society, however, Munby would probably see them as an affirmation of his argument for a secular society.

Economics, progress, and the secular society

The reader familiar with *The Idea of a Secular Society* may raise a sceptical eyebrow at this point and ask whether Munby's idea of a secular society is not based simply on the notion that economic progress in a market economy allows all members of society a greater array of choices; a case of prosperity breeding tolerance. Isn't the core of his argument to be found in the second lecture, entitled "Change, Specialization and Human Values"? Perhaps Munby's response to Eliot is more about accepting a form of social organization conducive to economic progress than it is about the society's neutrality to religion? Certainly, progress plays a significant role in Munby's argument; he uses it to counter Eliot's claim that secular change will always be destructive of human values. In his usual understated style, Munby says that, despite all the changes since the 1930s, "it is not at all clear that we are in any unambiguous or generally agreed sense 'worse off'" (Munby 1963: 48). But he does not make progress the core of his argument for a secular society.

In order to understand why, we need to return to the relation of liberal society and secularization, and begin to incorporate Munby's economic perspective.

Liberalism is often understood as a political philosophy that seeks to enable the members of a pluralistic society to function together while pursuing their various personal ends (Hall 1987). Munby's training in economics added an additional element to his understanding of liberal society, highlighted by his frequent reference to "specialization." The economics tradition in which Munby was trained made the radical claim that liberal society is held together by the mutual benefits that individuals find from exchange with one another. The *locus classicus* for this claim is the opening chapters of Adam Smith's *Wealth of Nations,* with their eloquent appeal to the division of labor. Specialization, via the division of labor, in an economy regulated by market processes enables the creation of wealth exceeding that available to a closed economy committed to self-sufficiency. While it is tempting to leap immediately to the prospects for the growth of wealth and incomes in a market economy, Smith makes a more subtle point. The market creates interdependencies among the members of such a society (and across societies that trade with each other) that bind people with disparate values, beliefs and commitments to each other. In a market economy, my prosperity depends upon my ability and willingness to serve you. (While Smith was right that we depend on the self-interest of the baker, butcher, and brewer for our supper, it is also the case that they depend on our self-interest for their income.) Interdependency builds upon specialization, and specialization requires trust in our interdependency. No underlying commonality is required to produce social order. It springs – as if by an "invisible hand" – from the self-regulating process implicit in market exchange.

Many people, including some economists, have resisted this economic version of the argument for liberalism. Apart from those who reject the argument on efficiency grounds, the most telling criticisms are two sides of the same coin. On one side is Eliot's argument that the market either destroys human values or supports the satisfaction of the "wrong" values. In either case, the market is said to leave us without an underlying philosophy that can animate a rich life for our society as a whole. This argument has a long tradition in British discourse, from Charles Dickens's novels and Thomas Carlyle's debates with J.S. Mill (see Levy 2001) to more recent postmodern accounts (Giddens 1991). It also appears in the North American literature, most forcibly in the work of Frank Knight (1923a) and Charles Taylor (1989). A new variant of the argument appears in the contemporary literature of environmentalism, which shares Eliot's distress at the fact that the market is unable to distinguish between "right" and "wrong" values and, hence, may allow individuals to make "bad" choices.

Munby's response to Eliot provides us with two counter-arguments to the claim that the market has a destructive effect on human values. I have treated the first of these arguments – his claim that market exchange widens the scope for the realization of human values. Those who wish to be "self-acclaimed spokespersons for humanity" (or the environment) often find it difficult to accept people's willingness to trade the benefits of living in a community with strong social or religious bonds for the benefits of living in a secular society that allows one to select among a larger range of values. But, if we agree with Knight that "the chief thing which the common-sense individual actually wants is not satisfaction for the wants which he has, but more, and better wants" (Knight 1922: 42), then we may wish to argue that widening the array of choices will allow individuals to adopt better values.

The possibility that people's values may change is the source of Munby's second counter-argument to Eliot. The possibility of new values being adopted provides a specialized mission for the church in a secular society. If the church truly believes that God is in the world, and not just that part of the world that lies outside the market, then the church's task in a secular society is to help its members construct lives within the secular society that are true to the Gospel (Munby 1963: 67–77, 85–9). This is not an Anabaptist call for a Christian counterculture (although Christians may adopt some values that others will not), but rather a recognition of the fact that it is in the ordinary business of life that the Gospel is lived out. This argument is also an appropriate response to the environmental movement's attack on the market's neutrality toward "bad" values.

The other side of the moral critique of the market is that a market society works best when its participants share strong common bonds, like religion. For example, Francis Fukuyama (1995) has argued that market exchange requires a non-market basis for trust among individuals who are not family members. Fukuyama provides a new version of the Weber thesis with his claim that certain forms of religion (among them Protestantism) build a basis for such trust, and therefore, enhance their societies' prosperity. Nelson extends Fukuyama's claim as far as to suggest that "investments in religion may be a more effective means than achieving higher levels of physical and human capital in advancing economic growth and development" (Nelson 2001: 301). Much earlier, Josiah Stamp (1926) made a similar argument about the role of the Christian ethic in promoting national wealth.

Munby never considers this second side of the moral critique of markets, but there is a fundamental flaw in it. Essentially, the problem is this: if we limit our trade to a group with whom we share common bonds, we may increase the prosperity of that group relative to other groups (notice Fukuyama's and Stamp's focus on *national* prosperity), but we will also curtail the total prosperity of all groups. This is a result that Smith would have appreciated, but that is best known today from game theory. The economist's argument, once again, is that people will trade where they judge there to be an advantage to do so, and that such trades will contribute to all participants' prosperity, regardless of national, regional, or even religious affiliation. Group-based differences – such as religion, ethnicity, or nationality – may alter one's estimation of the benefits or costs of trade, but where a net benefit is seen, trade will occur (and grow) if allowed. This argument is not heard enough today in the clamor over the benefits and costs of globalization.

Munby's discussion of progress and the positive aspects of change, therefore, emerge from the core of his argument about the secular society rather than the other way around. Neutrality does not only mean the absence of state privilege for any religion and toleration of diverse values. It also extends to the notion that trade will benefit not only one group but also all participants. Economic progress strengthens the argument for a secular society, but is not its foundation.

The core of Munby's argument for a secular society, then, can be restated this way: a market economy, combined with a liberal democratic political system, provides the social processes for the coordination of the available resources across existing human needs and wants. In such a society, the processes of social coordination are independent of, and remain neutral toward, the religious or other value systems that may inform the needs and wants of individuals in the society. Rather than seeking to avoid responsibility for our own choices, we as individuals can welcome a secular society because it provides a setting in which we not only can satisfy our needs most efficiently but also can explore values that we have not adopted before. The church need not fear the widening array of choices provided in a secular society, for God's presence in the world has not changed.

Does Munby's argument retain its currency today? Does the reappearance of religion as a major social and political force contradict Munby's idea of a secular society as it does the secularization thesis? The short answers are "Yes" to the first question and "No" to the second. Munby's argument is built around religious neutrality rather than religious decline, and hence his notion of a secular society can accommodate the emergence of religious movements with broad social appeal. What his defense of a secular society stands against is a *religious society*, in which the state gives social privilege to a particular religion. But that, of course, is what Eliot called for. In the midst of the reappearance of religious societies in various parts of the world, and the strident claims of some within liberal democratic market economies to give religious movements greater political control, the secular society remains an ideal worth pursuing, even by those with religious commitments.

Specialization and the relation between economics and theology

We have dealt at length with Munby's case for a secular society, and have found good reasons to support it. But the argument is not finished. Eliot, in his time, and Nelson, today, argue that economics and religion are not separate realms, as Munby assumed, but overlap in several ways. For Eliot, theology was the queen of the sciences, providing the glue that held all knowledge together. True economic knowledge could be built only upon an orthodox theological base. Nelson goes even further, claiming that economics provides an alternative theology, competing with traditional religious beliefs (and probably winning). Nelson's view is similar to that of theologian Harvey Cox. Cox recently wrote of reading the modern "signs of the time":

> The lexicon of *The Wall Street Journal* and the business sections of *Time* and *Newsweek* turned out to bear a striking resemblance to Genesis, the Epistle to the Romans, and Saint Augustine's City of God. Behind descriptions of market reforms, monetary policy, and the convolutions of the Dow, I gradually made out the pieces of a grand narrative about the inner meaning of human history, why things had gone wrong, and how to put them right. Theologians call these myths of origin, legends of the fall, and doctrines of sin and

redemption. But here they were again, and in only thin disguise: chronicles about the creation of wealth, the seductive temptations of statism, captivity to faceless economic cycles, and, ultimately, salvation through the advent of free markets, with a small dose of ascetic belt tightening along the way, especially for the East Asian economies.

(Cox 1999: 18)

Can Munby's argument for a distinction between economics and theology be sustained in the face of these claims?

To his credit, Munby does not build his case for the separation of economics and theology on the common notion that they deal with different fields of human knowledge. Scientific inquiry invariably seeks an explanation for every aspect of our world, natural or human, and attempts to barricade some aspect of human activity against the encroachment of science always fail. "There is no field left where we can exclude science and intrude God as an alternative explanation" (Munby 1963: 71). Insistence on interpreting religious knowledge as the same type of knowledge as scientific knowledge inevitably runs into difficulty. Munby argues that we can render "to Caesar the things that are Caesar's and to God the things that are God's" (Matthew 22.21) if we acknowledge that science and religion make different types of claims. He states:

The conclusion is clear. God does not provide explanations of events as does science, whether physical, social, or psychological sciences are in question. We are not to look for the hand of God in any particular fields of experience. He is in all or in none. Providence is universal or nowhere. It does not provide an explanation mat we can fall back upon when other explanations fail. [...] The tools that [the natural and social sciences have] provided for us, as well as those provided by philosophers in the analysis of language, are necessary and fundamental parts of our everyday life. There can be no conflict in principle between their use and the glory of God. The world they reveal to us has always been there, and it is God's world.

(Munby 1963: 71–2)

Munby's argument that science and religion provide different *types* of knowledge is reminiscent of Richard Whately's *Introductory Lectures on Political Economy* (1832). In his lectures, Whately distinguished between scientific and religious knowledge on epistemological grounds: that in order to defend the Christian use of the knowledge of political economy from those who would argue that its association with utilitarianism rendered it antithetical to a Christian world view (Waterman 1994). Munby's purpose, and conclusion, is similar. His early experiences with the Christendom movement convinced him that their attempts to establish a Christian sociology were either trivial or misguided. Where a Christian economics (to put it in our terms) agrees with the economic discipline's approach, there is no particular reason to identify it as uniquely Christian: it is simply good economics. And where a so-called Christian economics makes scientific claims that disagree with the findings of the discipline, its conclusions usually prove to be inadequate because its claims are not subjected to the same scientific process.

Whately's lectures provided the first recognition within economics of what is known today as the positive/normative distinction. Munby accepted that distinction, and suggested that it provided a basis for the division of labour between economics and religion. Like Whately before him, he argued that Christians could accept the knowledge of the economics profession as a positive tool to be used in advancing their normative ends. But he has little appreciation for organized church bodies that seek to issue statements about current economic policy. He does not say that such bodies are irrelevant, but he does point out that, in a secular world, the pronouncements of such bodies sound altogether too much like the dictates of an Anglican schoolmaster. A world that has come of age does not wish to be treated as a child again. Rather than putting its energy into public policy pronouncements, the church should turn to the task of assisting the laity in considering the responsibilities of their ordinary lives in light of the normative claims of the Gospel (Munby 1963: 85–8). Unfortunately, the tendency of church bodies to continue making pronouncements about public policy on the assumption that the secular world has a responsibility to listen to them has not diminished since Munby's time.

It is interesting to observe that Munby's discussion of the relation between economic and religious knowledge touches only lightly on the theological task. In fact, there is a strong antipathy toward contemporary theology in his lectures. "It is clear that we can expect little help from the theologians," he says (Munby 1963: 83), just after his discussion of our need to bring the positive knowledge of economics and the norms of Christian religion together. Specialization in theology, while necessary, has also led, he claims, to a discipline removed from the ordinary concerns of Christians. One wonders if he would have had the same concern about specialization in economics had he been writing 40 years later.

How, then, would Munby respond to Nelson and Cox today? I suspect his response would be twofold. First, he might argue that Nelson has mistaken commitment for religion. All humans have commitments, which range across the varieties of human knowledge, beliefs, and values. Scientists may be firmly committed to certain scientific propositions, such as those that undergird the theory of evolution or the theory of the market. They may seek to explain every aspect of natural or human activity in the terms of that theory. They may employ their scientific knowledge in support of particular social or economic policies. Yet the knowledge that their science generates is not the same as religious knowledge. Economics is not religion; religion is not economics. Cox's rhetoric creates a powerful analogy, but his conflation of economics and religion re-opens the door to the notion of a religious society that he rejected almost 40 years ago in *The Secular City*. We would do better to hold out the ideal of a secular society than to provide fodder for those who want us to return to a religious one.

But Nelson and Cox may persist in their argument, claiming that, whether or not the knowledge of economics constitutes religious belief, many economists not only accept, but also advocate, values that run counter to the basic human values articulated by many religions. Surely, the market's destructive power over basic human values should be restricted. Munby's twofold response to Eliot's claim that the secular society allows the market to destroy human values is clearly as relevant today as it was in his time. The greatest enemy of the secular society is not religion per se, but rather it is those who, with the best of intentions, seek to restrict the operation of the market and liberal democracy in the interest of promoting values that they believe all humans should adopt.

Conclusion

"The Church will be seen, if seen at all, in the thick of ordinary life" (Munby 1963: 89). Throughout *The Idea of a Secular Society,* Munby refers frequently to the activity of ordinary people going about their ordinary business. The connection to economics is obvious to those familiar with Alfred Marshall's famous definition of economics as "a study of mankind in the ordinary business of life." But Munby's focus on the ordinary things of life was also an explicit criticism of Eliot, who spoke disparagingly of modern culture as a "lower middle class culture" (Eliot 1939: 76) and called for a "Church within the Church" (Eliot 1939: 78), comprised of "consciously and thoughtfully practising Christians, especially those of intellectual and spiritual superiority" (Eliot 1939: 35) – to provide leadership for the church and the Christian society. Up against Eliot's select group of superior Christians, Munby set the knowledge of economics and the religious beliefs of ordinary people. He then asked the church to assume the role of assisting these people to live the Gospel in the ordinary business of life. In our secular society, what higher calling could there be?

Notes

2 Reflections on "breaking away": Economics as science and the history of economics as history of science

1 This section is a condensed version of a portion of the Introduction to Emmett (1991).
2 Quentin Skinner's maxim for historical reconstructions: "No agent can eventually be said to have meant or done something which he could never be brought to accept as a correct description of what he had meant or done" (Skinner 1969: 28).
3 For an alternative version of what *geistesgeschichte* might mean for the historian of economic thought see Blaug (1990), who identifies it with one element only of historical reconstruction: the identification of an author's relation to his intellectual context.
4 Two comments may moderate the harsh remarks about historicism made here. First, if one's goal is to re-historicize the discipline of economics, there are more attractive candidates to support than the history of economic thought. Historicist explanations have begun to reenter the discipline, and one could fashion a stellar career for the first part of the twenty-first century by coupling an interest in economic history, or organizational evolution, with any of a number of traditional subfields (witness the Nobel prizes of Ronald Coase, Douglass North, and Robert Fogel). Second, as already suggested, Mirowski (1989) has launched a reevaluation of the close association of economics and physics throughout the late nineteenth and early twentieth centuries.
5 Samuels (1974) on the history of economics as intellectual history outlines a number of ways in which the discipline can draw on other aspects of intellectual history.

3 The therapeutic quality of Frank H. Knight's *Risk, Uncertainty, and Profit*

1 Knight's dissertation, "A Theory of Business Profit" (Knight 1916a), was completed under the supervision of Allyn Young, who replaced Johnson after the latter departed from Cornell to help found *The New Republic*. After the dissertation won second prize in the Hart, Schaffner, and Marx competition for essays in economics in 1917 (under the title "Cost, Value, and Profit"), Knight set about the task of revising it for publication. In the process, he made a number of additions which helped to clarify the therapeutic purpose underlying the book (see the appendix). Most of the revisions were done under the direction of J.M. Clark at the University of Chicago, where Knight moved in 1917 to assume a job as an economics instructor. The final touches were probably added after he moved to the University of Iowa in 1919, however. In any case, the revised manuscript was published in 1921 under the title we know it by today.
2 When a quotation from Knight's dissertation is used, reference to the appropriate passage in *RUP* is also provided, unless no parallel passage exists.
3 F.A. Hayek (1967: 198) once remarked that, "It is hardly an exaggeration to say that nearly all the younger American economists who really understand and advocate a competitive market system have at one time been Knight's students."

4 During Knight's initial appointment at the University of Chicago, he met Clarence Ayres, with whom he became lifelong friends and disputants (Breit 1976; and Samuels 1977), and was active in a small group who met regularly to discuss the importance of Thorstein Veblen's work (Neill 1972: 12; for Knight's contribution, see Knight 1920a). Knight's association with economists at Chicago who were sympathetic to the objectivist program in the social sciences coalesced around a series of round table discussions on the scientific status of economics which took place between 1919 and 1922. Among the other participants in these round table discussions were Morris Copeland, Rexford Tugwell, Carl Parry, and Arthur Benedict Wolfe. The discussions eventually led to the publication of *The Trend of Economics*, a collection of essays edited by Tugwell, in 1924. The core section of Knight's contribution to the volume (Knight 1924a) was an only slightly expanded version of the first 15 pages of *RUP* (although the rest of the essay extended the argument in directions that Knight did not develop in *RUP*).

5 Knight works out the relations between risk and uncertainty, and the cost and organizational structure of a firm in part three of *RUP*, especially in chapters VII–X.

6 The articles by LeRoy and Singell (1987) and Lawson (1988) are good examples of the contrast between these differing perspectives.

7 One of the things Knight did not change during the process of revision was the rather self-assertive style, despite repeated pleas from Allyn Young to "avoid the *appearance* of bumptiousness" (Young, quoted in Stigler 1987, italics in original). There were, however, several important additions in the treatment of the theory of perfect competition. The analysis of the principle of diminishing returns was enhanced by the addition of the total product curve, which today forms the backbone of any first-year textbook's presentation of production theory (see Knight 1921a: 100). Another important theoretical addition appeared in the very last footnote of his analysis of perfect competition, where he summarized the central insight of what was to become the theory of the dominant firm (see Knight 1921a: 193, n.1).

8 Because the organization of *RUP* reflects Knight's efforts to preserve the tension between his systematic and therapeutic purposes, I disagree with George Stigler's suggestion that Knight should have published his systematic exposition of value and distribution theory (the second part of *RUP*) separately from his examination of the role of uncertainty in economic and social life (the third part of *RUP*) (Stigler 1971: ix–x). The two parts of the book were, for Knight, inextricably bound together, and he viewed *RUP* as a single whole.

4 The Economist and the Entrepreneur: Modernist impulses in Frank H. Knight's *Risk, Uncertainty, and Profit*

1 When the Entrepreneur does appear in modern economics, it is usually in work that resists the positivism which dominates mainstream theory, such as in Austrian economics and in Schumpeter's (1934, 1942) work.

2 In an alternative discussion of the archetypes of modernism, Alasdair MacIntyre (1984, 23–78) creates four modern "characters": the manager, the therapist, the bureaucrat, and the aesthete. The first three can be viewed as descriptions of the contemporary functions Hollinger's Knowers assume; the last corresponds to Hollinger's "Artificer" (see subsequent discussion). I thank Phil Mirowski for reminding me of MacIntyre's archetypes.

3 The studies of various disciplines by Bannister (1987), Hughes (1961), Kloppenberg (1986), Novick (1988), Purcell (1973), Ricci (1984), Rorty (1979), Ross (1991, 1994c), Seidelman and Harpman (1985), and Mark Smith (1994) all emphasize the centrality of this theme.

4 Actually, Knight introduces a different analytical change first (1921a: chapter 5). In the static world of perfect competition, there is no change in the underlying conditions of population, resources, and so on. In order to show that the instability of an uncertain world – not simply the existence of change – is the key to his analysis, Knight (1921a: 148) relaxes the static assumption first and shows that prediction is still possible in

a dynamic world if all the underlying conditions change according to stable (hence knowable) principles and laws: "The point for especial emphasis is that the really far-reaching effects of change are not the results of the fact of change itself, but of the uncertainty which is involved in a changing world. If any or all of these changes take place regularly, whether progressively or periodically or according to whatever known law, their consequences in the price system and the economic organization can be briefly disposed of ... They will not upset human calculations or destroy universal perfect equalization of alternatives. Hence, in particular, changes, if foreseeable, do not disturb the prerequisites for perfect competition for productive services, bringing about exact equivalence between costs and values, with absence of profit."

5 For Knight's purpose, it does not matter if the probability distribution depends upon a priori or statistical analysis – indeterminateness or randomness is the key (Knight 1921a: 224–5).

6 Edward Schlee (1992: 739 n) captures the Economist's dilemma – being faced with the subjectivity of individual action in the uncertain world – this way: under uncertainty, "two individuals, who are alike in every aspect except their degree of confidence in their (identical) probability judgments, could well act differently in the same situation, which is inconsistent with the expected utility hypothesis." Knight's rejection of probability theory as a solution to the Knower's problem of knowledge reappears at several points in his career, perhaps most clearly in his response to Henry Schultz's statistical demand theory (Knight 1944b).

7 Note the amount of space that Knight (Knight 1921a: 76–81, 174–94) devotes to constructing the list of conditions assumed by perfect competition.

8 The entrepreneurial tragedy presented by Knight parallels Max Weber's (1958) discussion of the changing role of the capitalist/entrepreneur in modernity. For Weber, the pre-modern entrepreneur is an adventurer, while the modern capitalist oversees a bureaucratic organization. Weber's discussion of the transformation of the premodern entrepreneur into the modern capitalist also parallels Knight's – the organization emerges from a rational process of consolidation in the face of uncertainty. I thank Richard Boyd for identifying this parallel between Weber and Knight.

5 Frank Knight's dissent from Progressive social science

1 I have restored here material originally written for this essay, but not included in the published version. The omitted materials are the first two paragraphs of this sub-section, including the quotations. The initial published version concluded the introductory section of the paper with the final two paragraphs of this sub-section. A brief note appeared in the initial published version, providing an abridged version of my discussion of English Dissent and a reference to Clark (1985).

7 Maximizers vs. good sports

1 Despite my own preference for gender-balanced language, I believe it is appropriate to describe the maximizing individual constructed by neoclassical theory as "rational economic man" because, as Knight says in the passage from "The Ethics of Competition" quoted later on, the real person who comes closest to the ideal type of the maximizing individual is "the unencumbered male in the prime of life" (Knight 1923a: 68). Although I have generally sought to use passages from Knight's work which do not use male-oriented language, when such language appears I have not changed it because of the close connection Knight sees between males and the ideal maximizer, and because male-oriented language was common in his time.

2 Two different accounts exist of American economic thought between the introduction of marginalism in the 1870s and the 1920s. The first, most recently surveyed by Ross (1991), assumes that the rise of neoclassical economics happened simultaneously

with the marginal revolution. The other, which I have followed here, separates the two events. For a fuller account of the second version see Goodwin (1973).

3 Perhaps the strongest published version of the critical side of his argument can be found by reading (consecutively) Knight 1922, 1923a, and 1935b.

4 The metaphor does *not* appear in Knight's dissertation (1916a), upon which *RUP* is based. Because the metaphor appears during the process of revision, during which time Knight was involved in a discussion group on Veblen's work at the University of Chicago, it is likely that he picked up the metaphor from Veblen. As was common for Knight, however, he adapted the borrowed concept to his own purposes.

5 Knight's employment of paradox as a rhetorical strategy lies behind the frequent references by his commentators to his constant questioning; for example, by Patinkin, who identifies Knight as "the eternal asker of questions" (Patinkin 1973: 46). Warner Wick (1973: 513–14) identifies the connection between Knight's questioning mode and the more positive quality I describe here when he observes that the old difference between moving *from* first principles and moving *toward* them could be applied to Knight. After pointing out that Knight was good at moving from first principles (as his theoretical contributions show), Wick goes on to say: "But no man of my acquaintance has been more concerned with movement in the opposite direction, asking questions of ... relatively established principles, noting in turn their presuppositions and their limitations, in the attempt to discern more clearly how they might fit together in some order according to principles more comprehensive and, of course, more elusive."

6 Knight sets out the basic framework of his understanding of economic method in the first half of *RUP* (Knight 1921a). Subsequent restatements of his methodological framework (e.g. Knight 1924a, 1930a, and 1940a) are probably best understood as attempts to strengthen the economist's awareness of the critical distance between theory and practice (see Emmett 1991: 212–20).

7 Those familiar with *RUP* may want to argue that Knight's theory of uncertainty does not represent an attack on the maximizing assumption; rather, it is either a (largely mistaken) attempt to identify the need for subjective probability theory (Friedman 1976: 282), or simply a recognition of the distinction between what is insurable and what is not (LeRoy and Singell 1987). Earlier (Emmett 1991: 182–93) I argued, in a manner similar to my presentation in this chapter, that these interpretations of Knight's theory of uncertainty are flawed because they fail to pay attention to how Knight employed the notion of uncertainty in his campaign to delineate the strengths and limitations of neoclassical theory.

8 Frank Knight on the conflict of values in economic life

1 The view that Knight opposed was summarized succinctly by his student Milton Friedman in the introduction to his famous essay on economic methodology when he said: " ... differences about economic policy among disinterested citizens derive predominantly from different predictions about the economic consequences of taking action – differences that in principle can be eliminated by the progress of positive economics – rather than from fundamental differences in basic values, differences about which (we) can ultimately only fight" (Friedman 1953: 5).

2 I cannot resist adding two asides at this point: First, Knight's arguments against the possibility of using absolute rules for the guidance of human conduct go a long way toward explaining his negative reaction to the monetary rules proposed by his student, Milton Friedman. Knight was never very much of a monetarist! Second, Knight once commented that the authors of great imaginative literature were "always indefinitely better psychologists than the psychologists so-called" (Knight 1922: 49). I cannot help but think that he would also believe that they were "always indefinitely better *ethicists* than the *ethicists* so-called."

3 "It is the nature of interests to conflict, ultimately, to be subject to a law of diminishing importance or power. The interest in truth is no exception. ... We cannot live on

truth alone, or the discussion and quest of truth" (Knight 1925a: 250). This theme was repeated in many of his later writings.
4 Knight often quoted with approval Lord Bryce's definition of democracy – that is, "government by discussion" – because it gave him a way to lead up to the idea that it is the continuation of the discussion, rather than the resolution of a particular disagreement, which is of central importance (Knight 1952: 5–7; 1955: 49–56).
5 Many share the view expressed by Ben Seligman (1962: 665): "Despite all his protestations to the contrary, Knight was more of a traditionalist than he knew."

10 Entrenching disciplinary competence

1 Histories of the Chicago curricular debates can be found in Dzuback 1991; McNeill 1991; and Orlinsky 1992.
2 The split between the college and the departments did emerge in Gideonese's time at Chicago, however. Despite their support for his tenure, the departmental faculty did not support Gideonese's appointment as a full professor on the grounds that he had done insufficient research for a Chicago professor (McNeill 1991: 84).
3 These changes were accompanied by several other changes that reflect the same movement but will not be described here: the separation of the Business School from economics; the arrival of the Cowles Commission in 1939; the simultaneous decline in the number of women students in economics and increase in the number of women students in the Schools of Social Service Administration and Home Economics; and the rise of collaborative research.
4 Information regarding degree requirements comes from the yearly *Announcements* of the University of Chicago.
5 Stigler (1941) is the most famous product of Knight's history of thought training and well represents the role of the history of economic thought in developing a disciplinary self-critique.
6 Copies of examinations from the 1930s to the 1950s can be found in the Department of Economics Records in the University of Chicago Archives. Evidence of the changed focus of examination is best found in stories told by former Chicago students.

11 De gustibus *est* disputandum: Frank Knight's response to George Stigler and Gary Becker's "De gustibus non est disputandum"

1 In a letter to Lionel Robbins, Knight put it this way:

> The more I think about it the more I am inclined to say that the fundamental principle stressed so much in your book, of an absolute contrast between judgments of facts and judgments of value, is actually the basic error. … Stating it another way, I am inclined squarely to reverse the maxim, *De gustibus non [est] disputandum*, in this regard, and hold that only judgments of value can be discussed, facts as such not at all. That is, when we disagree about a fact it seems to me we disagree about the *validity* of observation or evidence, and that every disagreement is essentially a difference in evaluation.
>
> (Knight 1934d; emphasis in original)

> The possibility of securing agreement is an absolutely essential feature of the scientific criterion of truth. Truth is not merely what is the same for all, but is what is known and recognized as the same. …
>   The point is that illusion is what we agree is illusion, and reality what we agree is reality, because in each case it is shown to be so by tests which we agree are valid. It is ultimately a matter of agreement, of common-sense. Truth is established by

consensus as much as by beauty. In both cases, to be sure, it is a consensus of the 'competent.' But the competent are selected by agreement, another consensus; and ultimately we must come to principles agreed upon by the great mass of mankind.

(Knight 1925a: 117–18)

Knight's notion of the value-ladenness of facts, along with his appreciation for the social nature of value theory makes his epistemology similar to contemporary social constructivism. See Hands (1996) and Hammond (1991) for recognition of this similarity.

2 A paraphrase of Knight (1923a: 66).

3 A paraphrase of Knight (1924a: 1).

4 Knight's defense of an economics based on the reality of human intentionality stretches over a number of articles. See for examples Knight (1922, 1924a, 1925a, and 1925b).

5 In *RUP*, Knight made the stability of tastes and preferences one of the foundations for the stability of knowledge which undergirded perfect competition: "We have, then, our dogma which is the presupposition of knowledge … : that the world is made up of *things*, which, *under the same circumstances*, always behave *in the same way*." (Knight 1921a: 204, emphasis in original). But the instability of these foundations in the real world was the source of uncertainty. During the 1920s, Knight introduced an ethical element to the argument:

> A science must have a 'static' subject matter; it must talk about things which will 'stay put'; otherwise its statements will not remain true after they are made and there will be no point to making them. Economics has always treated desires or motives as … sufficiently stable during the period of activity which they prompt to be treated as causes of that activity in a scientific sense. It has thus viewed life as a process of satisfying desires. If this is true then life is a matter of economics; only if it is untrue, or a very inadequate view of the truth, only if the 'creation of value' is distinctly more than the satisfaction of desire, is there room for ethics in a sense logically separable from economics.
>
> (Knight 1922: 41–2)

6 A paraphrase of Knight (1922: 51).

7 Paraphrase of Knight (1942: 277). See also Knight (1922: 51). For a slightly different version of the argument, see Knight (1924a: 28–33).

8 A paraphrase using Knight (1922: 42–3; 1942: 278; 1940a: 388–89).

9 A paraphrase of Knight (1922: 52).

10 A paraphrase of Knight (1922: 52–3; and 1924a: 19). See also Knight (1930b). On the need for studying history:

> The fundamental fact in the way of a science of human nature is a familiar characteristic shared by all the higher animals, that the reaction of an individual to an 'object' depends not only on or mainly on the individual and the object, but on the previous history of the individual. … Long before he is adult, a being with man's sensitiveness to passing experience and his capacity for conscious and unconscious memory has become such an unique aggregation of attitudes toward meanings that there is no use talking about accurate classification; he has to be treated as an individual.
>
> (Knight 1924a: 23–4)

11 "Furthermore, just as it is impossible to avoid recognizing that human beings are:

> observers in a sense ultimately separate from and opposed to perceived data, it is equally impossible to treat them as subjects to be "controlled" without recognizing them at the same time as controllers. Control in society is a mutual relation.

> Failure to take account of the obtrusive fact reduces most of the voluminous extant discussion of 'social control' to the level of word-churning. The wish and effort to control are present in all the other social units as well as in the 'scientist' who discusses them with lofty detachment; and he is subject to any "laws of behavior" which apply to them ... Recognition of this mutuality of interest and 'control' between our fellows and ourselves becomes of course the corner-stone of ethical relations, the treatment of humanity as such as an end and never as a means.
>
> (Knight 1925a: 126)

12 A paraphrase of Knight (1922: 55).
13 A paraphrase of Knight (1941b: 194–200). For different versions of the same argument, see Knight (1939a: 45–53; and Knight and Merriam 1945).
14 A paraphrase of Knight (1925a: 115).
15 See Knight (1924a).
16 "The real sociology and economics must be branches of literature as much as of science." Knight (1924a: 38–39). See also Knight (1922: 55–56).
17 Paraphrase of Knight (1922: 55–56).

12 "Did the Chicago School reject Frank Knight?

1 The standard version of the traditional account is Reder (1982). A slightly expanded version appears in Reder (1987).
2 Harberger added D.N. McCloskey's teaching of Econ 300 from the late 1960s to 1980 as another essential element of continuity in the teaching of price theory. Econ 300 was designed for students who did not have sufficient undergraduate background in economics to move directly into Econ 301. These three individuals did teach Econ 301 is significantly different ways.
3 The group of economists that Knight made the target of his criticism included Sumner Slichter (Knight 1932), John Maurice Clark (Knight 1925a), Clarence Ayres (Knight 1935f), John Maynard Keynes (Knight 1937), and even David Ricardo (Knight 1935c) – how does one read the past as a critique of the present, one asks? By making the goal of the history of thought the correction of the past's mistakes!
4 When I asked Harold Demsetz how he would characterize the Chicago tradition, he responded "Prove it" (Demsetz 2002).
5 The Industrial Organization workshop in the department led by Stigler and the Law & Economics workshop in the Law School run by Ronald Coase had reputations for the ruthless attacks on presenters. Not all the workshops had the same reputation.

14 Economics as religion

1 A review essay on Nelson (2001).

References

Adler, M. (1940) "God and the Professors," *Daily Maroon* (University of Chicago), 14, November supplement: 1–2.

American Economic Association (1973), "In Memoriam: Frank H. Knight, 1885–1972," *American Economic Review*, 63: 1047–48.

Anderson, G.M., Levy, D.M. and Tollison, R.D. (1988) "The Half-Life of Dead Economists," *Canadian Journal of Economics*, 22: 174–83.

Backhouse, R. (1992) "How Should We Approach the History of Economic Thought: Fact, Fiction, or Moral Tale?," *Journal of the History of Economic Thought*, 14: 18–35.

——(1994) "Why and How Should We Study the History of Economic Thought?," *History of Economic Ideas*, 2: 115–23.

Bannister, R.C. (1987) *Sociology and Scientism: The American Quest for Objectivity, 1880–1940*, Chapel Hill, NC: University of North Carolina Press.

Barber, W.J. (1985) *From New Era to New Deal: Herbert Hoover, the Economists, and American Economic Policy, 1921–1933*, Cambridge: Cambridge University Press.

Barzel, Y. (1987) "Knight's 'Moral Hazard' Theory of Organization," *Economic Inquiry*, 25: 117–20.

Becker, G.S. (1965) "A Theory of the Allocation of Time," *Economic Journal*, 75: 493–517.

——(1976) *The Economic Approach to Human Behavior*, Chicago, IL: University of Chicago Press.

——(1996) *Accounting for Tastes*, Cambridge, MA: Harvard University Press.

Becker, G.S. and Murphy, K.M. (2000) *Social Economics: Market Behavior in a Social Environment*. Cambridge: Belknap Press.

Bender, T. (1993) *Intellect and Public Life: Essays on the Social History of Academic Intellectuals in the United States*, Baltimore, MD: Johns Hopkins University Press.

Bellofiore, R. (1994) "History of Economic Thought as a Problem," *History of Economic Ideas*, 2: 124–46.

Bevir, M. (1999) *The Logic of the History of Ideas*, Cambridge: Cambridge University Press.

Bewley, T.F. (1989) "Market Innovation and Entrepreneurship: A Knightian View," unpublished discussion paper no. 905, Cowles Foundation for Economic Research in Economics, Yale University.

Blaug, M. (1980) *The Methodology of Economics: Or How Economists Explain*, Cambridge: Cambridge University Press.

——(1985) *Economic Theory in Retrospect*, Cambridge: Cambridge University Press.

——(1990) "On the Historiography of Economics," *Journal of the History of Economic Thought*, 12: 27–37.

Boland, L. (1982) *The Foundations of Economic Method*, London: George Allen & Unwin.

Bonhoeffer, D. (1953) *Letters and Papers from Prison*, London: SCM Press.

Boudreaux, D.J. and Holcombe, R.G. (1989) "The Knightian and Coasian Theory of the Firm," *Managerial and Decision Economics*, 10:147–54.

Boyd, R. (1996) "Re: Knight and Weber." E-mail (11 September).

——(1997) "Frank H. Knight, Talcott Parsons, and Max Weber," unpublished mss.

Breit, W. (1976) Clarence Edwin Ayres: An Intellectual's Portrait," in W. Breit and W.P. Culbertson, Jr. (eds) *Science and Ceremony: The Institutional Economics of C.E. Ayres*, Austin, TX: University of Texas Press.

Breit, W. and Ransom, R.L. (1982) *The Academic Scribbler*, rev. edn, Chicago, IL: Dryden Press.

Brennan, H.G. and Waterman, A.M.C. (eds) (2008) *Are Economists Basically Immoral? and other Essays on Economics, Ethics, Religion and Education by Paul Heyne*, Indianapolis, IN: Liberty Fund.

Bronfenbrenner, M. (1962) "Observations on the 'Chicago School,'" *Journal of Political Economy*, 70: 72–5.

Brouwer, M.T. (2002) "Weber, Schumpeter and Knight on Entrepreneurship and Economic Development," in J.S. Metcalfe and U. Cantner (eds) *Change, Transformation and Development*, Heidelberg: Physica Verlag.

Buchanan, J.M. (1967) "Politics and Science: Reflections on Knight's Critique of Polanyi," *Ethics*, 11: 303–10.

——(1968) "Frank H. Knight," in D. Sills (ed.) *The International Encyclopedia of the Social Sciences*, New York: Macmillan.

——(1979) "Natural and Artifactual Man," in *What Should Economists Do?*, Indianapolis, IN: Liberty Press.

——(1982) "Foreword," in F.H. Knight, *Freedom and Reform: Essays in Economics and Social Philosophy*, reprint edn, Indianapolis, IN: Liberty Press.

——(1987) "The Economizing Element in Knight's Ethical Critique of Capitalist Order," *Ethics* 98: 61–75.

Bulmer, M. (1984) *The Chicago School of Sociology: Institutionalization, Diversity, and the Rise of Sociological Research*, Chicago, IL: University of Chicago Press.

Butterfield, H. (1931) *The Whig Interpretation of History*, London: Pelican.

Caldwell, B.J. (1994) *Beyond Positivism: Economic Methodology in the Twentieth Century*, rev. edn, London: Routledge.

Camic, C. (1991) "Introduction: Talcott Parsons before *The Structure of Social Action*," in C. Camic (ed.), *Talcott Parsons: the Early Essays*, Chicago, IL: University of Chicago Press.

Cantor, N.F. (1991) *Inventing the Middle Ages: The Lives, Works, and Ideas of the Great Medievalists of the Twentieth Century*, New York: Morrow.

Caravale, G. (1992) "Comment," *History of Political Economy*, 24: 204–7.

Church, R.L. (1974) "Economists as Experts: The Rise of an Academic Profession in America, 1870–1920," in L. Stone (ed.) *The University in Society*, vol. 2, *Europe, Scotland, and the United States from the Sixteenth to the Twentieth Century*, Princeton, NJ: Princeton University Press.

Clark, C.M.A. (1994) "Werner Stark and the Historiography of Economics," *History of Economic Ideas*, 2: 97–108.

Clark, J.C.D. (1985) *English Society 1688–1832: Ideology, Social Structure and Political Practice during the Ancient Regime*, Cambridge: Cambridge University Press.

Coats, A.W. (1992) "Comment," *History of Political Economy*, 24: 208–11.

Collins, R. (1980) "Weber's Last Theory of Capitalism: A Systematization," *American Sociological Review*, 45: 925–42.

Collini, S. (2000) "General Introduction," in S. Collini, R. Whatmore and B. Young (eds) *Economy, Polity and Society: British Intellectual History 1750–1950*, Cambridge: Cambridge University Press.

Cowen, T. (1989) "Are All Tastes Constant and Identical?," *Journal of Economic Behavior and Organization*, 11: 127–35.

——(2008) "Is a Novel a Model?" in S. Peart and D. Levy (eds) *The Street Porter and the Philosopher: Conversations on Analytical Egalitarianism*, Ann Arbor, MI: University of Michigan Press.

Cowles Commission (1952) *Economic Theory and Measurement*, Chicago, IL: Cowles Commission for Research in Economics.

Cox, H. (1965) *The Secular City: Secularization and Urbanization in Theological Perspective*, New York: Macmillan, 1965.

——(1999) "The Market as God," *Atlantic Monthly* 283 (March):18–23.

Davis, J.R. (1974) "Three Days with Knight: A Personal Reminiscence," *Nebraska Journal of Economics and Business*, 13: 17–29.

Demsetz, H. (2002) Interview with R.B. Emmett, Chicago Economics Oral History Project, University of California, Los Angeles, February.

Derrida, J. (1976) *Of Grammatology*, Baltimore, MD: Johns Hopkins University Press.

Dewey, D. (1987) "The Uncertain Place of Frank Knight in Chicago Economics," paper presented at a joint session of the American Economic Association and the History of Economics Society, Chicago, December 1987.

——(1990) "Frank Knight before Cornell: some light on the dark years," in W.J. Samuels (ed.) *Research in the History of Economic Thought and Methodology*, 8: 1–38.

Dilthey, W. (1976) *Selected Writings*, Cambridge: Cambridge University Press.

Dzuback, M.A. (1991) *Robert M. Hutchins: Portrait of an Educator*, Chicago, IL: University of Chicago Press.

Ebner, A. (2005) "Re: Knight and Weber." E-mail (25 April).

Eliot, T.S. (1939) *The Idea of a Christian Society*, London: Faber and Faber.

Elster, J. (1984) *Ulysses and the Sirens: Studies in Rationality and Irrationality*, revised edn, Cambridge: Cambridge University Press.

Emmett, R.B. (1989) "The Therapeutic Quality of Frank H. Knight's *Risk, Uncertainty and Profit*," paper presented at History of Economics Society meeting, University of Richmond, June 1989; revised version published in this volume.

——(1991) "'The Economist as Philosopher': Frank H. Knight and American Social Science during the Twenties and Early Thirties," unpublished dissertation, University of Manitoba.

——(1992) "Frank H. Knight on the Conflict of Values in Economic Life," in W.J. Samuels (ed.) *Research in the History of Economic Thought and Methodology*, 9: 87–103; reprinted in this volume.

——(1994a) "Frank Knight: Economics vs. Religion," in H.G. Brennan and A.M.C. Waterman (eds), *Economics and Religion: Are They Distinct?*, Boston, MA: Kluwer Academic; reprinted in this volume.

——(1994b) "Maximizers vs. Good Sports: Frank Knight's Curious Understanding of Exchange Behavior," in N. De Marchi and M.S. Morgan (eds) *Higgling: Transactors and their Markets in the History of Economics*, Durham, NC: Duke University Press; reprinted in this volume.

——(1997a) "'What is Truth' in Capital Theory? Five Stories Relevant to the Evaluation of Frank Knight's Contribution to the Capital Controversy," in J.B. Davis (ed.) *New Economics and Its History*, Durham, NC: Duke University Press; reprinted in this volume.

——(1997b) "Reflections on 'Breaking Away': Economics as Science and the History of Economics as History of Science," in W.J. Samuels and J.E. Biddle (eds) *Research in the History of Economic Thought and Methodology*, 15: 221–36; reprinted in this volume.

——(1998a) "De Gustibus Non Est Disputandum," in J. Davis, D.W. Hands and U. Mäki (eds) *The Elgar Handbook of Economic Methodology*, Cheltenham: Edward Elgar.

——(1998b) "Entrenching Disciplinary Competence: The Role of General Education and Graduate Study in Chicago Economics," in M.S. Morgan and M. Rutherford (eds) *From Interwar Pluralism to Postwar Neoclassicism*, Durham, NC: Duke University Press; reprinted in this volume.

——(1998c) "Frank Knight's Dissent from Progressive Social Science," in S. Pressman and R. Holt (eds) *Economics and Its Discontents: Twentieth Century Dissenting Economists*, Cheltenham: Edward Elgar; reprinted in this volume.

——(ed.) (1999a) *Selected Essays by Frank H. Knight*, 2 vols, Chicago, IL: University of Chicago Press.

——(1999a) "Frank H. Knight (1885–1972): A Bibliography of his Writings," in Warren Samuels (ed.) *Research in the History of Economic Thought and Methodology*, Archival Supplement 9: 1–100.

——(1999b) "Frank Hyneman Knight Papers 1910–72: Finding Guide," in Warren Samuels (ed.) *Research in the History of Economic Thought and Methodology*, Archival Supplement 9: 101–273.

——(1999c) "The Economist and the Entrepreneur: Modernist Impulses in Frank H. Knight's *Risk, Uncertainty and Profit.*" *History of Political Economy* 31: 29–52; reprinted in this volume.

——(2003) "Is Economics a Religion?," in W.J. Samuels and J.E. Biddle (eds) *Research in the History of Economic Thought and Methodology*, 21-A: 229–38; reprinted in this volume.

——(2006a). "De Gustibus *Est* Disputandum: Frank H. Knight's Response to George Stigler and Gary Becker's 'De Gustibus Non Est Disputandum'," *Journal of Economic Methodology*, 13: 97–111; reprinted in this volume.

——(2006b) "Frank H. Knight, Max Weber, Chicago Economics, and Institutionalism," *Max Weber Studies*, Beiheft 1: Weber and Economics: 101–19; reprinted in this volume.

——(2007) "Knight's Challenge (to Hayek): Spontaneous Order is Not Enough for Governing a Liberal Society," in P. McNamara and L. Hunt (eds) *Governing the Great Society: Liberalism, Conservatism and Hayek's Idea of Spontaneous Order*, New York: Palgrave Macmillan.

——(2008) "The Religion of a Skeptic: Frank H. Knight on Ethics, Spirituality and Religion during His Iowa Years," in B. Bateman and S.Banzhaf (eds) *Keeping Faith: Religious Belief and Political Economy*, Durham, NC: Duke University Press.

Fish, S. (1980) *Is There a Text in This Class? The Authority of Interpretive Communities*, Cambridge, MA: Harvard University Press.

Fontaine, P. (1999) "Classical Political Economy between Two Fires: Jean-Baptiste Say and Frank Knight on the Enterprise Economy," *History of Political Economy*, 31: 1–28.

Foss, N.J. (1993) "More on Knight and the Theory of the Firm," *Managerial and Decision Economics*, 14: 269–76.

Foucault, M. (1972) *The Archaeology of Knowledge*, London: Tavistock.

Friedman, M. (1953) "The Methodology of Positive Economics," in *Essays in Positive Economics*, Chicago, IL: University of Chicago Press.

——(1974) "Schools at Chicago," *University of Chicago Magazine*, August: 11–16.

——(1976) *Price Theory: A Provisional Text*, Chicago, IL: Aldine.

Fukuyama, F. (1991) *The End of History and the Last Man*, New York: Free Press, 1991.

——(1995) *Trust: The Social Virtues and the Creation of Prosperity*, New York: Free Press.

Furner, M.O. (1975) *Advocacy & Objectivity: A Crisis in the Professionalization of American Social Science, 1865-1905*, Lexington, KY: University Press of Kentucky.

Gadamer, H.G. (1989) *Truth and Method*, 2nd edn, New York: Crossroad.

Geertz, C. (1973) *The Interpretation of Culture: Selected Essays*, New York: Basic Books.

Geiger, R.L. (1986) *To Advance Knowledge: The Growth of American Research Universities, 1900–1940*, New York: Oxford University Press.

Gerrard, B. (1993) "The Significance of Interpretation in Economics," in W. Henderson, Dudley-Evans, T., and Backhouse, R. (eds), *Economics and Language*. London: Routledge.

Giddens, A. (1991) *Modernity and Self-Identity*, Palo Alto, CA: Stanford University Press.

Gideonese, H. (1937) *The Higher Learning in a Democracy: A Reply to President Hutchins' Critique of the American University*, New York: Farrar and Rinehart.

Golinski, J. (1998) *Making Natural Knowledge: Constructivism and the History of Science*, Cambridge: Cambridge University Press.

Gonce, R.A. (1972) "Frank H. Knight on Social Control and the Scope and Method of Economics," *Southern Economic Journal*, 38: 547–58.

——(1996) "F.H. Knight on Social Philosophy and Economic Theory: the Beginnings," in W.J. Samuels and J.E. Biddle (eds) *Research in the History of Economic Thought and Methodology*, 14: 1–22.

Goodin, R.E. (1990) "Comment: De Gustibus Non Est Disputandum," in K. Schweers Cook and M. Levi (eds) *The Limits of Rationality*, Chicago, IL: University of Chicago Press.

Goodwin, C.D. (1973) "Marginalism Moves to the New World," in R.D.C. Black, A.W. Coats and C.D. Goodwin (eds) *The Marginal Revolution in Economics*, Durham, NC: Duke University Press.

Grundberg, E. (1957) Review of *On the History and Method of Economics: Selected Essays,* by Frank H. Knight, *Journal of Economic History*, 17: 276–79.

Hahn, F. (1993) "Autobiographical Notes with Reflections," in M. Szenberg (ed.) *Eminent Economists*, Cambridge: Cambridge University Press.

Hall, J.A. (1987) *Liberalism: Politics, Ideology and the Market*, London: Paladin.

Hammond, J.D. (1991) "Frank Knight's Antipositivism," *History of Political Economy*, 23: 359–81.

Hands, D.W. (1994) "The Sociology of Scientific Knowledge: Some Thoughts on the Possibilities," in R.E. Backhouse (ed.) *New Directions in Economic Methodology*, London: Routledge.

——(1996) "Frank Knight's Pluralism," in A. Salanti and E. Screpanti (eds) *Pluralism in Economics*, Aldershot: Edward Elgar.

Harberger, A.C. (2002) Interview with R.B. Emmett, Chicago Economics Oral History Project, University of California, Los Angeles, February.

Harrison, L.E. and Huntington, S.P. (2000). *Culture matters: How Values Shape Human Progress*, New York: Basic Books.

Hawthorn, G. (1987) *Enlightenment and Despair: A History of Social Theory*, 2nd edn, Cambridge: Cambridge University Press.

Hayek, F.A. (1934) "On the Relationship between Investment and Output," *Economic Journal*, 44: 207–31.
——(1936) "The Mythology of Capital," *Quarterly Journal of Economics*, 50: 199–228.
——(1937) "Economics and Knowledge," *Economica* (n.s.), 4: 33–54.
——(1941) *The Pure Theory of Capital*, London: Macmillan
——(1967) "The Transmission of the Ideals of Economic Freedom," in S*tudies in Philosophy, Politics, and Economics*, Chicago, IL: University of Chicago Press.
——(1978) "Two Kinds of Minds," in *New Studies in Philosophy, Politics, Economics and the History of Ideas*, Chicago, IL: University of Chicago Press.
Heidegger, M. (1962) *Being and Time,* revised edn, New York: Harper & Row.
Henderson, J.P. (1996) "Whig History of Economics is Dead – Now What?," HES List. Online posting. Available http://eh.net/pipermail/hes/1996-November/004822.html (accessed 19 June 2008).
Hildreth, C. (1986) *The Cowles Commission in Chicago, 1939–1955,* New York: Springer-Verlag.
Hirsch, E. and Hirsch, A. (1976) "The Heterodox Methodology of Two Chicago Economists," in W.J. Samuels (ed.) *The Chicago School of Political Economy*, East Lansing, MI: Michigan State University.
Hodgson, G. (2001) "Frank Knight as Institutionalist Economist," in J.E. Biddle, J.B. Davis and S.G. Medema (eds) *Economics Broadly Considered: Essays in Honor of Warren J. Samuels*, London: Routledge.
Hollander, S. (1979) *The Economics of David Ricardo*, Toronto: University of Toronto Press.
——(1992) "Comment," *History of Political Economy*, 24: 212–14.
Hollinger, D. (1985) *In the American Province: Studies in the History and Historiography of Ideas*, Bloomington, IN: Indiana University Press.
——(1994) "The Knower and the Artificer, with Postscript 1993," in D. Ross (ed.) *Modernist Impulses in the Human Sciences, 1890–1930*, Baltimore, MD: Johns Hopkins University Press.
Hughes, H.S. (1961) *Consciousness and Society: The Reorientation of European Social Thought, 1890–1930*, New York: Vintage Books.
Huntington, S.P. (1996) *The Clash of Civilizations and the Remaking of World Order*, New York: Simon and Schuster.
Hynes, A. (2001) "Economies' Past and Present: Historical Analysis and Current Practice," *Journal of the History of Economic Thought*, 23: 181–95.
Iannacone, L.R. (1998) "Introduction to the Economics of Religion," *Journal of Economic Literature*, 36: 465–95.
Ingrao, B. (1994) "History of Economics: Meaning and Method," *History of Economic Ideas*, 2: 147–64.
Johnson, A.S. (1952) *Pioneer's Progress: An Autobiography*, New York: Viking Press.
Joravsky, D. (1994) "Knowing Ourselves: Literary Art versus Social Science," in D. Ross (ed.) *Modernist Impulses in the Human Sciences, 1890–1930*, Baltimore, MD: Johns Hopkins University Press.
Kaldor, N. (1937) "Annual Survey of Economic Theory: The Recent Controversy on the Theory of Capital," *Econometrica*, 5: 201–33.
Kasper, S.D. (1993) "Frank Knight's Case for Laissez Faire: The Patrimony of the Social Philosophy of the Chicago School," *History of Political Economy*, 25: 413–33.
Kern, W.S. (1988) "Frank Knight on Preachers and Economic Policy: A 19th Century Liberal Anti-Religionist, He Thought Religion Should Support the Status Quo," *American Journal of Economics and Sociology*, 47: 61–9.

Kessel, R.A. and Alchian, A.A. (1960) "The Meaning and Validity of the Inflation-Induced Lag of Wages behind Prices," *American Economic Review*, 50: 43–66.

Keynes, J.M. (1933) *Essays in Biography*, London: Macmillan; reprinted in *The Collected Writings of John Maynard Keynes*, vol. 10 (1972), London: Macmillan.

Keyssar, A. (1992) "Comment," *History of Political Economy*, 24: 215–17.

Klamer, A. (1993) "Modernism in Economics: An Interpretation beyond Physics," in N. de Marchi (ed.) *Non-Natural Social Science: Reflecting on the Enterprise of More Heat than Light*, Durham, NC: Duke University Press.

Kloppenberg, J.T. (1986) *Uncertain Victory: Social Democracy and Progressivism in European and American Thought, 1870–1920,* New York: Oxford University Press.

——(1998) "Democracy and Disenchantment: From Weber and Dewey to Habermas and Rorty," in *The Virtues of Liberalism*, New York: Oxford University Press.

Knight, F.H. (1911) "The Problem," Frank H. Knight Papers, Box 55, Folder 15, Special Collections Research Center, University of Chicago Library.

——(1913) "Causality and Substance," unpublished paper for Philosophy 30, Empiricism and Rationalism, Cornell University, Frank H. Knight Papers, Box 55, Folders 2–3, Special Collections Research Center, University of Chicago Library.

——"The Ethical Basis for Socialism," presentation for the Cornell University Philosophy Club, February 1914, Frank H. Knight Papers, Box 55, Folder 27, Special Collections Research Center, University of Chicago Library.

——(1916a) "A Theory of Business Profit," unpublished dissertation, Cornell University.

——(1916b) "Neglected Factors in the Problem of Normal Interest," *Quarterly Journal of Economics* 30: 279–310.

——(1917) "The Concept of Normal Price in Value and Distribution," *Quarterly Journal of Economics* 32: 66–100.

——(1919a) Review of *Proposed Roads to Freedom: Socialism, Anarchism and Syndicalism*, by B. Russell, *American Journal of Sociology* 25: 227–28.

——(1919b) Review of *Cooperation and the Future of Industry*, by L.S. Woolf, *Journal of Political Economy* 27: 805–6.

——(1920a) Review of *The Place of Science in Modern Civilization*, by T. Veblen, *Journal of Political Economy* 28: 518–20.

——(1920b) "Social Organization: A Survey of Its Problems and Forms from the Standpoint of the Present Crisis," Frank H. Knight Papers, Box 31, Folders 6–7, Special Collections Research Collection, University of Chicago Library.

——(1921a) *Risk, Uncertainty, and Profit*, Boston, MA: Houghton Mifflin.

——(1921b) "Traditional Economic Theory–Discussion," *American Economic Review*, 11, supplement: 143–46.

——(1921c) "Cost of Production over Long and Short Periods," *Journal of Political Economy* 29: 304–35; reprinted in *The Ethics of Competition* (1935), New York: Harper; and also in R.B. Emmett (ed.) (1999) *Selected Essays by Frank H. Knight*, vol. 1, Chicago, IL: University of Chicago Press.

——(1921d) "Cassel's *Theoretische Sozialökonomie*," *Quarterly Journal of Economics*, 36: 145–53.

——(1922) "Ethics and the Economic Interpretation," *Quarterly Journal of Economics* 36: 454–81; reprinted in *The Ethics of Competition* (1935), New York: Harper; and also in R.B. Emmett (ed.) (1999) *Selected Essays by Frank H. Knight*, vol. 1, Chicago, IL: University of Chicago Press.

——(1923a) "The Ethics of Competition," *Quarterly Journal of Economics* 37: 579–624; reprinted in *The Ethics of Competition* (1935), New York: Harper; and also in

R.B. Emmett (ed.) (1999) *Selected Essays by Frank H. Knight*, vol. 1, Chicago, IL: University of Chicago Press.

——"The Concept of Spirituality," presentation to the Midwest regional association of Unitarians, October 1923b, Frank H. Knight Papers, Box 4, Folder 23, Special Collections Research Center, University of Chicago Library.

——"Discussion Group in Religion," Notes for Iowa City Unitarian Church group, Iowa City, 30 September – 2 December 1923c, Frank H. Knight Papers, Box 47, Folder 25, Special Collections Research Center, University of Chicago Library.

——(1924a) "The Limitations of Scientific Method in Economics," in R.G. Tugwell (ed.) *The Trend of Economics*, New York: Knopf; reprinted in *The Ethics of Competition* (1935), New York: Harper; and also in R.B. Emmett (ed.) (1999) *Selected Essays by Frank H. Knight*, vol. 1, Chicago, IL: University of Chicago Press.

——(1924b) "Some Fallacies in the Interpretation of Social Cost," *Quarterly Journal of Economics* 38: 582–606; reprinted in *The Ethics of Competition* (1935), New York: Harper; and also in R.B. Emmett (ed.) (1999) *Selected Essays by Frank H. Knight*, vol. 1, Chicago, IL: University of Chicago Press.

——(1924c) "Love and Force," unpublished manuscript, Frank H. Knight Papers, Box 21, Folders 16–18, Special Collections Research Center, University of Chicago Library.

——(1925a) "Fact and Metaphysics in Economic Psychology," *American Economic Review* 15: 247–66; reprinted in R.B. Emmett (ed.) (1999) *Selected Essays by Frank H. Knight*, vol. 1, Chicago, IL: University of Chicago Press.

——(1925b) "Economic Psychology and the Value Problem," *Quarterly Journal of Economics*, 39: 372–409; reprinted in *The Ethics of Competition*, New York: Harper & Bros.

——(1925c) "A Note on Professor Clark's Illustration of Marginal Productivity," *Journal of Political Economy* 33: 550–53.

——(1925e) letter to J. Viner, 9 September, Jacob Viner Papers, Public Policy Papers, Department of Rare Books and Special Collections, Princeton University Library.

——(1927) "Translator's Introduction," in M. Weber, *General Economic History*, New York: Greenberg.

——(1928) "Historical and Theoretical Issues in the Problem of Modern Capitalism," *Journal of Economic and Business History*, 1: 119–36; reprinted in *On the History and Method of Economics* (1956), Chicago, IL: University of Chicago Press; and also in R.B. Emmett (ed.) (1999) *Selected Essays by Frank H. Knight*, vol. 1, Chicago, IL: University of Chicago Press.

——(1929) letter to F.D. Kershner, 30 March, Frederick D. Kershner Papers, Christian Theological Seminary Library, Indianapolis.

——(1930a) "Statik und Dynamik: zur Frage der Mechanischen Analogie in den Wirtshaftswissenschaften," trans. A. Mahr, *Zeitschrift für Nationalökonomie*, 2: 1–26; reprinted as "Statics and Dynamics: Some Queries Regarding the Mechanical Analogy in Economics," in *The Ethics of Competition* (1935), New York: Harper; and also in R.B. Emmett (ed.) (1999) *Selected Essays by Frank H. Knight*, vol. 1, Chicago, IL: University of Chicago Press.

——(1930b) "Fact and Interpretation in Economics," Special Lectures on Economics, Washington, DC: US Department of Agriculture, Graduate School.

——(1931) "Professor Fisher's Interest Theory: A Case in Point," *Journal of Political Economy*, 39: 176–212.

——(1932) "The New Economics and the Control of Economic Activity," *Journal of Political Economy* 40: 433–76; reprinted in R.B. Emmett (ed.) (1999) *Selected Essays by Frank H. Knight*, vol. 1, Chicago, IL: University of Chicago Press.

——(1933a), "Preface to the Re-issue," in *Risk, Uncertainty, and Profit*, reprint edn, London: London School of Economics and Political Science.

——(1933b) "Capitalistic Production, Time and the Rate of Return," in *Economic Essays in Honour of Gustav Cassel*, London: George Allen and Unwin; reprinted in R.B. Emmett (ed.) (1999) *Selected Essays by Frank H. Knight*, vol. 1, Chicago, IL: University of Chicago Press.

——(1933c) *The Economic Organization*, Chicago: University of Chicago Press; reprinted in *The Economic Organization: with an Article, "Notes on Cost and Utility"* (1951), New York: A.M. Kelley.

——(1933d) letter to E. Graue, 5 October, Frank H. Knight Papers, Box 59, Folder 26, Special Collections Research Center, University of Chicago Library.

——(1934a) "Capital, Time and the Interest Rate," *Economica* (n.s.) 1: 257–86.

——(1934b) "Social Science and the Political Trend," *University of Toronto Quarterly*, 3: 407–27; reprinted in *Freedom and Reform: Essays in Economics and Social Philosophy* (1947), New York: Harper.

——(1934c) "Modern Thought: Is it Anti-Intellectual?," *University of Chicago Magazine*, November, 20–21, 23; reprinted in R.B. Emmett (ed.) (1999) *Selected Essays by Frank H. Knight*, vol. 1, Chicago, IL: University of Chicago Press.

——(1934d) letter to L. Robbins, 17 February, Frank H. Knight Papers, Box 61, Folder 17, Special Collections Research Center, University of Chicago Library.

——(1934e) letter to F.A. Hayek, December, Frank H. Knight Papers, Box 60, Folder 10, Special Collections Research Center, University of Chicago Library.

——(1935a) *The Ethics of Competition*, New York: Harper.

——(1935b) "Economic Theory and Nationalism," in *The Ethics of Competition*, New York: Harper.

——(1935c) "The Ricardian Theory of Production and Distribution," *Canadian Journal of Economics and Political Science* 1: 3–25, 171–96; reprinted in *On the History and Method of Economics* (1956), Chicago, IL: University of Chicago Press; and also in R.B. Emmett (ed.) (1999) *Selected Essays by Frank H. Knight*, vol. 1, Chicago, IL: University of Chicago Press.

——(1935d) "Professor Hayek and the Theory of Investment," *Economic Journal* 45: 77–94.

——(1935e) "Bemerkungen über Nutzen und Kosten," trans. G. Lovasy, *Zeitschrift für Nationalökonomie*, 6: 28-52, 315-36; reprinted in *The Economic Organization: with an Article, "Notes on Cost and Utility"* (1951), New York: A.M. Kelley.

——(1935f) "Intellectual Confusion on Morals and Economics," *International Journal of Ethics*, 45: 200–220.

——(1935g) "Value and Price," in E.R.A. Seligman (ed.) Encyclopedia of the Social Sciences, New York: Macmillan; reprinted in *The Ethics of Competition* (1935), New York: Harper.

——(1936a) "The Place of Marginal Economics in a Collectivist System," *American Economic Review*, 26: 255–66.

——(1936b) "The Quantity of Capital and the Rate of Interest," *Journal of Political Economy* 44: 433–63, 612–42; reprinted in R.B. Emmett (ed.) (1999) *Selected Essays by Frank H. Knight*, vol. 1, Chicago, IL: University of Chicago Press.

——(1936c) "Capital as Round-Aboutness," unpublished manuscript, Frank H. Knight Papers, Box 1, Folder 23, Special Collections Research Center, University of Chicago Library.

——(1936d) letter to T. Parsons, 1 May, Talcott Parsons Papers, Harvard University Archives, HUG(FP) 42.8.2, Box 2, Pusey Library.

——(1936e) letter to A.L. Harris, 27 May, Frank H. Knight Papers, Box 60, Folder 6, Special Collections Research Center, University of Chicago Library.

——(1937) "Unemployment: And Mr. Keynes's Revolution in Economic Theory," *Canadian Journal of Economics and Political Science* 3:100–123; reprinted in R.B. Emmett (ed.) (1999) *Selected Essays by Frank H. Knight*, vol. 1, Chicago, IL: University of Chicago Press.

——(1939a) "Ethics and Economic Reform," *Economica*, 6: 1–29, 296–321, 398–422; reprinted in *Freedom and Reform: Essays in Economics and Social Philosophy* (1947), New York: Harper; and also in R.B. Emmett (ed.) (1999) *Selected Essays by Frank H. Knight*, vol. 2, Chicago, IL: University of Chicago Press.

——(1939b) letter to R.H. Tawney, 28 April, Frank H. Knight Papers, Box 62, Folder 9, Special Collections Research Center, University of Chicago Library.

——(1940a) "'What is Truth' in Economics?" *Journal of Political Economy*, 48: 1–32; reprinted in *On the History and Method of Economics* (1956), Chicago, IL: University of Chicago Press; and also in R.B. Emmett (ed.) (1999) *Selected Essays by Frank H. Knight*, vol. 1, Chicago, IL: University of Chicago Press.

——(1940b) "Socialism: The Nature of the Problem," *Ethics*, 50: 253–89; reprinted in *Freedom and Reform: Essays in Economics and Social Philosophy* (1947), New York: Harper; and also in R.B. Emmett (ed.) (1999) *Selected Essays by Frank H. Knight*, vol. 2, Chicago, IL: University of Chicago Press.

——(1940c) "God and Professor Adler and Logic," *Daily Maroon* (University of Chicago) 14, November supplement: 5; reprinted in R.B. Emmett (ed.) (1999) *Selected Essays by Frank H. Knight*, vol. 1, Chicago, IL: University of Chicago Press.

——(1941a) "Social Science," *Ethics*, 51: 127–43; reprinted in *On the History and Method of Economics* (1956), Chicago, IL: University of Chicago Press.

——(1941b) "Religion and Ethics in Modern Civilization," *Journal of Liberal Religion*, 3: 3–22; reprinted in (1947) *Freedom and Reform: Essays in Economics and Social Philosophy*, New York: Harper.

——(1941c) "Anthropology and Economics," *Journal of Political Economy*, 49: 247–68; reprinted in R.B. Emmett (ed.) (1999) *Selected Essays by Frank H. Knight*, vol. 2, Chicago, IL: University of Chicago Press.

——(1942) "Fact and Value in Social Science," in R. Anshen (ed.) *Science and Man*, New York: Harcourt Brace; reprinted in (1947) *Freedom and Reform: Essays in Economics and Social Philosophy*, New York: Harper.

——(1943) "The Meaning of Freedom," in C.M. Perry (ed.) *The Philosophy of American Democracy*, Chicago, IL: University of Chicago Press; reprinted in R.B. Emmett (ed.) (1999) *Selected Essays by Frank H. Knight*, vol. 2, Chicago, IL: University of Chicago Press.

——(1944a) Diminishing Returns from Investment," *Journal of Political Economy*, 52: 26–47.

——(1944b) "Realism and Relevance in the Theory of Demand," *Journal of Political Economy*, 52: 289–318; reprinted in R.B. Emmett (ed.) (1999) *Selected Essays by Frank H. Knight*, vol. 2, Chicago, IL: University of Chicago Press.

——(1944c) "Human Nature and World Democracy," *American Journal of Sociology*, 49: 408–20; reprinted in *Freedom and Reform: Essays in Economics and Social Philosophy*, (1982), Indianapolis, IN: Liberty Press.

——(1946) "The Sickness of Liberal Society," *Ethics*, 56: 79–95; reprinted with substantial additions in *Freedom and Reform: Essays in Economics and Social Philosophy* (1947), New York: Harper; and also in R.B. Emmett (ed.) (1999) *Selected Essays by Frank H. Knight*, vol. 2, Chicago, IL: University of Chicago Press.

——(1947a) *Freedom and Reform: Essays in Economics and Social Philosophy*, New York: Harper.

——(1947b) "Salvation by Science: The Gospel according to Professor Lundberg," *Journal of Political Economy*, 55: 537–52; reprinted in *On the History and Method of Economics* (1956), Chicago, IL: University of Chicago Press.

——(1948) "Free Society: Its Basic Nature and Problem," *Philosophical Review*, 57: 39–58; reprinted in *On the History and Method of Economics* (1956), Chicago, IL: University of Chicago Press.

——(1949) "Virtue and Knowledge: The View of Professor Polanyi," *Ethics* 59: 271–84; reprinted in R.B. Emmett (ed.) (1999) *Selected Essays by Frank H. Knight*, vol. 2, Chicago, IL: University of Chicago Press.

——(1951a) "Economics and Ethics of the Wage Problem," in D.M. Wright (ed.) *The Impact of the Union*, New York: Harcourt Brace; reprinted in R.B. Emmett (ed.) (1999) *Selected Essays by Frank H. Knight*, vol. 2, Chicago, IL: University of Chicago Press.

——(1951b) "The Role of Principles in Economics and Politics," *American Economic Review* 41: 1–29; reprinted in *On the History and Method of Economics* (1956), Chicago, IL: University of Chicago Press; and also in R.B. Emmett (ed.) (1999) *Selected Essays by Frank H. Knight*, vol. 2, Chicago, IL: University of Chicago Press.

——(1952) "Economic Freedom and Social Responsibility," Emory University School of Business Administration, Studies in Business and Economics, No. 7.

——(1953) "Theory of Economic Policy and the History of Doctrine," *Ethics* 63: 276–92.

——(1955) "Economic Objectives in a Changing World," in *Economics and Public Policy*, Washington, DC: The Brookings Institution.

——(1956a) *On the History and Method of Economics: Selected Essays*, Chicago, IL: University of Chicago Press.

——(1956b) "Science, Society, and the Modes of Law," in L. White (ed.) *The State of the Social Sciences*, Chicago, IL: University of Chicago Press; reprinted in R.B. Emmett (ed.) (1999) *Selected Essays by Frank H. Knight*, vol. 2, Chicago, IL: University of Chicago Press.

——(1960a) *Intelligence and Democratic Action*, Cambridge, MA: Harvard University Press.

——(1960b) "Social Economic Policy," *Canadian Journal of Economics and Political Science* 26: 19–34.

——(1961) "Methodology in Economics—Part I," *Southern Economic Journal*, 27: 185–93.

——(1962) "Philosophy and Social Institutions in the West," in C.A. Moore (ed.) *Philosophy and Culture: East and West*, Honolulu, HI: University of Hawaii Press; reprinted in R.B. Emmett (ed.) (1999) *Selected Essays by Frank H. Knight*, vol. 2, Chicago, IL: University of Chicago Press.

——(1963) "Christian Ethics and Social Betterment," Pulpit Address, First Unitarian Church, Chicago, 18 August, Frank H. Knight Papers, Box 4, Folder 6, Special Collections Research Center, University of Chicago Library.

——(1967) "Laissez-Faire: Pro and Con," *Journal of Political Economy*, 75: 782–95; reprinted in R.B. Emmett (ed.) (1999) *Selected Essays by Frank H. Knight*, vol. 2, Chicago, IL: University of Chicago Press.

——(1991) "The Case for Communism: From the Standpoint of an Ex-Liberal," in Warren J. Samuels (ed.) *Research in the History of Economic Thought and Methodology*, archival supplement 2: 57–108.

——(n.d.) "Non-Economistic Value," unpublished manuscript, Frank H. Knight Papers, Box 24, Folder 11, Special Collections Research Center, University of Chicago Library.

Knight, F.H. and Merriam, T.W. (1945) *The Economic Order and Religion*, New York: Harper.

Kolb, D. (1986) *The Critique of Pure Modernity: Hegel, Heidegger, and After*, Chicago, IL: University of Chicago Press.

Langlois, R.N. and Cosgel, M. (1993) "Frank Knight on Risk, Uncertainty, and the Firm: A New Interpretation," *Economic Inquiry*, 31: 456–65.

Latour, B. (1987) *Science in Action*, Cambridge, MA: Harvard University Press.

Lavoie, D. (ed) (1991) *Economics and Hermeneutics*, London: Routledge.

Lawson, T. (1988) "Probability and Uncertainty in Economic Analysis," *Journal of Post-Keynesian Economics*, 11: 38–65.

Lazear, E.P. (2000) "Economic Imperialism," *Quarterly Journal of Economics*, 115: 99–146.

LeRoy, S.E. and Singell, L.D., Jr. (1987) "Knight on Risk and Uncertainty," *Journal of Political Economy*, 95: 394–406.

Levy, D.M. (2001) *How the Dismal Science Got Its Name: Classical Economics & the Ur-Text of Racial Politics*, Ann Arbor, MI: University of Michigan Press.

Lewis, H.G. (n.d.) Memorandum, Department of Economic Records, Box 41, Folder 1, University of Chicago Archives, Special Collections Research Center, University of Chicago Library.

Lippmann, W. (1914) *Drift and Mastery: An Attempt to Diagnose the Current Unrest*, New York: Mitchell Kinnerley.

Lundberg, G.A. (1947) *Can Science Save Us?*, New York: Longmans, Green.

Lutz, F.A. (1967) *The Theory of Interest*, Chicago, IL: Aldine.

Machlup, F. (1935a) "Professor Knight and the 'Period of Production,'" *Journal of Political Economy*, 43: 577–624.

——(1935b) "The 'Period of Production': A Further Word," *Journal of Political Economy*, 43: 808.

MacIntyre, A. (1984) *After Virtue*, 2nd edn, Notre Dame, IN: University of Notre Dame Press.

Marshall, A. (1890) *Principles of Economics*, London: Macmillan.

Marshall, L.C. (n.d.) "Situations of Chicago," memorandum, Department of Economics Records, Box 5, Folder 17, University of Chicago Archives, Special Collections Research Center, University of Chicago Library.

May, H.F. (1949) *Protestant Churches and Industrial America,* New York: Harper.

McCloskey, D.N. (1994) *Knowledge and Persuasion in Economics*, Cambridge: Cambridge University Press.

——(1998) *The Rhetoric of Economics*, 2nd edn, Madison, WI: University of Wisconsin Press.

——(2001) Interview with R.B. Emmett, Chicago Economics Oral History Project, Chicago, May.

McKinney, J.W. (1967) "A Critique of Frank H. Knight's Economic Philosophy," unpublished dissertation, Columbia University.

McNeill, W.H. (1991) *Hutchins' University: A Memoir of the University of Chicago, 1929–1950*, Chicago, IL: University of Chicago Press.

Megill, A. (1985) *Prophets of Extremity: Nietzsche, Heidegger, Foucault, Derrida*, Berkeley, CA: University of California Press.

Ménard, C. (1987) "Why Was There no Probabilistic Revolution in Economic Thought?" in L. Krüger, G. Gigerenzer, and M.S. Morgan (eds) *The Probabilistic Revolution*, vol. 2, Cambridge, MA: MIT Press.

——(1992) "Comment," *History of Political Economy*, 24: 218–20.

Michael, R.T. and Becker, G.S. (1973) "On the New Theory of Consumer Behavior," *Swedish Journal of Economics*, 75: 378–95.

Michelfelder, D.P. and Palmer, R.E. (eds) (1989) *Dialogue and Deconstruction: The Gadamer-Derrida Encounter*, Albany, NY: State University of New York Press.

Mill, J.S. (1967) "On the Definition of Political Economy; and on the Method of Investigation Proper to It," in J.M. Robson (ed.) *Collected Works of John Stuart Mill*, vol. 4, Toronto: University of Toronto Press.

Miller, H.L., Jr. (1962) "On the 'Chicago School of Economics,'" *Journal of Political Economy*, 70: 64–9.

Mirowski, P. (1989) *More Heat Than Light*, Cambridge: Cambridge University Press.

——(1992) "Comment," *History of Political Economy*, 24: 221–3.

Moggridge, D.E. (1992) "Comment," *History of Political Economy*, 24: 224–6.

Morgan, M.S. (1990) *The History of Econometric Ideas*, Cambridge: Cambridge University Press.

——(1994) "Marketplace Morals and the American Economists: The Case of John Bates Clark," in N. De Marchi and M.S. Morgan (eds) *Higgling: Transactors and Their Markets in the History of Economics*, Durham, NC: Duke University Press.

Morgan, M.S. and Rutherford, M. (1998) *From Interwar Pluralism to Postwar Neoclassicism*, Durham, NC: Duke University Press.

Munby, D.L. (1963) *The Idea of a Secular Society: And its Significance for Christians*, London: Oxford University Press.

Negishi, T. (1992) "Comment," *History of Political Economy*, 24: 227–9.

Neill, R. (1972) *A New Theory of Value: The Canadian Economics of H.A. Innis*, Toronto: University of Toronto Press.

Nelson, R.H. (1991) *Reaching for Heaven on Earth: The Theological Meaning of Economics*, Lanham, MD: Rowman and Littlefield.

——(2001) *Economics as Religion: From Samuelson to Chicago and Beyond*, University Park, PA: Pennsylvania State University Press.

Nietzsche, F.W. (1993) *The Birth of Tragedy*, New York: Penguin Classics.

Nopenney, C. (1997) "Frank Knight and the Historical School," in P. Koslowski (ed.) *Methodology of the Social Sciences, Ethics and Economics in the Newer Historical School: From Max Weber and Rickert to Sombart and Rothacker*, Berlin: Springer.

Norman, A.L. and Shimer, D.W. (1994) "Risk, Uncertainty, and Complexity," *Journal of Economic Dynamics and Control*, 18: 231–49.

Novick, P. (1988) *That Noble Dream: The "Objectivity Question" and the American Historical Profession*, Cambridge: Cambridge University Press.

Orlinsky, D.E. (1992) "Not very Simple, but Overflowing: A Historical Perspective on General Education at the University of Chicago," in J.J. MacAloon (ed.) *General Education in the Social Sciences: Centennial Reflections on the College of the University of Chicago*, Chicago, IL: University of Chicago Press.

Parsons, T. (1927) letter to P.H. Douglas, 13 November, Talcott Parsons Papers, Harvard University Archives, HUG (FP) 42.8.2, Pusey Library.

——(1930) *The Protestant Ethic and the Spirit of Capitalism*, New York: Charles Scribner's Sons.

——(1947) *The Theory of Social and Economic Organization*, New York: Oxford University Press.

Patinkin, D. (1973) "Frank Knight as Teacher," *American Economic Review*, 63: 787–810; reprinted in *Essays on and in the Chicago Tradition* (1981), Durham, NC: Duke University Press.

——(1981) "Introduction: Reminiscences of Chicago, 1941–47," in *Essays on and in the Chicago Tradition*, Durham, NC: Duke University Press.

——(1982) *Anticipations of The General Theory?*, Oxford: Blackwell.

——(1992) "Comment," *History of Political Economy*, 24: 230–3.

Pocock, J.G.A. (1962) "The History of Political Thought: A Methodological Enquiry," in P. Laslett and W. Runciman (eds) *Philosophy, Politics and Society*, second series, Oxford: Blackwell.

——(1971) *Politics, Language and Time: Essays on Political Thought and History*, New York: Atheneum.

——(1985) "State of the Art," in *Virtue, Commerce and History*, Cambridge: Cambridge University Press.

Porta, P.L. (1994) "The Present as History in Economic Analysis," *History of Economic Ideas*, 2: 165–72.

Porter, T.M. (1992) "Comment," *History of Political Economy*, 24: 234–6.

Proctor, R.N. (1992) "Comment," *History of Political Economy*, 24: 237–9.

Purcell, E.A., Jr. (1973) *The Crisis of Democratic Theory: Scientific Naturalism and the Problem of Value*, Lexington, KY: University Press of Kentucky.

Quasten, J. (1953) *Patrology*, Utrecht: Spectrum.

Raines, J.P. "Frank Knight on Religion, Ethics and Public Policy," paper presented at a joint session of the American Economic Association and the History of Economics Society, Chicago, December 1989.

Raines, J.P. and Jung, C.R. (1986) "Knight and Religion and Ethics as Agents of Social Change: An Essay to Commemorate the Centennial of Frank H. Knight's Birth," *American Journal of Economics and Sociology*, 45: 429–39.

Ramsey, A.M. (1969) *God, Christ and the World: A Study in Contemporary Theology*, London: SCM Press.

Reder, M.W. (1982) "Chicago economics: Permanence and Change," *Journal of Economic Literature*, 20: 1–38.

——(1987) "Chicago School," In J. Eatwell, M. Milgate and P. Newman (eds) *The New Palgrave Dictionary of Economics*, New York: Stockton Press.

Ricci, D.M. (1984) *The Tragedy of Political Science: Politics, Scholarship, and Democracy*, New Haven, CT: Yale University Press.

Ricoeur, P. (1970) *Freud and Philosophy: An Essay on Interpretation*, New Haven, CT: Yale University Press.

——(1981) *Hermeneutics and the Human Sciences*, Cambridge: Cambridge University Press.

Rieff, P. (1961) *Freud: The Mind of the Moralist*, Garden City, NY: Doubleday Anchor.

Rodgers, D.T. (1982) "In search of Progressivism," *Reviews in American History*, 10: 113–32.

Roncaglia, A. (1996) "Why Should Economists Study the History of Economic Thought?," *European Journal of the History of Economic Thought*, 3: 296–309.

Rorty, R. (1979) *Philosophy and the Mirror of Nature*, Princeton, NJ: Princeton University Press.

——(1984) "The Historiography of Philosophy: Four Genres," in R. Rorty, Schneewind, J.B. and Skinner, Q. (eds), *Philosophy in History: Essays on the Historiography of Philosophy*, Cambridge: Cambridge University Press.

Rosenberg, A. (1979) "Can Economic Theory Explain Everything?," *Philosophy of Social Science*, 9: 509–29.

——(1980) *Sociobiology and the Preemption of Social Science*, Baltimore, MD: Johns Hopkins University Press.

——(1985) "Prospects for the Elimination of Tastes from Economics and Ethics," *Social Philosophy and Policy*, 2: 48–68.

——(1992) *Economics: Mathematical Politics or Science of Diminishing Returns?*, Chicago, IL: University of Chicago Press.

Ross, D. (1991) *The Origins of American Social Science*, Cambridge: Cambridge University Press.

——(ed.) (1994a) *Modernist Impulses in the Human Sciences, 1870–1930*, Baltimore, MD: Johns Hopkins University Press.

——(1994b) "Modernism Reconsidered," in D. Ross (ed.) *Modernist Impulses in the Human Sciences, 1890–1930*, Baltimore, MD: Johns Hopkins University Press.

——(1994c) "Modernist Social Science in the Land of the New/Old," in D. Ross (ed.) *Modernist Impulses in the Human Sciences, 1890–1930*, Baltimore, MD: Johns Hopkins University Press.

Runde, J. (1988) "Clarifying Frank Knight's Discussion of the Meaning of Risk and Uncertainty," *Cambridge Journal of Economics*, 22: 539–46.

Rutherford, M. (1994a) *Institutions in Economics: The Old and the New Institutionalism*, Cambridge: Cambridge University Press.

——(1994b) "Predatory Practices or Reasonable Values? American Institutionalists on the Nature of Market Transactions," in N. De Marchi and M.S. Morgan (eds) *Higgling: Transactors and Their Markets in the History of Economics*, Durham, NC: Duke University Press.

——(1997) "American Institutionalism and the History of Economics," *Journal of the History of Economic Thought*, 19: 178–95.

——(2003) "American Institutional Economics in the Interwar Period," in W.J. Samuels, J. Davis and J.E. Biddle (eds) *A Companion to the History of Economic Thought*, Oxford: Blackwell.

——(2004) "Institutional Economics: The Term and its Meanings," in W.J. Samuels and J.E. Biddle (eds) *Research in the History of Economic Thought and Methodology*, 22-A: 179–84.

Samuels, W.J. (1974) "The History of Economic Thought as Intellectual History," *History of Political Economy*, 6: 305–23.

——(ed.) (1976) *The Chicago School of Political Economy*, East Lansing, MI: Michigan State University.

——(1977) "The Knight-Ayres Correspondence: The Grounds of Knowledge and Social Action," *Journal of Economic Issues*, 11: 485–525.

——(ed.) (1990) *Economics as Discourse: An Analysis of the Language of Economists*, Boston, MA: Kluwer.

Samuelson, P.A. (1987) "Out of the Closet: A Program for the Whig History of Science," *History of Economics Society Bulletin*, 9: 51–60.

Samuelson, P.A., Patinkin, D. and Blaug, M. (1991) "On the Historiography of Economics: A Correspondence," *Journal of the History of Economic Thought*, 13: 144–58.

Schabas, M. (1992) "Breaking Away: History of Economics as History of Science," *History of Political Economy*, 24: 187–203.

Schelling, T. (1984) *Choice and Consequences*, Cambridge, MA: Harvard University Press.

Schlee, E.E. (1992) "Marshall, Jevons, and the Development of the Expected Utility Hypothesis," *History of Political Economy*, 24: 729–44.

Schmidt, C. (1996) "Risk and Uncertainty: A Knightian Distinction Revisited," in C. Schmidt (ed.) *Uncertainty in Economic Thought*, Aldershot: Edward Elgar.

Schmidt, I.L.O. and Rittaler, J.B. (1989) *A Critical Evaluation of the Chicago School of Antitrust Analysis*, Boston, MA: Kluwer.

Schumpeter, J.A. (1934) *The Theory of Economic Development*, Cambridge, MA: Harvard University Press.
——(1942) *Capitalism, Socialism and Democracy*, New York: Harper.
Schweitzer, A. (1975) "Frank Knight's Social Economics," *History of Political Economy*, 7: 279–92.
Screpanti, E. (1994) "Epistemic Relativism, the Post-Modern Turn in Philosophy, and the History of Economic Thought," *History of Economic Ideas*, 2: 173–205.
Seidelman, R. and Harpman, E.J. (1985) *Disenchanted Realists: Political Science and the American Crisis, 1884–1984*, Albany, NY: State University of New York Press.
Seligman, B. (1962) *Main Currents on Modern Economics*, vol. 3, Glencoe: Free Press.
Sen, A. (1977) "Rational Fools: A Critique of the Behavioral Foundations of Economic Theory," *Philosophy and Public Affairs*, 9: 317–44.
Sent, E.M. (1998) *The Evolving Rationality of Rational Expectations: An Assessment of Thomas Sargent's Achievements*, Cambridge: Cambridge University Press.
Shils, E. (1981) "Some Academics, Mainly in Chicago," *American Scholar* 50: 179–96.
Simons, H.C. (1934) *A Positive Program for Laissez Faire: Some Proposals for a Liberal Economic Policy*, Public Policy Pamphlet no. 15, Chicago, IL: University of Chicago Press.
Singal, D.J. (1991) *Modernist Culture in America*, Belmont, CA: Wadsworth Publishing.
Skinner, Q. (1969) "Meaning and Understanding in the History of Ideas," *History and Theory*, 8: 3–33; reprinted in J. Tully (ed.) (1988) *Meaning and Context: Quentin Skinner and His Critics*, Princeton, NJ: Princeton University Press.
Smith, A. (1795) "History of Astronomy," in W.P.D. Wightman and J.C. Bryce (eds) (1982) *Essays on Philosophical Subjects*, vol. 3 of Glasgow Edition of the Works and Correspondence of Adam Smith, Indianapolis, IN: Liberty Fund.
Smith, M.C. (1994) *Social Science in the Crucible: The American Debate over Objectivity and Purpose, 1918–1941*, Durham, NC: Duke University Press.
Smith, D. (1988) *The Chicago School: A Liberal Critique of Capitalism*, New York: St. Martin's Press.
Sraffa, P. (1951) "Introduction," in *The Works and Correspondence of David Ricardo*, Cambridge: Cambridge University Press.
Stamp, J. (1926) *The Christian Ethic as an Economic Factor*, London: Epworth Press.
Stein, H. (1994) "Chicago Economics," in W. Outhwaite and T. Bottomore (eds) *The Blackwell Dictionary of Twentieth-Century Social Thought*, London: Blackwell.
Stigler, G.J. (1941) *Production and Distribution Theories*, New York: Macmillan.
——(1961) "The Economics of Information," *Journal of Political Economy*, 69: 213–25.
——(1962) "Comment," *Journal of Political Economy*, 70: 70–71.
——(1965) "Textual Exegesis as a Scientific Problem," *Economica*, 32: 447–50.
——(1971) "Foreword," in F.H. Knight, *Risk, Uncertainty, and Profit*, reprint edn, Chicago, IL: University of Chicago Press.
——(1973) "Frank Knight as Teacher," *Journal of Political Economy*, 81: 518–20.
——(1976) "The Scientific Uses of Scientific Biography, with Special Reference to J. S. Mill," in Robson, J.M. and Laine, M. (eds) *James and John Stuart Mill: Papers of the Centenary Conference*, Toronto: University of Toronto Press; reprinted in Stigler, G.J. (1982) *The Economist as Preacher and Other Essays*, Chicago, IL: The University of Chicago Press.
——(1982) "The Ethics of Competition: The Friendly Economists," in *The Economist as Preacher and Other Essays*, Chicago, IL: University of Chicago Press.
——(1987) "Frank Hyneman Knight," in J. Eatwell, M. Milgate and P. Newman (eds) *The New Palgrave: A Dictionary of Economics*, New York: Stockton Press.

Stigler, G.J. and Becker, G.S. (1977) "De Gustibus Non Est Disputandum," *American Economic Review*, 67: 76–90.

Sylla, E.D. (1992) "Comment," *History of Political Economy*, 24: 240–2.

Taylor, C. (1989) *Sources of the Self: The Making of Modern Identity*, Cambridge, MA: Harvard University Press.

Tugwell, R.G. (ed.) (1924) *The Trend of Economics*, New York: A.A. Knopf.

Tully, J. (ed.) (1988) *Meaning and Context: Quentin Skinner and His Critics*, Princeton, NJ: Princeton University Press.

University of Chicago Research Center in Economic Development and Cultural Change (1952) Minutes of the Faculty Seminar on "The Role of Ideologies in Economic Development," 11 March, on back of draft in Frank H. Knight Papers, Box 24 Folder 24, Special Collections Research Collection, University of Chicago Library.

Valdes, J.G. (1995) *Pinochet's Economists: The Chicago School in Chile*, Cambridge: Cambridge University Press.

Van Horn, R. and Mirowski, P. (2008) "The Rise of the Chicago School of Economics and the Birth of Neoliberalism," in P. Mirowski and D. Plehwe (eds) *The Making of the Neoliberal Thought Collective*, Cambridge, MA: Harvard University Press.

Vaughn, K. (1993) "Why Teach the History of Economics?," *Journal of the History of Economic Thought*, 15: 174–83.

Veblen, T. (1899) *The Theory of the Leisure Class*, New York: Macmillan.

——(1904) *The Theory of Business Enterprise*, New York: Scribner's.

Vidich, A.J. and Lyman, S.M. (1985) *American Sociology: Worldly Rejections of Religion and Their Directions*, New Haven, CT: Yale University Press.

Walker, D.A. (1992) "Comment," *History of Political Economy*, 24: 243–5.

Waterman, A.M.C. (1987) "Economists on the Relation between Political Economy and Christian Theology: A Preliminary Survey," *International Journal of Social Economics*, 14: 46–68.

——(1988a) "Malthus on Long Swings: A Reply," *Canadian Journal of Economics,* 21: 206–7.

——(1988b) "Denys Munby (1919–76) on Economics and Christianity," *Bulletin of the Association of Christian Economists*, 12: 5–10.

——(1994) "Whately, Senior, and the Methodology of Classical Economics," in H.G. Brennan and A.M.C. Waterman (eds) *Economics and Religion: Are They Distinct?*, Boston, MA: Kluwer.

——(2008) "The Changing Theological Context of Economic Analysis since the Eighteenth Century," in B. Bateman and S. Banzhaf (eds) *Keeping Faith: Religious Belief and Political Economy*, Durham, NC: Duke University Press.

Weber, M. (1927) *General Economic History,* trans. F.H. Knight, New York: Greenberg.

——(1958) *The Protestant Ethic and the Spirit of Capitalism*, New York: Charles Scribner's Sons.

Weintraub, R. (1991) *Stabilizing Dynamics: Constructing Economic Knowledge*, Cambridge: Cambridge University Press.

Weintraub, R., Meardon, S. J., Gayer, T., and Banzhaf, H. S. (1998) "Archiving the History of Economics," *Journal of Economic Literature,* 36: 1496–1501.

Whately, R. (1832) *Introductory Lectures on Political Economy*, London: Fellowes.

Wick, W. (1973) "Frank Knight, philosopher at large," *Journal of Political Economy*, 81: 513–15.

Wilde. O. (1969) "Phrases and Philosophies for the Use of the Young," in R. Ellman (ed.) *The Artist as Critic: Critical Writings of Oscar Wilde*, New York: Random House.

Winch, D. (1996) *Riches and Poverty: An Intellectual History of Political Economy in Britain, 1750–1834*, Cambridge: Cambridge University Press.

——(2000) "Does Progress Matter?," *European Journal of the History of Economic Thought,* 7: 465–84.

Wise, M.N. (1992) "Comment," *History of Political Economy*, 24: 246–7.

Wolfe, A.B. (1924) "Functional Economies," in R. Tugwell (ed.) *The Trend of Economics*, New York: F.S. Crofts.

Wood, G.S. (1979) "Intellectual History and the Social Sciences," in J. Higham and P.K. Conkin (eds) *New Directions in American Intellectual History*, Baltimore, MD: Johns Hopkins University Press.

Working, H. (1927) "The Use of the Quantitative Method in the Study of Economic Theory," *American Economic Review*, 17, supplement: 18–24.

Yonay, Y.P. (1998) *The Struggle over the Soul of Economics: Institutionalist and Neoclassical Economists in America between the Wars*, Princeton, NJ: Princeton University Press.

Young, A.A. (1927) letter to F.H. Knight, 25 February, Frank H. Knight Papers, Box 62, Folder 24, Special Collections Research Center, University of Chicago Library.

Yu, T.F-L. (2002) "The Economics of Frank H. Knight: An Austrian Interpretation," *Forum for Social Economics*, 31: 1–23.

Index

218   *Index*

Rodgers, D. T. 34, 66
Rorty, R. xxv, xxvi, 8–9, 23, 33, 51, 103–4
Rosenberg, A. 138–9
Ruskin, J. 95

Samuels, W. J. xiii, xix–xxiii, 190 n. 2.5
Samuelson, P. A. 12, 51, 172, 173–4
Schabas, M. 16–7, 20, 24, 25–6, 27
Schlee, E. E. 192 n. 4.6
Schultz, H. 192 n. 4.6
Schultz, T. W. 146, 148, 153
Schumpeter, J. A. 191 n. 4.1
The Secular City 188
secular society 180–3, 185–6, 188–9
secularization 181–3
Seligman, B. 194 n. 8.5
Singell, L. *see* LeRoy, S.
Simons, H. C. xix, 129, 132, 146, 147;
    positive program for laissez-faire 145;
    Simons' syllabus 131, 148
Skinner, Q. xxv, xxvi, 8, 14–5, 190 n. 2.2
Smith, A. xix, xxvii, 10, 177, 185; see also
    Wealth of Nations
social action 97
Sombart, W. 114, 121
Stamp, J. (Baron) 185
Stigler, G. J. xxi, xxiii, 31, 51, 154, 173,
    191 n. 3.8, 194 n. 10.5; hermeneutic
    principles xxvi, 4–7, 10, 11–12,
    13–5; methodological principle xv,
    xxix, 70, 99, 135, 137–43, 151–2; on
    Knight 98–9, 140, 146, 168; on *Risk,
    Uncertainty, and Profit* 32, 48; role in
    Chicago School 146, 147, 173, 196
    n. 12.5
successive approximation 76, 82, 118

Tawney, R. 107
Taylor, C. 184
thick description 15
The Trend of Economics 191, n. 3.4
trust: and markets 177
Tugwell, R. 127, 191 n. 3.4

uncertainty 14, 66–7, 76, 191 n. 3.5, 193
    n. 7.7; in *Risk, Uncertainty and Profit*
    20–3, 31, 41–3, 45, 48–9, 52, 55–8, 62,
    91, 191–2 n. 4.4; role in capital theory
    82, 85;
University of Chicago 39, 63, 74–5,
    116–17, 123, 124–5, 127–8, 170, 190
    n. 3.1, 191 n. 3.4, 193 n. 7.4; educational
    reform 83–5, 125, 128–30, 194 n. 10.1
University of Iowa 74, 114, 190 n. 3.1
Usher, A. P. 114

value theory 68–70, 75, 94, 99–102,
    105–6, 143, 167–8, 195 n. 11.1
Veblen, T. 35, 87–8, 96, 114, 191 n. 3.4,
    193 n. 7.4
Verry, E. 74
verstehen 118, 165
Vidich, A. J. xxxi, 159, 169–70, 171, 175
Viner, J. xiv, xix, 75, 116, 131, 132, 145,
    146, 148, 151

Wagner, R. 111
Wallis, W. A. 146
Waterman, A. M. C. 8–9, 164–5, 180
Wealth of Nations xxiii, 184
Weber, M. xix, 28, 62, 111–12, 118, 128,
    178, 192 n. 4.8; and religion 185; *see
    also General Economic History and
    Knight, F. H. and Weber and verstehen*
Werenfels, S. 4
what is truth? 73
Whately, R. 29, 176, 187–8
Whig history 11–12
Wick, W. 103, 193 n. 7.5
Wilcox, W. 39
Wilde, O. 53, 61
Wittgenstein, L. 33, 103
Wolfe, A. B. 68, 191 n. 3.4
workshop model 133–4, 153–4, 195 n. 12.5

Young, A. A. 35, 39, 114, 116, 190 n. 3.1,
    191 n. 3.7

For Product Safety Concerns and Information please contact our EU
representative GPSR@taylorandfrancis.com
Taylor & Francis Verlag GmbH, Kaufingerstraße 24, 80331 München, Germany

www.ingramcontent.com/pod-product-compliance
Ingram Content Group UK Ltd.
Pitfield, Milton Keynes, MK11 3LW, UK
UKHW021615240425
457818UK00018B/578